REFLECTIONS OF THE CHRIST MIND

DOUBLEDAY

New York

London

Toronto

Sydney

Auckland

REFLECTIONS

OF THE

CHRIST MIND

The Present-day Teachings
of Jesus

PAUL FERRINI

WITH AN INTRODUCTION
BY NEALE DONALD WALSCH

PUBLISHED BY DOUBLEDAY
a division of Random House, Inc.
1540 Broadway, New York, New York 10036

DOUBLEDAY and the portrayal of an anchor with a dolphin are
trademarks of Doubleday, a division of Random House, Inc.

Library of Congress Cataloging-in-Publication Data

Ferrini, Paul.
Reflections of the Christ mind: the present-day teachings
of Jesus Christ/Paul Ferrini; with an introduction by
Neale Donald Walsch—1st ed.
p. cm.
1. Spiritual life.   2. Jesus Christ—Miscellanea.   I. Title.

BL624.F465 2000
232.9—dc21
00-026685

ISBN: 0-385-49952-3

3 5 7 9 10 8 6 4 2

BOOK DESIGN BY JENNIFER ANN DADDIO

CONTENTS

INTRODUCTION

Everywhere I go since the publication of the trilogy of books called *Conversations with God,* I have been asked one question more often than any other: "Why you?" People want to know—and quite understandably—why I was "chosen" to bring such astonishing and heartwarming truth through to the human race.

Always I have given the same answer to this question: "It is not I who have been *chosen.* It is all of us." That is, in fact, the primary message of the *Conversations with God* trilogy. Each of us is a "converser" with God. And each of us has the ability to receive the most extraordinary wisdom from the Source to which we are most open. What is needed to "tap into" this Source of wisdom and truth is simply to be a person who has the will to do so.

Paul Ferrini is such a person. His earnest desire to know the answers to the largest questions lying within the deepest reaches of his mind, and nestled in the softest places in his heart, has produced the remarkable document that you are holding in your hands. I have read this material, and I am both moved and inspired by it.

It is not necessary that you or I agree with every single sentence or word that Paul has brought through. Indeed, I am sure that Paul would not want us to. For none of us should swallow whole the truths of another, but rather, allow the sharing of those truths to clear a path and open a dialogue that leads us to our own truth.

That is the gift, of course. That is the real treasure. And for that "opening to our own truth," we owe Paul an enormous thanks. For he has done something quite risky. He has shared with us his most personal process, and taken us to the most vulnerable places within his soul. And he has done so—as have all of those who have ever chanced to inspire us through the ages—without regard to what we might think of him. May I tell you, please, that I know what this has required.

Receive this gift, as I have, with gratitude and love. And open yourself now to the wisdom of Jesus, as Paul has brought it through. These words can inspire you to greater insights and understandings, to more clarity and a grander resolve to make changes in your life that can truly change the world.

NEALE DONALD WALSCH
AUTHOR OF CONVERSATIONS WITH GOD

AUTHORS' PREFACES

PREFACE BY JESUS

You need not accept the authority of the teachings in this book just because they are attributed to me. Listen to these words and be with them. You will know if they speak to your heart. Like a string being plucked on a guitar, truth always resonates in the heart of the listener.

If these words resonate in your heart, embrace them. Work with them in your life.

This is a living teaching. It lives through you if you accept it. Your acceptance is our covenant. It is our agreement to live and move and breathe together in the spirit of love and truth.

While reading this book may be a first step into communion with me, know that meeting me in your heart is an ever-present possibility. These words are one door that you walk through into that friendship.

This book invites you into a living communion with one who loves you and accepts you without conditions. If you learn to receive my love, you will attune to it. Like one torch lighting another, my love will ignite yours and our love will become a single blazing fire. It will burn away every obstacle to peace in your consciousness.

As it burns, your brother and sister will approach you, drawn by the light of the fire that rages in your heart. If they let your love in, they too will be set ablaze. In this way, the fire of love and truth will continue to burn until it consumes every fearful thought. Only then will its job be done. Only then will my work here be complete.

Our fire of light and love will give you the strength to face your fears, as well as the fears of other people. It will let you know in every situation that you are loved. It will remind you to let others know that you love them without conditions. When you are scared, it will give you the courage to say "I'm scared." When you make mistakes, it will give you the courage to say "I am mistaken, please forgive me."

My teaching is not difficult to understand. I did not say, "Love only blacks or Jews or Muslims." I did not say, "Love only people who dress like you, speak like you and share your beliefs." I said, "Love everyone. No exceptions. Even your enemy deserves your love." This concept is easy to understand, is it not? Even a child can understand it. Yet, it will challenge you every day of your life. This teaching will require all of your insight, all of your understanding, all of your willingness to practice if it is to become embodied in your life.

And embodiment is what I ask for. I ask you to embody the truth, not just to speak it. I ask you to live it every day. And when you forget, I ask you to become aware that you have forgotten. When you are afraid, I ask you to recognize the fact that you have fear rising and that fear shuts down your heart. I ask you to take a deep breath and remember. Remember me. Remember your brother and sister. Remember who you really are. You are not the ogre created by your fear.

You are the one who is completely loved and accepted. That is the truth. Let it come into your heart. Take my hand and walk with me through your fear. It is a journey you must all take, again and again, moving from fear to love, from weakness to strength, from resistance to acceptance. That journey is your redemption. It waits for you in every moment.

Please do not wait for Sunday to take the journey into love's embrace. Please take it right now. For there is only this moment, my friend. There is no past or future. Now is the only time in which we can meet. Are you ready to hear me now? Are you ready to take my hand and walk through the door of your fear?

I await your invitation. Knock and I will answer the door. Open your heart and my love will enter you.

I am the one you know as Jesus. While I am not in a body, I live in the hearts of those who remember me. Remember me, and I will abide with you. This is my promise.

PREFACE BY PAUL FERRINI

There was a time when the very thought of Jesus turned me off. It took me a while to realize that it was not Jesus that I needed to reject. It was the untruth attached to the Christian teaching. It was the untruth embodied in thousands of acts of brutality committed in his name.

It took me a while to realize that he was not responsible for the choices made by other people. He was not responsible for the lies or the acts of cruelty. He was responsible only for what he thought, what he said and what he did.

Some of what he taught and demonstrated has come down to us unobscured. That is our great blessing. Yet other parts of the teaching have become lost or twisted. The fear of other men and women has consistently stood between him and us. It is hard to see him through that fear.

Jesus never taught a single fearful principle. He taught only about the power of love and forgiveness. But even the purest words can be distorted.

I had to forgive that distortion to see him as he really is. I had to let him into my heart.

Over and over again, I heard a voice in my mind saying "I want you to acknowledge me" but I resisted. I didn't want to acknowledge Jesus. I heard his words deep in my soul, but I did not want to name him.

You see, naming him would change everything. Naming him would mean that I acknowledged him, not as some great teacher who lived the past, but as a presence living in my awareness. It would mean accepting his love as an active ingredient in my life and my awakening process. It would mean that I had a teacher.

Back then, I didn't want a teacher. I was comfortable with spirituality as an abstract concept, an impersonal energy. I was not comfortable with the idea of a personal relationship with a teacher and a teaching. I needed to keep my teachers at arm's length. That's what felt safe to me.

Naming him meant letting him in. It meant acknowledging him as a here and now teacher. It meant I had to give up my safe, intellectual distance. I had to let go of my need to be in control.

Naming him meant accepting my relationship with him personally and publicly. It wasn't an easy thing to do.

But I did it because I felt his love. Even before I knew who he was, I felt his energy. He was joining me in my emotional body long before he asked me to acknowledge him mentally.

I wasn't opening the door to a stranger. I was opening the door to the Friend.

If you are like I was and want to keep your safe, intellectual distance, your hands-off skepticism, you better think twice about reading this book. Reading these words may open a door you want to keep closed. Better turn back before it's too late.

Words are not just words but containers of energy. Although some words and sentences in this book may fall short of capturing the precise meaning he intends, I know that taken as a whole this book carries the energy of his intention.

As you read this book, you will attune to Jesus and begin to feel his love in your heart. Then, you will know in the core of your being that you are not alone. You will accept the Friend into your life. That is a blessing that cannot be taken away.

For those of you who want to know more about my encounter with Jesus before reading his teachings, I refer you to the appendix. But for the rest of you, please start at the beginning and let him speak now for himself.

I send you my love and my blessings.

PAUL FERRINI

NOTES ON EDITING
AND SELECTION

For the most part, the material in this book has been taken from the previous four books in the *Reflections of the Christ Mind* series. These books are:

> *Love Without Conditions* (Part I), 1994
> *The Silence of the Heart* (Part II), 1996
> *Miracle of Love* (Part III), 1997
> *Return to the Garden* (Part IV), 1998

At the end of every selection in this book you will find an abbreviation in parenthesis that indicates the book from which the selection was taken (e.g., LWOC, SOTH, MOL, and RTG).

In order to create a sense of flow in the current book, some sections have been edited and new transitional paragraphs have been added. The result is a book that very much stands on its own.

Even if you own the other four volumes in the *Christ Mind* series, you will find this book valuable as it synthesizes the teachings in a single volume. If this is your first *Christ Mind* book and it speaks to your heart, you might want to consider reading one or more of the previous volumes. Each one of those books contains a great deal of material not included in this book. A complete list of books with ordering information is included in the back of this volume.

1.

I AM NOT
THE ONLY CHILD
OF GOD

THE SOURCE OF THIS INFORMATION

With all of the fanfare about channeling, it seems important to be clear that this is not a channeled book. The information in this book does not come from some entity or personality apart from the mind of the listener. Indeed, this book is the result of one listener's joining with the *Christ Mind,* of which he and you are essential parts.

To think of me as being outside of and independent of your mind is to miss the point. For it is in your mind that I address you. I am your most intimate friend speaking to you, sometimes in words, often beyond words. Your communication and communion with me are essential to your practice of my teaching. (LWOC)

The Second Coming
A teaching lives only to the extent that people understand it and live it. It is like a musical composition. It doesn't come alive until someone performs it.

When you understand my teaching and practice it in your daily life, you become a beacon for others. Through you, my teaching comes alive. Through your life, I live.

This is my Second Coming. I will not come again in a physical body. I will come through your heart/mind and your life as you attune to me, just as I have always done.

There was a time when I had twelve apostles. Now I have thousands.

Every time a person turns to me in complete surrender, he becomes my instrument. Through his hands and heart I work to spread love in the world. (MOL)

I Am Not the Only Child of God

It is nearly 2,000 years since my birth and my teaching—which was once like a raging stream—has shrunk to barely a trickle of water. You have rationalized me and put me in my place: an exalted place perhaps, but a distant one. You have placed me above you where I will not challenge you. By making me a deity, an only Son of God, you excuse yourself from having to live up to my example. Yet my example is the heart of my teaching. If you do not try to emulate me, what is the meaning of your belief in me? (RTG)

Crucifixion and Resurrection (1)

You think I am special because I was crucified. Yet you are nailed to the cross every day. And when you are not being nailed, you are doing the nailing. There is nothing special about being crucified.

Some of you believe that I alone was resurrected. Yet you are raised from death by the power of love every time you remember who you are or who your brother is. Every time love is given or received, death is vanquished. For everything dies, except love. Only the love you have given or received lives forever.

You may think that by believing in me you are guaranteed some special place in the afterlife. That is not true, unless your belief in me has inspired you to give love or receive it. If you have not opened to love in your life, your belief in me or in anyone else means very little. (MOL)

Crucifixion and Resurrection (2)

You think your hurtful actions condemn you for all time. You think that God is vengeful and will punish you for your mistakes. But that is not the God I know. That is the God created out of human fear and guilt.

You think that I died for your sins. That is a misunderstanding of my life and my teaching. I came to teach that no sin is unforgivable, that every being deserves love, including those who strike out against others in their fear and their pain.

I did not die to save you from your sins, nor did I die to condemn you for crucifying me. I died, quite simply, because you could not recognize me in yourself.

You think you are attending my crucifixion when in truth you are attending your own. But remember, like me, you too will be resurrected from the prison of pain. My Passion play is just a metaphor for your own. (RTG)

Do Not Think That I Alone Am Christ

Do not think that I alone am Christ or you will miss the entire point of my teaching. Every one of you is the anointed one. Every one of you is chosen.

But to be chosen is not enough. Some of my Jewish brothers and sisters were chosen, yet they chose to worship idols nonetheless. Some of my Christian brothers and sisters were chosen, yet they chose to make idols of me and mother Mary. You see, it is not enough to be chosen. You too must choose.

I made my choice and so must you. Choosing to put God first does not mean that you are perfect or mistake free. I was not perfect, although you believe me to be. That, of course, is the problem.

If you believe that I was perfect, then how can you measure up to me? My friends, you are not talking about Jesus here. You are talking about some abstract idol, an intellectual concept to which you will nail yourself as though it were a cross. The story of the crucifixion is not over. You keep it alive through your perfectionism and relentless self-judgment.

Knowing that I was an imperfect human being like you, you can muster a bit of hope for yourself. Salvation is not for those who are mistake free, but for those who make mistakes and desire to atone for them. (MOL)

I Did Not Die for Your Sins

If I died for your sins, then there is nothing left for you to do. Why then not ascend to heaven on the strength of your belief in me?

I will tell you why. Because, in spite of your belief, you are not happy. You are not at peace.

Take me down from the pedestal, my brother or sister, and place me at your side, where I belong. I am your absolute, unconditional equal. What I have done, you too will do.

You will not be saved by my thoughts and actions, but by your own. Except you become the Christ, peace will not come to the world. If you would see me as king, then king must you yourself be.

Do not put distance between us, for I am no different from you. Whatever you are—a beggar or thief, a holy man or a king—that I am too.

There is no pedestal I have not been lifted upon, nor any gutter I have not lain in. It is only because I have touched the heart of both joy and pain that I can walk through the doors of compassion. (MOL)

You Are the Teaching

My teaching is about remembering. It is about becoming conscious of the truth and living it. It is not enough just to know the words. Words are easily forgotten. Words must become practice. And practice must become spontaneous action.

You have focused so much on how great I am, you have forgotten your own greatness. You have neglected the fact that forgiveness cannot be offered to the world except through you. And you cannot offer it, unless you have accepted it for yourself. (MOL)

The Myth of the Virgin

I was born to a simple woman in a barn. She was no more a virgin than your mother was. You make her special for the same reason that you make me special: to put distance between us, to claim that what we did you cannot do.

If our lives have any meaning to you at all, you must know that we do not claim a special place. Neither Mary nor I is more spiritual than you are. We are like you in every way. Your pain is our pain. Your joy is our joy. If this were not true, we could not come to teach.

Do not hold us at arm's length. Embrace us as your equal. Mary could have been your mother. I could have been your son. (MOL)

Communion

When you commune with me, it is not my body and my blood that you consume, but the spirit of forgiveness, which uplifts your hearts. When you raise the cup, remember your innocence and that of all other beings. That is my lifeblood, the legacy of truth that you must remember and extend. (MOL)

Miracle of Love

When you think of me, remember what I have empowered you to do in your life, and do not dwell on the "miraculous" things I have done. The power of love will make miracles in your life as wonderful as any attributed to me. For love is the only miracle, not you or I.

We are here to embrace the miracle of love and pass it on to others. Let us not take credit for what love has done or will do. The credit belongs to the one who loved us without conditions long before we knew what love was, or what its absence would mean to us.

We have all strayed from the fold. We have all forgotten the Creator's love. I come to you as a reminder of that love. When you remember my birth into this world, remember my purpose for coming. It is your purpose too.

Your birth into this embodiment is no less holy than mine. Nor will the love you extend to others be any less important than the love that has been offered to you through me. We are all doors to the infinite and eternal and each time your heart opens, Spirit makes its appearance in the world.

You are the light of the world. You are the lamb of God come to remind us that we are loved. (MOL)

The Jewel

Each of you is one facet in the many-faceted jewel of God's love and grace. Each one of you has your own simple dignity of expression.

The beauty of one facet does not interfere with the splendor of another, but adds to it in both breadth and intensity. What makes one facet shine is available to all. The light that is in me is also in you.

I am no more beloved by God than you are. This, you must come to know in your own heart. No amount of teaching or preaching will cause you to believe it. (LWOC)

A Personal Relationship

Each of you has available to you a personal relationship with me. That relationship comes into being simply as you begin to want it and trust it. There is no technology, no invocation, no esoteric spiritual practice involved in it. The simple but authentic need for my friendship is all that is required. (LWOC)

God Within Is the Only Authority

I do not wish to become an authority figure for you. Indeed, I stand against all authority save God's. I ask merely that you take my hand as an equal, and that you reach out to each one of your brothers and sisters with the same mutual respect and intention of equality.

My teaching may be simple, but it will require all of your attention, all of your energy, all of your commitment. To intend to "be equal with" each person in your experience is a revolutionary teaching. It is a teaching that will take you a lifetime of practice to master. (LWOC)

Communicating with Me

The desire to communicate with me is essential to opening the door to my presence. I will not force myself upon anyone. The relationship with me is voluntary and must be initiated by each person when s/he is ready.

I am as close to you as you would have me be. That is because I am already a thought within your mind. And everything that I am proceeds from that thought, just as everything which is not I proceeds from a different thought. This you must learn through experience.

Some claim that I speak through them, yet it is neither my voice that they hear nor my thoughts that they speak. I never condemn or make fearful. My intention is only to bless and uplift. (LWOC)

You Are Not the Body

You are not the body, for the body is born and dies. Who you are—the essential Self—is not born, nor does It die. It exists without limitation, for It is ever expanding into the formlessness of God. There is no form that can contain It.

It has joined with God in perfect forgiveness. It is free of guilt. It is free of grievances. It does not believe that It can be wronged, nor does It believe that It has the power to wrong another. (LWOC)

Thoughts

It is in your thoughts that you choose to walk with me or to walk away from me. If you would be like me, you must learn to think like me. And if you would think like me, you must place every thought you think in my hands. I will tell you if it is helpful or not. Unhelpful thoughts must be witnessed lovingly and gently released. Then, only thoughts that bless and recall you to truth will remain. (LWOC)

Surrendering to Me

Surrendering to me is unlike any act of surrender you can know in the world. For the world would use your surrender harshly to control you, but I would use it gently to release you from falsehood and give you back your true Self. (LWOC)

Those Who Work Against Me

Those who work against me find many faults with you, which they would fix. They would make you dependent on them for your salvation. Do not accept such lies. Learn to discriminate. No one on earth has a better answer for you than the one you will find through trust in yourself and in me. (LWOC)

Distortions in My Teaching

My teaching has been and will continue to be distorted because it threatens every thought that is false. And so threatened, false thoughts take hold of the teaching and seek to mold it to fit their ends. It does not take long before the words attributed to me are the opposite of the ones that I have said.

This is why I ask you to be vigilant. Do not resist this distortion, attack it or seek to discredit it, for that will just make it stronger. But be clear in your own mind and reject the false for the sake of truth.

A single false idea can bring the mind that thinks it to despair. But a single true thought restores the kingdom. (LWOC)

Inverting the Truth

You are all masters at taking truth and inverting it. You have the creative ability to make anything mean what you want it to mean. You can take yes and make it no, wrong and make it right. That is how strong your beliefs are.

But just because you have inverted truth does not mean the truth ceases to be true. It means only that you have succeeded in hiding the truth from yourself. (LWOC)

Truth Is an Open Door

Truth is a door that remains open. You cannot close this door. You can choose not to enter. You can walk in the opposite direction. But you can never say: "I tried to enter, but the door was closed." The door is never closed to you or anyone else. (LWOC)

Joy and Pain

This world is a birthing place for the emotional and mental body. Physical birth and death simply facilitate the development of a thinking/feeling consciousness that is responsible for its own creations.

It is absurd to deny the importance of this birthing work. And it is equally absurd to glorify it. Every human being who participates in the journey of birth and death experiences both joy and pain.

Are both necessary?

Absolutely. Without pain, the mother would not expel the baby from the birth canal. And without the joy of the newborn life, the pain would have no meaning.

My experience here was no different from yours. I did not conquer pain. I surrendered to it. I did not overcome death. I went willingly through it. I did not glorify the body, nor did I condemn it. I did not call this world heaven or hell, but taught that both are of your own making.

I entered the dance of life as you have entered it, to grow in understanding and acceptance, to move from conditional love to the experience of love without conditions. There is nothing that you have felt or experienced, dear brother and sister, that I have not tasted. I know every desire and every fear, for I have lived through them all. And my release from them came through no special dispensation.

You see, I am no better dancer than you are. I simply offered my willingness to participate and to learn, and that is all that I ask of you. Be willing. Participate. Touch and be touched. Feel everything. Open your arms to life. That is why you are here. (LWOC)

Walking Through the Door

An open heart and an open mind are the doors that open to love's presence. Even when the door is closed, it bids you open it. Even when you are judging and feeling separate from another, love calls to you from within.

I have told you that—no matter how many times you have refused to enter the sanctuary—you have only to knock and the door will be opened to you. I have said to you, "Ask, and it shall be given you," but you refuse to believe me. You think that someone is counting your sins, your moments of indecision or recalcitrance, but it is not true. You are the only one counting.

I say to you, brother and sister, "Stop counting, stop making excuses, stop pretending that the door is locked. I am here at the threshold. Reach out and take my hand and we will open the door and walk through together."

I am the door to love without conditions. When you walk through, you too will be the door. (LWOC)

2.

WORDS AND CONCEPTS CANNOT OPEN YOUR HEART

YOU AND GOD

You have heard me say, "I am the way, the truth and the life." That statement is equally true for you. The truth, the path to the divine, the life of the witness runs through your heart. There is no way, no truth, no life, except through you.

Please understand this. It is the core of my realization and my teaching.

God does not exist apart from you. God is the essence of your being. God dwells within your heart and within the hearts of all beings. (RTG)

Seeking God

It is not necessary to seek God, because God is already the essence of who you are. To connect with God, simply remove all judgments and thoughts that do not bless you and others. These are not your essence. They are false ideas that you carry around. They are the veils, the illu-

sions that appear to separate you from your own heart and the heart of
God. Remove the illusions, lift the veils and you will rest in the heart.
Rest in the heart, and God will abide with you. (RTG)

Healing

All healing happens thus: as illusions are surrendered, truth appears.
As separation is relinquished, the original unity emerges unchanged.
When you stop pretending to be what you are not, what you are can
be clearly seen. (RTG)

I Am an Example

I ask you to look to my example, not because I want you to worship me
or put me on a pedestal, but because I want you to understand what is
possible for you. It is through you that the word will become flesh.

I offer you a living teaching, not just a set of abstract beliefs. Following me means more than preaching my words. It means following
my example.

There is nothing special about who I am or what I have done. If
you insist on calling me "Lord," do so out of the awareness that this
same "Lord" is within you. Power is not separately vested in me or in
you, but abides in what we experience together when our hearts are
open. (RTG)

The Friend

The Friend is the Christ within you. It doesn't matter what you call
him or her. The Friend is the one who has your greatest good at heart.
The Friend is the one who also has the greatest good of others at
heart.

The Friend is the one who is free of judgment, the one who accepts you and everyone else unconditionally. This Friend is within
every mind and heart. S/He embodies essence. S/He is the voice of
God in your experience.

Some people call the Friend Christ. Some call the Friend Buddha,

Krishna, or Ram. Names do not matter. The Friend is the embodiment of love. S/He has many names and faces.

God and the Friend are always one. When you approach the Friend within, God hears your footsteps. (RTG)

The Spark of Light

Each of you has a tiny spark of light that illuminates the darkness of your unconsciousness. This divine spark of awareness keeps your connection with God alive; it connects you to the divine teacher in your tradition and to the divinity within your brothers and sisters. Were you to see only that spark of light within yourself and others, all perception of darkness in your experience would dissolve. (LWOC)

In the Beginning

In the act of Creation, love becomes embodied. Out of oneness comes diversity.

In every form born of love, the spark of love inheres. In each of the ten thousand things, the original essence remains. Thus, within your heart and mind right now is the original spark of Creation. It belongs to you and can never leave you. No matter where your life takes you, no matter how far you stray from the path, you cannot extinguish the spark of divinity within your own consciousness. It was and is God's gift to you.

You can forget about the gift but you cannot give it back. You can ignore or deny it, but you cannot un-create it. The deeper the darkness through which you walk, the more visible the tiny spark becomes. It calls to you like a beacon reminding you of your essence and your place of origin.

When you acknowledge the spark and nurture it, the light within you grows. The more attention you give to it, the more it expands until your whole being is surrounded by light. Even total strangers feel the rays of your love touching them.

You enter the spiritual path when you acknowledge the spark

within and begin to attend to it. That is the moment when you stop being a victim and begin to take full responsibility for your life. The spiritual path culminates when you fully realize your God nature and that of all the other beings around you. Then you too become the Friend, the Christ, the Buddha, the Compassionate One. (RTG)

The End of Suffering

Ultimately, the end of human suffering comes when you decide that you have suffered enough, when each of you, in your own lives, begins to ask for a better way.

Do you think the little spark in your heart will shrink and grow dim, a casualty of your fear, your guilt and your pain?

Not so!

Because the light is within you, it cannot refuse to shine when you call upon it. The light of Christ is within each one of you. Let us invoke it together, in the name of love. (LWOC)

The Dark Night of the Soul

The light of truth lives even in the darkest of places. There is no such thing as total absence of light. Darkness cannot exist except in reference to the light. No matter how great your pain, it is measured in the degree to which you feel love's absence or loss. All darkness is a journey toward light. All pain is a journey toward love without conditions.

You are here to enter the darkness you perceive in yourself and others and to find the light that lives there. Once you find the light, no matter how tiny or insignificant it seems, your life will never be the same. A light-bearer never questions the light s/he carries. And so s/he can offer it to others patiently and without fear. (MOL)

I Am Just the Messenger

Some of you think that because you have my ear you do not have to dialogue with God. That is absurd. Without God, I am nothing. It is precisely because I dwell in respect and rapture at the feet of God that I am able to extend the divine blessing to you. (MOL)

The Universal Teaching of Love

Do not make the mistake of thinking that I seek anything other than the establishment of the kingdom of love in your minds and hearts. This is my single goal.

This is also the goal of all spiritual guides. St. Francis works for this. The Baal Shem Tov works for this. Rumi works for this.

Divisions into religions are relics of the past. Such boundaries do not exist in the Christ Mind, where all beings join in this single goal. (LWOC)

Religious Tolerance

My followers practice love and forgiveness for all beings, including themselves. They embrace the Jew, the Muslim and the Hindu as their brothers. They do not seek to convert others, but rest securely in their own faith. They don't believe that those who choose a different path will be denied salvation, for they know that God has many ways of bringing us home. (LWOC)

Love Is Not Dogmatic

Anyone who practices being loving returns to the divine home. It does not matter what path s/he takes or what s/he calls it.

No one way is better than another. You will not get home faster if you believe in me than you will if you believe in Krishna or Buddha. The man or woman who loves the most makes the most progress. That is the simple truth.

Religions, sects, dogmas are nothing but obstacles on the journey home. Anyone who thinks he has the one and only truth builds his house on quicksand. It will not take long before he discovers that his pride, narrow-mindedness and lack of tolerance toward others are the cause of his undoing. (MOL)

Other Ways of Remembering

Be easy with your neighbor's form of spirituality, even if it differs substantially from your own. What helps him remember God can only benefit you.

Words and beliefs that separate you from others must be put aside. If you wish to walk a path of Grace, overlook the differences you see, find what you can share with others and focus on these things.

Truth comes in all shapes and sizes, but it remains one simple truth. You must learn to see the truth in every form, in each situation. That is what a man or woman of peace must do. (LWOC)

Universal Spiritual Experience

All forms of spiritual practice invite you to the experience of unconditional love and grace here and now. They invite you into silent communion with yourself and others. Throw out all the dogma and empty ritual and you will come to the core spiritual experience. This essential invitation to worship—to commune, to give thanks and to celebrate—is there in every tradition. (LWOC)

The Language of Love

If you are a loving person, does it matter if you are Jewish, or Muslim, or Taoist? That love expresses itself regardless of what you believe. The language of love is not a language of words.

Words and concepts will not open your heart. Only love can open your heart.

When you open to the love that is available to you and extend it freely to others, the words that you need will be given to you. You will not have to struggle to know what to say or to do.

When love is in your heart, the path opens before you. Actions flow spontaneously from you. There is no self-consciousness, ambivalence or deliberation. For these are not the qualities of love.

Love is unconditional and direct. It always finds the beloved, even when s/he is hiding. (MOL)

Love Is the Only Teacher

Love gives without thought of return. It does not ask people to change, but accepts them as they are. No one can minister in my name and withhold love and acceptance.

You must recognize your own fallibility, as I was forced to recognize mine. When you make up the rules, love is constricted or denied. No one is as great as love, not you or I.

Love is and will always be our teacher. Will we be its students and learn what it has to teach us? Or will we insist on writing the syllabus and interpreting the text? (MOL)

What Is Spirituality?

Spirituality and religion are not necessarily the same thing. Religion is the outer form; spirituality is the inner content. Religion is the husk; spirituality is the seed. Religion is a set of beliefs; spirituality is a continuum of experience.

One can be spiritual and not attend church or temple. One can find one's spirituality in intimate sharing with others, in communion with nature, in being of service. Spiritual experience is simply that which relaxes the mind and uplifts the heart. Meditating, walking in the woods or by the ocean, holding an infant or looking into a lover's eyes—these are all spiritual experiences. When there is love and acceptance in your heart, your spiritual nature is manifest and you can see the spiritual nature of other people.

To be spiritual is to see without judgment, to see not just with the eyes, but also with the heart. When you look with the heart, you see beauty everywhere, even in suffering. Wherever people are touched by the poignancy of life, there is beauty. There is beauty in the rain and clouds, and beauty in the sunlight. There is beauty in aloneness and in intimacy, in laughter and in tears.

When you look with the heart, you do not dwell on behaviors that appear to be ugly, cruel or manipulative. You know that these behaviors are coming from a lack of love. You learn to give love when it is asked for, even if it is requested in a fearful or aggressive way.

Spirituality is the consciousness that life is okay the way it is. It doesn't need to be changed or fixed. When you accept your experience, you don't hold on to the past or look for happiness in the future. You dwell in the present moment. And that is where love abides. That is where the miracle of life unfolds. (MOL)

3.

NOT ONE OF GOD'S CHILDREN IS EVIL

ACCEPT YOUR INNOCENCE

You are God's child, even as I am. All that is good and true about God is good and true about you. Accept this fact, even for an instant, and your life would be transformed. Accept this about your sister, even in this single moment, and all conflict between you would end. (LWOC)

Recognizing Goodness
Conflict is erased from the mind that recognizes its own goodness. Having recognized your goodness, you cannot maintain it except by extending that recognition to others. (LWOC)

Doubt and Fear
Your life is made up of goodness assaulted by doubt and fear. How many times during the course of a day do doubt and fear challenge your perception of your goodness? How many times do they challenge your perception of your neighbor's goodness?

Consciously acknowledge your doubts and fears instead of projecting them onto your brother or sister. Then, you will be practicing real compassion. (LWOC)

Not Judging Others
In your interactions with others, you have a simple choice: to find them innocent or to find them guilty. This choice occurs over and over again, every day, every hour, every moment. Thought by thought, you imprison other people or release them. And as you choose to treat them, so do you deliver the same judgment upon yourself. (LWOC)

Freedom
Release other people from every grievance you have toward them. Do not withhold love from them in any way. Holding them back from their happiness only pushes happiness away from you. (LWOC)

You Are the One You Judge
Every judgment you make about your brother or sister states very specifically what you cannot accept about yourself. You never judge or dislike another person unless s/he reminds you of yourself. (LWOC)

Forgiving Yourself
You have only one person to forgive in your journey and that is yourself. You are the judge. You are the jury. And you are the prisoner. (LWOC)

Withholding Forgiveness
When you withhold forgiveness from others, you also withhold it from yourself. Every nail you pound into your brother's hand holds you to the cross. (LWOC)

The Circle of Blame

There is no way out of the circle of blame but to stop blaming. (LWOC)

Looking in the Mirror

Until you look in the mirror and see your own beliefs reflected there, you will be using every brother or sister in your experience as a mirror to show you what you believe about yourself. (LWOC)

Inequality

As soon as there is the slightest perception of inequality between you and another person, you must understand that you have left your heart. You have abandoned the truth.

I have told you many times that your good and that of your brother or sister are one and the same. You cannot advance your life by hurting another, nor can you help another by hurting yourself. All attempts to break this simple equation lead to suffering and despair. (RTG)

Support and Empowerment

You cannot get to heaven by holding your brother down, nor will you get there if you try to carry him. Acknowledge your brother and bless him upon his journey. If he asks for your help, give it gladly. But do not try to do for your brother what he must do for himself. (LWOC)

The Golden Rule

Make others equally important. Do not sacrifice for them or ask them to sacrifice for you, but help them when you can and receive their help gratefully when you need it.

More than this is too much. Less than this is too little. (LWOC)

There Is No Evil

Not one of God's children can be evil. At worst he is hurt. At worst he attacks others and blames them for his pain. But he is not evil.

Yes, your compassion must go this deep. There is no human being who does not deserve your forgiveness. There is no human being who does not deserve your love. (LWOC)

Original Sin

People aren't born with error. It is something they learn. Take any baby and love it and nurture it and give it wings and it will be a beacon of love. But take the same baby and withhold love from it and refuse to encourage it, and you will be sowing the seeds of discontent. (MOL)

Admitting Your Mistakes

There is no one who does not make mistakes. Trespass, one against another, with or without intention, is commonplace.

I urge you to acknowledge your mistakes. Your awareness of your mistakes is a gift because it brings you to correction.

When you justify your mistakes, you hang on to them, forcing yourself to defend your actions over and over again. This takes a great deal of time and energy. Indeed, if you are not careful, it can become the dominant theme of your life.

Have the courage to admit your mistakes so that you can forgive them and release yourself from pain, struggle and deceit. There is no mistake that cannot be corrected. There is no trespass that cannot be forgiven. That is my teaching. (LWOC)

Being Wrong Does Not Mean Being Bad

To be mistaken is not so terrible a thing. It will not deprive you of love and acceptance. You think that it will, but that is a fiction. What deprives you of love is your insistence on being right when you are not. That prevents correction from being made.

Being wrong does not mean being "bad" and being right does not mean being "good." Every one of you will be both right and wrong hundreds of times in a single day.

This world is a school and you have come here to learn. Learning means making mistakes and correcting them. Learning does not mean being right all the time. If you were right all the time, why would you need to come to school?

Be humble, my friend. Unless you recognize that you have made a mistake, how can you correct it?

But admit your mistake and correction will be there, along with forgiveness. That is the path I have set out for you. (LWOC)

Mistakes Are Opportunities for Learning

Mistakes are opportunities for learning. To condemn your sister for making mistakes is to pretend to be mistake free, which you are not. I have asked you before and I will ask you again: Which one of you will throw the first stone?

Instead of condemning your sister for her mistakes, release her from your judgment. To release her is to love her, for it places her where love alone lies, beyond judgment of any kind. (LWOC)

Not Making Wrong

To make wrong is to teach guilt and perpetuate the belief that punishment is necessary. To make right is to teach love and demonstrate forgiveness. To put it simply, you are never right to make wrong, or wrong to make right. To be right, make right.

You cannot love in an unloving way. You can't be right and attack what's wrong. (LWOC)

Correction Is Gentle

You have heard the expression "two wrongs do not make a right." That is the essence of my teaching. All wrongs must be corrected in the right manner. Otherwise correction is attack. (LWOC)

The Willingness to Forgive

The willingness to forgive yourself and release others from your judgments is one of the greatest powers you can experience in this embodiment. The only power that is greater is the power of love itself. (LWOC)

Confession and Atonement

Why do you suppose I asked you to confess your sins? I asked you to confess your sins so that you might lighten your load and release the judgments you make about yourself and others. You cannot walk next to me so long as you carry those judgments with you. They are too heavy a load.

So confess your sins and your pain in a private place where no other man or woman enters. Forgive your mistakes. Vow to learn and to do better by yourself and others. Connect with love in the private place where you pray and confess, and take that love with you when you leave.

When you become burdened by the affairs of the world and your attachment to them, find this inner temple and take sanctuary there. Release your worries, your fears, your guilt about what you have said and done and let your heart be mended. Then you can go forth and make amends with anyone you have slighted or treated unkindly.

By confessing your sins, you free yourself from unnecessary suffering and guilt. Neither your suffering nor your guilt feeds the hungry or heals the sick.

Accept the forgiveness I offer you so that you can come back into your life with a clear vision and a strong heart. I offer you freedom, not for yourself alone, but also for the sake of those who need your love and your service.

Come and take the branch of peace and carry it forth into the neighborhoods where people need empowerment and hope. Your love can heal all the wounds of the past, if you will only believe in it. (MOL)

Divinity

You open to divinity when you see your good and that of your brother or sister as one and the same. Divinity is always shared. It is never exclusive. (LWOC)

The Power of Love

Everything in your experience can be endowed with spiritual qualities by bringing your love, acceptance or forgiveness to it. Even a terminal illness, a rape or a murder can be transformed by the power of your love. (LWOC)

Pain

Much of your pain is caused by your erroneous belief that you are cut off from the Source of love. Give up that belief and love will find you instantly. (LWOC)

The Purpose of Experience

All experience happens for one purpose only: to expand your awareness. Any other meaning you see in your life experience is a meaning that you made up. (LWOC)

The World

When you see the world in its utter neutrality, you will understand that it exists only as a tool for your learning. (LWOC)

4.

LOVE OTHERS
AS YOURSELF

LOOKING WITH YOUR HEART

Do not let the differences in your beliefs, your culture or skin color keep you apart from each other. For these things are simply exterior garments covering the truth that you are. If you want to know the truth, you must learn to look beyond appearances. You must learn to look not just with your eyes, but with your heart. When you do that, you will not see an adversary, but a brother, a sister, a friend.

When you look with the heart, you feel your friend's pain and confusion. You feel compassion for the universal experience of suffering, which you both share. From that compassion, love is born—not the love that wants to fix or change others, but the love that accepts, affirms, reaches out, befriends and empowers. (MOL)

Hold Your Brother in Your Heart
Whenever you take another person into your heart, you open the door to me as well. There is no person who is not dear to me. For I see into

the soul of both the criminal and his victim. I see both calling for love and acceptance, and I will not refuse them. Do not be shocked that I ask the same of you, who are my hands, my feet and my voice in the world. (LWOC)

To Walk with Me

To walk with me is to be a servant of God and man simultaneously. You serve man by showing him that God remembers him and cares about him. You bring him food and drink and solace in his suffering. You embrace him and allow him to lay his head on your shoulder. And you encourage him to weep, because he feels abandoned by his parents, his children, his lover and by God. And as he weeps, you comfort him. For how long has it been since you too felt abandoned and shed gut-wrenching tears of sorrow and regret?

That is the nature of the human experience. It is only appropriate that you should have compassion for your brother. For you share the same experience of suffering and you share the same release. (LWOC)

Upholding the Good of Others

To honor and care for yourself is your responsibility. But to act in a selfish way, placing your good above another's, invites conflict and resentment.

The ways of the world are harsh in this regard. One who takes advantage of others may be feared but he is not loved. When his fortune changes, which it invariably does, others are more than happy to help pull him down.

When you attack others, you must live defensively. You are always looking over your shoulder to see who or what might be sneaking up on you. Your fearful thoughts and actions call forth the fearful thoughts and actions of others. This is not a particularly satisfying or dignified way to live.

On the other hand, consider the good of others along with your own good and you feel peaceful and content. You may not have riches, but you don't have to live with regrets. (SOTH)

Not Withholding Love

Only by recognizing the worthiness of others is your own worthiness confirmed. When you withhold your love, your enemy is not the only one who is denied that blessing. You are denied it too.

So think twice before you react to someone else's trespass and cast that person out of your heart. Stand up for yourself in a loving way. Tell the person how you feel. Ask to be treated fairly. But don't attack back and don't withhold your love.

When you recognize the other person's worthiness, you establish the climate in which understanding and forgiveness thrive. Then the resentment and guilt from your mutual trespasses won't be carried into the future. (LWOC)

Love Even Your Enemy

Even those who oppose you deserve your love and your blessings. They are your absolute equals too. You cannot love me and hate them. If you hate them, then you offer me the same hatred.

There is no brother or sister who is unworthy of my love. If there were one such, then my awakening would not be complete.

That is why I have told you that there are no exceptions to the law of equality. If you would condemn any one of my brothers or sisters or withhold your love from them, then you are not following my teaching or my example. (RTG)

Unselfish Actions

When you have given birth to Christ in a single relationship with another human being, you have taken the first step into the circle of grace. Having experienced what it is like to hold one person's happiness equally with your own, you can learn to do this in other relationships.

You can practice doing unselfish acts for others without expecting anything in return. And you can experience the joy that comes from giving without strings attached.

When you give without thought of return, the law of grace manifests through you. You become the vehicle through which God's love expresses in this world.

Obviously, you cannot give unconditionally to others unless you are feeling loved yourself. True giving is an overflowing of your love. You don't feel that you are being depleted when you give in this way. In fact, you feel energized, because the love you give away returns to you through the gratitude of others whom you have touched.

Seeing the innocence and the beauty in others is the greatest gift that you can give them. When you can see that innocence and beauty not just in those who treat you well, but also in those who misunderstand or judge you, then you know that you are anchored in the consciousness of unconditional love.

My teachings are very clear on this point. Your responsibility is not just to love the people you like and admire. I ask you to love your enemies too. Indeed, there is no one who is unworthy of your love.

This is a simple, but uncompromising teaching. Recognizing that you are being challenged, you learn to dig down to find that ever-deepening Source of love within you. Those who challenge you are, in this sense, your greatest teachers. They push you to the limit, forcing you to move through your own walls of fear and judgment.

As you follow this path, you look less and less to see how you are being treated, and more and more to see how you are treating others. You learn to be loving toward others even when they are not being loving toward you. You don't focus on their words and actions. You focus on your own.

There is no greater understanding on the spiritual path than this. When you learn to respond to the fears of others in a loving way, you can be sure that your own fears rest in the most compassionate embrace. You are no longer emotionally reactive or ambivalent, but patient and steady, knowing that only love is real. Everything else is illusion. (RTG)

Turning the Other Cheek (1)

I have advised you that if someone injures you, you should turn the other cheek. This does not mean that you condone the attack or that you are inviting the other person to attack you again. Quite the contrary, by turning the other cheek, you are inviting your brother or sister to make a different choice.

Usually, your fear triggers the fear of others and their fear triggers yours. Often you think your opponents are blocking your access to the love you want. In fact, they are the doorways to the love that you want.

Your enemy is your ally in disguise. If you offer your enemy love, you will make peace not only with him or her, but with yourself as well.

Attack happens because you dehumanize the object of your attack. The more you see each other's humanness with compassion, the more difficult it will be for you to attack each other.

To turn the other cheek does not mean that you refuse to stand up against injustice. Quite the contrary. I encourage you to oppose injustice wherever you encounter it. Take issue with actions that are uncaring, hurtful, disrespectful to you or others, but do so in a loving way. Do so in a way that respects the people whose actions you oppose. For they are your brothers and sisters too. (RTG)

Don't Play At Being a Victim

Don't play at being a victim. It is a game of mirrors, in which the one who trespasses on you is but a reflection of your own lack of self-worth, as you are a reflection of his. Holding grievances against him will not help you.

Do not hold him to you with thoughts of retribution, but release him with love, knowing that as you release him, you release yourself. (LWOC)

Turning the Other Cheek (2)

When I said to turn the other cheek, I instructed you to demonstrate to your brother that he could not hurt you. If he cannot hurt you, he cannot be guilty for his attack on you. And if he is not guilty, then he does not have to punish himself.

When you turn your cheek, you are not inviting your brother to hit you again. You are reminding him that there is no injury. You are telling him that you know that you cannot be unfairly treated. You are demonstrating to him your refusal to accept attack, for you know you are worthy and lovable in that moment. And knowing your worthiness, you cannot fail to see his. (LWOC)

Love Your Enemy

I did not tell you to "love your enemy" to be perverse or difficult. I said this for an important reason. It is easy for you to love your friend. Most of the time your friend agrees with you and supports you. So it is not hard to love him.

But your enemy disagrees with you. He believes that you are wrong. He sees your weaknesses and would do his best to exploit them. If you have a blind spot, you can be sure he sees it. To put it simply, your enemy is not willing to give you the benefit of the doubt. He is therefore your very best teacher.

Your enemy reflects back to you everything that you do not like about yourself. He shows you exactly where your fears and insecurities lie. If you listen to what your enemy is saying to you, you will know exactly where you are in need of healing. Only one who opposes you thus can be such an effective teacher.

When you learn to love your enemy, you demonstrate your willingness to look at all of the dark places within your mind. Your enemy is a mirror into which you look until the angry face that you see smiles back at you. (LWOC)

Making Peace with Your Enemy

Peace does not come through the agreement of egos, for it is impossible for egos to agree. Peace comes when love and mutual respect are present.

When love is present, your enemy becomes like a friend who is not afraid to disagree with you. You do not cast her out of your heart just because she sees things differently from you. You listen carefully to what she has to say.

The cause of human conflict is simple: people dehumanize each other. Each side sees the other side as unworthy. As long as people who disagree perceive each other this way, even the simplest details cannot be negotiated. But let each person bring to the other the attitude of respect and acceptance, and even difficult details can be resolved. In human affairs, the willingness to love—to regard each other as equals—is the essence behind all miracle-making. (LWOC)

Answering the Call for Love

When your brother acts inappropriately toward you, you turn away from him. You withhold your love from him.

Your brother only wants your love, but he does not know how to ask for it. Indeed, he is confused about what love is. So he asks for money, or sex, or something else. He tries to manipulate you to get what he wants.

Of course, you don't want to be manipulated. You don't want to reinforce his inappropriate behavior by giving in to his demands. But you don't want to reject him either. So what do you do?

You say "yes" to loving him and "no" to being manipulated. You say "no" to his demands, but you do not cast him out of your heart. You do not judge him, or separate from him. You refuse to be a victim or a victimizer. You offer him love in response to his fearful thoughts.

You say: "No, friend, I cannot give you what you ask, but I will find a way to support you that affirms both of us. I will not reject you. I will not pretend that you are less worthy than I am. Your need for love is as important as mine and I honor it."

This is how the lover talks to the beloved. He does not say, "I will do anything you want." He says, "I will find a way to honor us both." The lover is equal to the beloved. They are the mutual expression of love. (LWOC)

Love Without Conditions

If loving others is based on agreeing with them, there will be very few people you can love. Fortunately, love runs deeper than that.

When you love without conditions, you support the freedom of others to choose their own way, even when you disagree with them. You trust them to make the best choice for themselves. You trust God's plan for their awakening. You know that they can never make a mistake that will cut them off from God's love or from yours. (LWOC)

Forgiving the Criminal

If you can forgive yourself for having thoughts of revenge, why can't you forgive the man or woman who acts with vengeance?

I am not justifying the act of vengeance. I cannot justify any attack, nor do I suggest that you do. I am simply asking you, "Why do you cast this brother out of your heart? He is perhaps even more desperate for love and forgiveness than you are. Would you withhold it from him?"

Your brother has been wounded deeply. He has grown up without a father. He has been addicted to drugs since he was nine years old. And he has lived in a ghetto where he has never felt safe. Do you not feel some compassion for the wounded boy in the man who commits the crime?

If you were to step into his shoes, would you do that much better? Be honest, my friend. And in that honesty, you will find compassion, if not for the man, for the boy who became the man.

And I will tell you right now it is not the man who pulls the trigger, but the boy. It is the boy who is overwhelmed and scared. It is the little one who does not feel loved and accepted. It is the wounded boy who strikes out, not the man.

Do not let your sight be distorted by the angry, disdainful face of the man. Beneath that hard exterior is overwhelming pain and self-judgment. Beneath the mask of mismanaged manhood and vicious anger is the boy who does not believe he is lovable.

If you cannot embrace the boy in him, how can you embrace the boy or the girl in yourself? For his/her fear and yours are not so different.

Let the boy or girl in you look out at the boy or girl in the criminal, the outcast, the homeless person. That is where love and acceptance begin. That is where forgiveness has its roots. (LWOC)

Untouchables

Criminals are just one group of untouchables in your society. You do not want to look at their lives. You do not want to hear about their pain. You want to put them away where you do not have to deal with them. You do the same with the elderly, the mentally ill, the homeless and so forth.

You see, my friend, you do not want the responsibility to love your sister. Yet without loving her, you cannot learn to love and accept yourself. Your sister is the key to your salvation. She always was and always will be.

Just as the individual denies and represses the negative tendencies she does not want to accept in herself, society denies and institutionalizes the problems it does not want to face. Both the individual and collective unconscious are filled with unspeakable wounds.

Forgiveness brings a searchlight into these dark, secret places in self and society. It says to guilt and fear "Come out and be seen. I need to understand you." And it says to the criminal "Come out, meet the victims of your crime, make amends, begin the process of healing."

Acknowledging the wound is always the first step in the healing process. If you are not willing to face the fear behind the wound, individually and collectively, the healing process cannot begin.

It is hard for you to look at your own repressed pain. It is hard for society to look at the pain of its outcasts. But this must be done.

Everybody lives in a prison of reactivity until the wound is made conscious. It is not just the criminal who is behind bars. The men and women who put him there live behind different bars.

If you don't bring your unconscious material into awareness it will express on its own distorted terms. If you don't work intentionally with the criminal to help him come to love and accept himself, he will re-enter society with the same anger and vindictiveness.

Building more prisons or putting more police on the streets will not make your neighborhoods safer. These actions just exacerbate the situation by raising the level of fear.

If you want to improve these situations, bring the work of forgiveness into the prisons and the neighborhoods. Hire more teachers and counselors and social workers. Feed people, challenge them emotionally and mentally. Offer them experiences of safe emotional bonding. Provide them with opportunities for education and training. Give them hope. Give them acceptance. Give them love.

And please remember, in giving to others, you will be giving to yourself. Nobody gives love without receiving it. Nobody gives a gift he does not simultaneously receive.

It is time that you stopped trying to punish the sinner in yourself and the criminal in your society. Punishment simply reinforces rejection. That is the opposite of what is needed.

Those who strike out at others feel that they have no choice. This is the key. Show them the choices they have and they will not commit crimes.

The only way out of the vicious cycle of violence is for society to drop the agenda of ostracism and punishment and commit to healing. Every person in pain must be asked to help himself. He must be helped to consciously identify his unworthiness and guilt. And he must be assisted in transforming these negative emotions and beliefs about himself into positive ones.

The lepers of your society are no different from the lepers of my time. They bear everyone's wounds on their skin. They are bold witnesses to the pain you do not want to deal with. Society should be grateful to them, for they are way-showers. They point to the path of healing all human beings must take. (LWOC)

Redemption, Not Punishment

Your "eye for an eye" system of justice perpetuates the cycle of abuse. By making the perpetrator into a victim, you hope to discourage him from brutalizing others in the future. You don't understand that all of his rage comes from his perception of himself as a victim and it is that which you are reinforcing by punishing him.

If you want to change the criminal, you must stop punishing him and begin to love him. Nothing else will work.

Love is not a reward for his trespass. It is the redeemer of his soul. It recalls him to himself. It shifts him out of the reactive cycle in which he dehumanizes himself and others. In the face of genuine love and caring, even the most vicious criminal softens.

You cannot stop hate by fighting it with revenge. Every act of violence begets a counter-act. By now you should know this.

The only approach that can bring freedom from violence is one that is itself free of violence. Only a spiritual solution works. You can't solve a problem on the level on which you perceive it. You must go to a higher level, see the big picture, see the cause of the problem and address that. (SOTH)

Resist Not Error

To oppose, seek to overpower or argue with a false idea is to strengthen it. That is the way of violence. My way, on the other hand, is nonviolent. It demonstrates the answer in its approach to the problem. It brings love, not attack, to the ones in pain. Its means are consistent with its ends. (LWOC)

The Root of Error

The root of error is fear, and love is the only response that undoes fear. This is true, not so much because love is an antidote to fear, but because fear is "the absence of love." It therefore cannot exist whenever love is present. (LWOC)

The Myth of Evil

You perceive certain people as evil and, indeed, their actions seem to confirm this. But, although their actions may be unloving and cruel, they are not evil.

If you can change the consciousness of a person so that his actions are loving instead of unloving, is he evil? Of course not! Therefore, you must allow for the possibility of redemption.

"So," you ask, "how do you deal with people who cause suffering for others?"

You ask them to be responsible for their actions, but you don't seek to reinforce their guilt. You don't want them to believe that they are evil. Instead, you tell them that they are essentially "good." You tell them that they are mistaken about who they are. Others are mistaken too. Those who abused, neglected or humiliated them did not know who they were. But you know. And you are willing to treat them in a respectful way and help them rebuild their lives.

Can you imagine your society saying this to its hardened criminals: its rapists and murderers? Yet that is what it must do or it will reinforce their guilt and keep the cycle of violence intact.

If you want someone to act in a loving way, you must be willing to love him. Only your love for him will teach him the meaning of love. Empty words and promises will not do.

You, my friend, must learn to love your enemy—the one on whom you project your own fears and inadequacies—the one you blame for your problems. In each devil you perceive, there is an angel you must discover, an angel who has fallen and needs your love to ascend. When you offer that love, you will find that you too have risen.

Don't wait for heaven to come to spread your love around. Do it now. For heaven is here right now. It is in your eyes when you see with acceptance and compassion. It is in your hands when you reach out to help. It is in your mind when you see good instead of evil. (MOL)

An Open Heart

You can't find peace in the world. You can find it only in your heart, when it is open.

An open heart invites the beloved in. It invites the stranger in, and yes, even the criminal. An open heart is a sanctuary where all are welcome. It is a temple where the laws of Spirit are practiced and celebrated. It is the church you must enter again and again to find redemption.

Crucifixion happens when your heart closes to your brother. Resurrection happens when you open your heart to him, when you stop blaming him for your problems and punishing him for his mistakes, when you learn to love him as you love yourself. Only this will bring release from the prison of fear. Only this!

Love is the only miracle. All other "miracles" are frosting on the cake. Look beneath the surface of every one of them and you will see a shift from fear to love, from self-protection to self-expansion, from judgment of others to acceptance of them.

Love says: "I accept you as you are. I consider your good equally with my own." Do you have any idea how powerful this statement is? To every person you address in this way, you offer freedom from suffering. And by offering it to him, you offer it to yourself.

If you do not seek equality, then you will never learn how to give love without conditions. If you do not offer equality, you will never learn how to receive unconditional love.

What you seek, you will find. As you offer, so will you receive. The law has not changed. (SOTH)

5.

RELATIONSHIP AS A

SPIRITUAL PATH

TRUE EQUALITY

True equality requires individuation. Until you know the contours of your own heart you can't learn those of another. So don't leave home before you are ready. Don't become entangled in relationships before you know who you are or your chances of waking up are not strong.

The world will be only too happy to give you a role and a responsibility. Other people will be only too happy to assign you a role in their drama. Let's face it, some roles are seductive. They promise a lot. It's hard to say no.

"Leave your lonely wilderness and come and live with me. I will love you and take care of you." These are the words the homeless child has been waiting to hear. At last, direction has come. The missing parent has materialized. All will be well. Or will it?

Hardly! Rather, this is how the self is betrayed.

Live with someone before you have learned to live with yourself and you will make a mockery of relationship. Find home inside your heart first.

Only one who knows and accepts herself can find equality with another. Anyone else gives herself away. And then she wakes up and wonders, "Why did I trade one dream for another? The original dream was lonely, but it was on track."

Unless you commit to your own awakening, others can offer you only detours, side trips, running in place. Time goes by, but nothing changes. The pain doesn't lift. The old dissatisfaction is still there.

The sheets have been changed, but the bed still sags. The problem is not a cosmetic one. The problem is in the foundation itself. That is what must be addressed.

Your dissatisfaction says one thing and one thing only: "You are not honoring yourself." If you were honoring yourself, there would be energy and commitment to a vision in your life. You would not be bored. You would not be lonely. You would not be anxious to trade your dream for someone else's.

You are the one, my brother or sister, who opts for the detour. Don't blame the companion who accompanies you. It is not her fault. It is not his fault.

It was simply your choice. Don't beat yourself up over it. Make a different choice. Choose to honor yourself, to step fully into your life.

When you fully inhabit your life, you are drawn to others who are doing the same thing. Then, one person does not have to give up his life for another. Both people can be in their lives and explore how it feels to come together. That is the beginning of a different dance, a dance that happens only when both people are congruent and living in their own truth. (SOTH)

Not Giving Yourself Away

There is a tendency when people go into relationship to "go limp," the way an animal goes limp when it is caught by a predator. There is a kind of "false surrender," a giving away of one's power to the other person. This sets the stage for later violation.

I urge you to go slowly and consciously into relationships so that you do not give yourself away. The desire to please the other, to be liked and accepted, to be loved and adored easily and quickly crosses the line and becomes self-betrayal.

You must realize that relationships can be addictive. They can offer you the opportunity to escape from self, to avoid feeling your feelings.

If you are unhappy with your life, a relationship may provide a temporary escape from your troubles, but sooner or later your problems will return. When they do, the demands and expectations of your partner will not make them any easier to deal with.

The emotional high of a new relationship promises more than it can ever deliver. If you experience "falling in love," you can be sure that you will experience "falling out of love." The very expression "falling in love" should tell you that this experience is about self-betrayal.

In what other area of life would you allow yourself "to fall" and be whimsical about it? The whole romantic tradition suggests a socially acceptable, nearly institutionalized form of self-betrayal.

Just as the child creates a false self to cope with the unreasonable demands and expectations placed on him early in life, so does the adult create a "false surrender" to a lover to ease the pain of personal and social isolation. The reason the surrender is false is that it does not withstand the eruption of the dark side. As soon as unconscious fears arise in the partners, the feeling of "being in love" quickly disappears.

A conscious partnership is at odds with "falling in love," because it is not a giving away of oneself. It is rather a commitment to be present with oneself and the other person through the ups and downs of experience.

Most relationships fall apart as soon as trouble comes along. The promise "to have and to hold, in sickness and in health" is for most people an exercise in absurdity, for many people go to the altar without having taken the time to get to know each other.

For this reason, formal marriage should be discouraged until couples have lived together for at least three years. During this time they can discover if they have a mutual commitment to be present for each other.

Most relationships will not survive this three-year period of mutual exploration. Indeed, many relationships do not survive the "falling in love" stage. That is because many relationships are initiated by the mutual desire of the partners to "feel good" and avoid the pain, fragmentation and isolation of self. As soon as two people encounter their differences and reveal their fears, they stop "feeling good" all the time. They experience emotional ups and downs in the relationship just as they did when they were alone. If they are afraid to face their inner conflict and ambivalence, they are likely to leave the relationship and begin looking for a new person to fall in love with. This is clearly an addictive pattern.

Relationship is never a panacea for the wounds and traumas of the individual psyche. At best, it is an incubation chamber.

Emotional safety is not to be found in most relationships, which end in mutual distrust and/or abandonment. Yet when you "fall in love," you have the expectation that your partner is offering you not only safety, but perpetual bliss.

If there ever were a setup in life, this would have to be it! The question, of course, is how do you avoid this scenario of "falling in love" and betraying yourself?

The answer is to go into relationship with open eyes, seeing not just what you want to believe, but the fears and judgments that arise too. By staying awake through the process, you can avoid the pain and disappointment of waking up a month or a year later and finding out that the relationship was just a self-created fantasy.

It all comes down to one question: "How honest are you willing to be?" Are you willing to be with your feelings and tell the truth to yourself? Are you willing to be with your feelings and tell the truth to your partner?

All masks must be peeled away if you are to stand face-to-face.

Until then, this is just a carnival, the sad ending of which has been temporarily forgotten. (SOTH)

Commitment to Self Attracts the Beloved

There is only one way that you will find genuine fulfillment in your life and that is to learn to love and accept yourself. With that as a foundation, relationships cease to be traumatic. Perhaps that is because one does not bring such intense expectations to them.

If you want to dance with another, root yourself first. Learn to hear your own guidance. Dialogue with the hurt child and the divine host within. Practice forgiveness and compassion for yourself. Be with your experience and learn from it.

Stay in the rhythm of your life. Be open to others, but do not go out of your way to find them. Those who know how to dance will meet you halfway. It will not be a struggle.

Sometimes you are attracted into relationships that are inappropriate for you to be in. Such relationships exacerbate the abuse patterns of the past. Learning in such meetings is painful. A better choice can and should be made. But in order to make that choice, you must be able to ask unabashedly for what you want. If you let another dictate the terms of the relationship, don't be surprised if you remain stuck in a situation that does not honor you.

You know what feels good to you and what does not. Say what you need, speak your truth and be firm in your commitment to your own healing. Only through your commitment to honor yourself can you attract a partner willing to do the same.

These are simple truths, but they are not practiced. Over and over again, you compromise, play by other people's rules, and betray yourself. By now, you should be tired of repeating the lesson and exacerbating the wound.

I will say this to you as clearly as I can: If you do not take care of yourself, nobody else will take care of you. Your lack of love and commitment to yourself attracts people with similar lessons into your vibrational field. Then you simply mirror back to each other that lack of self-understanding and self-commitment.

Few meet the beloved in this life, for few have learned to honor themselves and heal from the inside out. However, you can be one of these few if you are willing to commit to your own healing.

Take this simple vow: I pledge that I will no longer betray myself in any relationship. I will communicate how I think and feel honestly, with compassion for the other, but without attachment to how s/he receives my communication. I trust that by telling the truth and honoring myself, I am in communion with the beloved. I will no longer try to "make a relationship work" by sacrificing myself to try to meet my partner's needs. (SOTH)

Choosing a Partner

Nothing is more confusing in a relationship than the cycle of mutual, reactive projections. While the mirroring process—seeing your own fears in the other person—may be helpful, most people are not aware enough to use this kind of feedback skillfully. For most people, projection results not in greater consciousness, but in greater unconscious reactivity. While the pain of this may eventually lead to greater consciousness, there are gentler ways to learn.

To learn gently, choose a partner who does not push all of your buttons at once. Choose a partner who desires a conscious relationship and is willing to take responsibility for facing his or her fears. Choose a partner you like and respect, a partner who can hold a safe, loving space for you. Do not settle for less. (SOTH)

Notice the Unassuming One

If you want to succeed in your relationships with others, take the time to get to know yourself. Then it will be clear when and to whom you must say no and when and to whom you can say yes. Remember, what comes to you is not always what it seems. The knight in shining armor may be an insecure abuser in disguise and the one offering comfort and support may be a wolf in sheep's clothing.

Always look beyond appearances, for nothing is as it seems to be. When you know what you want and what you need, be patient and wait for it. Many will come to you claiming to be the one you asked for, but only one will be authentic. Usually, it won't be the one who comes with lots of smoke and mirrors. More often than not, it will be the simple unassuming one, the one who doesn't use big words or promise great gifts, but who takes your hand and looks into your eyes without fear. (MOL)

A Spiritual Partnership

Imagine living with another person without trying to change him or her in any way. Imagine that your only calling is to accept where that person is, at any time, and to accept where you are in that same moment. Imagine not having to put pressure on others to meet your needs or expectations and knowing that others will not put pressure on you.

Imagine feeling connected in your heart to your partner in the same way that you feel connected to your own breathing. When your breath becomes shallow, you automatically become aware of it and take a deep breath. When your attention to your partner becomes attenuated, you make eye contact and allow the mutual consciousness of your love to flow back between your hearts.

Imagine that your relationship is a continual dance in which moving in a complementary way is the only goal. Each one of you is constantly making little adjustments so that you can stay together in a comfortable way. None of these adjustments takes much thought. It is just what you do when you are dancing.

Imagine a dance in which each person takes turns leading. Sometimes one person feels the music more deeply than the other and takes the lead. Another time the other person is more tuned in and leads the way. This happens by itself, out of the mutual regard and attunement of the partners, not because of some prearranged agreement about "equal time."

Imagine feeling that your most profound gift as a human being is to honor your partner with every breath and every step. Imagine considering your partner's thoughts and feelings every time you consider your own.

Imagine having a "we" awareness, where you once had an "I" awareness. Imagine being as devoted to your partner's comfort, pleasure and well-being as you are to your own.

Imagine not disconnecting from your partner as a way of connecting with yourself. Imagine understanding that any disconnection with your partner is a disconnection with yourself.

Your unconditional love and acceptance of your partner is your best and easiest pathway to God-communion. With your partner, you learn to be both lover and beloved. You learn to give and receive unconditional love and acceptance.

When you have learned to do this with one person, you become capable of doing it with all people. That is when Christ is born in you. Then, no one can be excluded from your love. What you give to one, you give to all.

The Christ Mind is the end of separate thoughts, separate agendas, separate wills. The Christ Heart is the end of disparate feelings and special love. The Christ Consciousness has one thought, one agenda, one will, one love for all beings.

But none of this will mean anything to you until you learn to love one person as you love yourself. So choose your partner well. If you choose one who dances too slowly, you may be held back. If you choose one who dances too fast, you may break your ankle trying to keep up with him or her.

Find a partner who dances at the same speed that you do, one who will complement you and help you realize your potential. Find a partner you can empower and assist. Then, together you can help each other anchor in the truth of your experience. (MOL)

Autonomy and Shared Vision in Relationship

If you do not do what is necessary to create and maintain your happiness, who will do it? Do you expect your partner to do it?

Of course not! You must make your own choices. You are responsible for your own happiness.

So give yourself permission to move toward your joy and express your gifts. Your willingness to do this is essential to your creative fulfillment. Nobody else can do this for you, not even your partner.

In a healthy relationship, both people support each other in taking responsibility for their own happiness and creative fulfillment. They offer each other encouragement and positive feedback. And then they let go. They trust the other person to find her own way. They don't judge her goals or interfere with her attempts to realize them.

In a healthy relationship, people are not enmeshed in each other's creative process. Even when they work together, they find a way to support each other's autonomy.

Unless each person has this autonomy and the time and space to grow, he won't command his partner's respect. But autonomy is only one ingredient. Equally important is a shared vision.

Both people must have dreams, values and aspirations that they hold in common. They must have a vision of a shared life in which they move together as a couple.

When either the autonomy or the shared vision of the partners is weak, the relationship will not prosper. In some relationships, the shared vision is strong, but the autonomy is not sufficient. The couple does not thrive because the individuals are not being challenged to grow. In other relationships, autonomy is strong, but the shared vision and experience is weak. The partners express themselves well as individuals, but do not spend sufficient time together. Their emotional connection is attenuated, and they begin to lose sight of their reason for being together.

Neither of these extremes is helpful. Partners need to work both on expressing themselves as individuals, as well as on expressing their sense of common purpose. In a healthy partnership, the commitment to self and the commitment to the relationship are equal in depth and intensity. (MOL)

The Challenge of a Spiritual Relationship

It is tragic when two people stay together without individuating. It is equally tragic when people stay together without ever creating a shared purpose.

One should not have to sacrifice becoming an authentic person in order to create a shared purpose with another. Nor should one have to sacrifice creating a shared reality in order to pursue one's own creative potential. These are not mutually exclusive propositions. They are inclusive and contemporaneous ones. Much of the tension and therefore challenge in relationship lies in the attempt to honor and balance these equally important commitments.

While each one of you must learn to love and accept yourself, this is only half of your purpose here. The other half is to learn to extend that love and acceptance to another person. You are asked not only to give yourself permission to move toward your joy in spite of the obstacles that are placed in your way, but also to give your partner permission and support to move toward his or her joy, regardless of its perceived impact on you.

To pretend that any of this is easy is absurd. There are lifelong lessons here to which each person must submit in order to find fulfillment and completion.

Relationships offer you a profound spiritual path. Your partner is not only your friend, your lover and your companion, but also your teacher. S/he reflects back to you all the beauty that lies within you, as well as all the fear, doubt and ambivalence which lies buried deeply within your soul. As you come to accept your partner's apparent imperfections, you begin to address your own unacknowledged fears.

There is perhaps no more rapid path to psychological wholeness and spiritual awakening than the path of relationship. It is also one of the most challenging paths.

You must be realistic if you choose to walk this path. While your partnership may occasionally be fun and free of pain—and this is a great goal to aspire to—there may be just as many times when you and your partner are wounded and defensive. Your great accomplishment as a couple is not your ability to navigate around your pain, but your ability to move through your pain together without making the other person responsible for it.

By all means have fun together and celebrate each other's beauty. But do not think you have failed when your fears come up and you begin to see each other as adversaries rather than friends. For this is the moment when your real work together begins. If you can do this work of inner and outer reconciliation, while still holding on to your joy and mutual reverence, you will build a union which is strong and deep. This is the ground love must be anchored in to grow its brightest flower. (MOL)

Asking Your Partner for What You Want

You cannot force another person to love you the way you want to be loved. Demanding specific expressions of love will only make it more difficult for others to respond to you in good faith.

To be sure, you can ask for what you want. However, once you have communicated what you want, give your partner the time and the space to honor your request to the best of his or her ability.

Don't find fault with your partner's efforts to please you because they aren't perfect or don't match your pictures of the way things should be. Praise your partner's efforts. That makes it easier for him or her to give to you.

When you don't receive what you asked for, acknowledge what you did receive, and ask again for what you did not receive. Ask in a kind and respectful way, anticipating that your partner would love to be able to please you. Then, give your partner the time and space to respond to you in an authentic way. (MOL)

Choosing Whether or Not to Stay Together

Sometimes you can ask in all the right ways, and your partner is still unable to respond to you. When you know you have done your part to communicate your wants and surrender your expectations, you must face the fact that your partner may be unwilling or unable to meet your needs. Usually, when your partner is honest with you, you find that s/he shares your disappointment and frustration.

In this case, you have a choice. You can part ways and look for another partner who might be more responsive to you. Or you can renew your commitment to your present partner with an increased willingness to love and accept him or her as s/he is. The latter choice is generally the preferred one, since most relationships can be moved to higher ground when both people stop focusing on what they are not receiving from each other, and instead focus on what they can give to each other.

In the event you and your partner decide to separate, please do so in a loving way, without holding on to resentments or grievances. Send each other love and support as often as possible. It is not easy when a relationship ends or changes form, and gentleness on both sides is extremely important if healing is to happen for both people.

When you complete a relationship, consider what you have learned from the other person and be grateful for your experience together. Be cognizant of the issues that separated you and take responsibility for your part in them. When you begin another relationship, be aware of how similar issues arise and see if you can deal with these issues in a more generous and responsible way. Moreover, consider the possibility that something needs to shift inside of you before these issues can be resolved in the context of a relationship. (MOL)

Relationship as a Spiritual Path

Some of you think you can be happier with someone else than you can be with yourself. If you think about it, this expectation is unrealistic.

The truth is that you can be only as happy with another person as you can be with yourself. If you like who you are, being with your partner can be an extension of your happiness. But, if you do not like yourself, being with your partner can only exacerbate your unhappiness.

Your decision to enter into partnership should not be based on a desire to avoid looking at yourself, but on a willingness to intensify that process. When you live with other people, you are likely to trigger their unhealed wounds and they are likely to trigger yours.

Becoming aware of the unhealed parts of you is neither pleasant nor easy. However, it is a necessary part of the journey to psychic wholeness.

While you may be able to avoid looking at the unconscious aspects of your psyche while living alone, you won't be able to avoid looking at them when you are in relationship. Relationship is like a giant backhoe. It digs down through the superficial layers of consciousness and exposes your deepest fears and insecurities.

If you aren't willing to look this deeply, you might want to question your desire to be in an intimate relationship. You can't get close to another person without coming face-to-face with yourself. (RTG)

6.

HEALING TOGETHER
AND APART

MARRIAGE IS NOT A TIE THAT BINDS

All committed relationships have one thing in common: you wish the best for your partner. You are willing even to give your partner up if s/he could thereby find a greater happiness. Contrary to popular belief, marriage is not a tie that binds but one that releases.

You want the greatest happiness for your partner in the same way that you want the greatest happiness for yourself. You love your partner as you love yourself, with an equal love.

Your partner's needs are as important as your own. Not more important. Not less important. But equally important.

Marriage is not a promise to be together throughout all eternity, for no one can promise that. It is a promise to be present "now." It is a vow that must be renewed in each moment if it is to have meaning.

In truth, you can be married in one moment and not in the next. Marriage is a process, a journey of becoming fully present to yourself and your partner. (SOTH)

Dealing with Your Partner's Negative States

When your partner is happy and loving toward you, it is easy to think positively about your relationship. But when s/he is drained, introspective, expressing negative thoughts and emotions, it is not so easy to stay positive.

When your partner finds fault with you or withholds love from you, realize that s/he does not feel loved. That isn't your fault and you don't have to accept blame for it. But try not to react to your partner's negativity. Be as patient and as loving as you can be in that moment.

If you can't be patient and loving, excuse yourself from the situation. Go into another room. Take a walk by yourself. And work on bringing love and acceptance to yourself. When your love for yourself fills you up, you can reconnect with the other person.

Remember, love does not complain, argue or blame. Love simply embraces the other exactly as s/he is. Love overlooks fear, because fear is not ultimately real. It is a temporary wrinkle in the fabric of life. Wrinkles do not last forever. In the next moment the fabric can be pulled tight and the wrinkles will disappear. Love honors the fabric and knows that it is flexible enough to adjust to new conditions.

No partner is happy all of the time. Don't allow your happiness to be dependent on your partner's happiness. That will just drag both of you down. Tend to your own garden, and offer your partner a rose to smell. Refusing to tend your garden and complaining that your partner never gives you roses will not make either one of you feel better.

When one person is cranky or sad, the other must dig deep inside to find the source of love. When she finds the light within, she must carry it for both people for a while. That way the other person does not forget that the light is there, even if he can't see it in himself.

This does not mean that one person should do all the supporting. Relationships require a give-and-take. But it does mean that there will be times when each partner will have to rise to the occasion and maintain the connection to Source in the face of the other person's fear and mistrust. That is never an easy thing to do. But it is often necessary in the course of a committed relationship. (MOL)

Working Through Conflict

As soon as you and your partner feel separate from each other, correction is needed. It's time to stop, take a deep breath, step back and look at what's happening.

Don't blame yourself or the other person. Don't try to be right or make the other person wrong. Just acknowledge the separation you feel and understand that it cannot be bridged while fear is coming up for you.

Take some time alone and get clear about what you are afraid of, what you feel you need to defend, what your hurt or anger is about. And try to tune into what positive reassurance or affirmation you need from your partner. Then, when you are both feeling peaceful, take turns asking each other directly for the desired validation.

Almost all fear, anger and hurt stem from the fact that you're feeling unloved or unappreciated. When someone acts in a way that triggers you, you usually interpret that behavior as meaning that the person doesn't care. Then, if you react in a hurt or angry way, the other person feels invalidated by you. The downward spiral of mutual attack and invalidation continues until you are both thoroughly disgusted with each other.

When you recognize that you and your partner are moving into the game of "I'll hurt you because you hurt me," you must stop immediately. Tell your partner, "I don't want to do this. Let's take some time to tune into what's going on inside before this situation escalates beyond control and we turn off our love completely."

Just stop and say, "I'm going to take a walk. I'll be back when I understand better what's happening inside. I want to talk with you when I'm feeling okay, not when I'm feeling hurt or angry."

When you walk, realize that what you are feeling—unloved and unappreciated—goes very deep. It is not just a response to this particular incident with your partner. It is a response to every experience you've ever had in which you felt attacked, judged, rejected, abandoned or betrayed. When the emotional body is triggered, even though the trigger seems insignificant, many past memories and levels of experience are contacted. The sadness that comes from feeling the loss of love can be intense.

Obviously, your partner is not responsible for the depth of sadness you feel. S/he was just the trigger. So take him or her off the hook, and see that the job of bringing love to the sad and wounded parts of you belongs primarily to you. Spend some time being gentle and loving with yourself. Understand that all you want from your partner is reassurance that s/he loves you and wants to be with you. When you return to your partner, ask for that reassurance. Ask for specific words that will help you remember that you are loved. Ask for a hug, some cuddling, a back rub or some eye contact.

Listen to what your partner needs from you. And remember, the issue is always that s/he needs to feel loved and accepted by you, whatever the specific request for validation is.

When you and your partner have difficulty validating each other, the relationship goes into crisis. When you criticize and invalidate each other, negative patterns are set into motion which destroy the trust and block the love you have for each other.

There are many times in the course of a relationship when you and your partner may appear to want different things. But that is just the symptom of a more radical problem. If you look deeply enough, you will see that neither one of you feels validated by the other.

When love is present in your relationship, the question is always "What are *we* going to do?" not "What am I going to do?" You and your partner are committed to finding a shared reality and staying connected to your love for each other. In the process, you grow beyond narrow self-interest and learn to serve the higher purpose of your union. (MOL)

Forgiveness

In any intimate relationship, no matter how good it is, people forget to honor each other. They get stressed out and project their pain onto each other. They attack and defend, give and receive guilt, and generally make a mess of things. I want you to know this not so you can make excuses for yourself, but so you will not give up on your relationship when it is asking you to grow in wisdom and emotional strength.

Since there are no perfect partners out there, your challenge is to accept and honor the imperfect one who stands before you and, yes, to honor yourself, even though your life also is riddled with mistakes. If you and your partner can forgive each other's transgressions and reestablish your trust in each other, then you can deepen in your love and your capacity for intimacy.

Anyone can enter into relationship. Falling in love is easy, especially when hormones are at work. And leaving isn't much harder, especially when people are blindly projecting their fears onto each other. But what most people don't seem to be willing to do is to practice forgiveness together. And that is why so many partnerships fail.

Forgiveness is the key to success in every relationship. Indeed, if you and another person are committed to practicing forgiveness you can live together successfully, even if you don't have a lot in common.

On the other hand, if the two of you are not willing to practice forgiveness, then nothing you try will work. No, not religion, or psychotherapy or relationship workshops.

If you decide to leave one relationship because you are unwilling to forgive, what makes you think that you can succeed in another? It's true, people are different and some people push your buttons more than others, but everyone is imperfect and everyone is going to push your buttons at one time or other. Your ability to create a successful relationship depends not so much on your choice of partner, but on your willingness to forgive yourself and the partner you choose.

By all means, hold out for the partner you want. Insist on common goals, shared interests and mutual attraction. Abandon any relationship that promises to be abusive, even though you might eventually learn something there. Don't play the game of love with half a deck.

But realize, my friends, that no matter how well or how poorly you choose a mate, the practice of forgiveness will be necessary. It is the one constant. It is the key to your ultimate happiness and that of your partner.

Through the practice of forgiveness, imperfect people become whole, and broken relationships are healed and strengthened. You learn what real love and real essence are all about. (MOL)

Forgiving Your Parents' Mistakes

The fears that come up for you and your partner do not just stem from your interactions with each other. They are rooted in the unconscious wounds of childhood. Your compulsive behaviors and those of your partner are learned at a very young age in reaction to the conditional love of your parents.

No parent can honor you totally unless s/he has learned to honor him or herself completely. And no one who takes physical embodiment has reached that stage of self-forgiveness.

You entered physical embodiment with your parents and siblings because they provided the best available classroom in which you could learn to honor yourself and others equally. All the ways in which you had to bargain with your family for love were lessons in integrity and equality.

Until you have forgiven your parents and siblings for their unconscious, compulsive and abusive actions toward you, you are the one who will suffer, because you are holding on to the violation. You are holding on to the shame. And you and your partner will continue to replay your father and mother wounds until you have made them conscious and begin to forgive them.

When you come to peace with your parents and accept them as equals, you no longer wish them to change to meet your expectations, nor do you feel any desire to change to meet their expectations. You no longer accept any claims of authority from them nor do you make any claim of authority over them. You bless them as equals. You respect their achievements and have compassion for their challenges and mistakes.

When you are complete with your parents, you stop creating parental lessons in your intimate relationships. If you are a man, you stop finding your mother in your wife and trying to be her husband. If you are a woman, you stop finding your father in your husband and trying to be his wife. Unconscious, abusive relationships come to an end and the stage is set for the journey of conscious, committed intimacy. (SOTH)

Father and Mother
The Father and Mother of Creation ask only for what contributes to your awakening. Their love for you is both gentle and fierce. One type of love is not enough. The love of both father and mother is necessary.

Father's love teaches courage; Mother's love teaches gentleness. With courage, you walk through your fears. With gentleness, you open your heart.

Problems with the Father translate as an inability to understand and fulfill your creative life purpose. Problems with the Mother translate as an inability to develop loving, intimate relationships.

When there is lack of learning on one side of the equation, there is usually overcompensation on the other. Balance can be restored only by learning the lesson brought by the more challenging parent. (SOTH)

Holding on to the Love
You come into relationship to each other in different ways: as children, parents, siblings, friends, workmates, teachers, students. What is important is not the form of the relationship, but the love that abides within the form.

Relationships constantly change form. Children grow up and become parents; parents surrender their bodies to the next adventure; friends move apart; lovers break up; and so it goes. No form remains the same.

Growth must continue. Forms must come and go. That is the bittersweet quality of life. If you become attached to the form or throw away the love just because the form is changing, you will suffer unnecessarily. The challenge is to let the form go, but hold on to the love.

To love another is a spiritual act. It is an unconditional gesture. When I love you now, there is no limit placed on that love. It is timeless and eternal. When you feel my love in this moment, you don't have to be concerned for the next moment, because love naturally extends. It continues to be itself. If it is here now, it will be here always. Love does not change. The form love takes may change, but love itself will not change.

Too often you deny the love you have for each other when the form changes. That is just another kind of attachment to form. It says: "I must have love in this particular way or I do not want it at all." That is childish. When you grow up, you realize that you can't always have things exactly the way you want them, especially when other people are involved.

When one person no longer wants to keep an agreement, the agreement is off. You can't hold another person against his or her will. If you try to do so, you will push love away. Love survives the ending of agreements, if you will allow it to.

Love and freedom go hand in hand. Love cannot be contained forever in a specific form. It must break free of all forms, all conditions, if it is to become itself fully.

Grant to the other person the freedom to be who s/he is and the form will take care of itself. Try to take away that freedom and the form will become a prison for both of you.

True relationship happens only between people who regard each other as equals. It happens only between those who honor and respect each other. It happens only when people are present for each other right now.

If love is present now, then you need take no thought for the future. You need to think about the future only when you aren't fully present right now.

When you are in harmony with each other now, no plans or external agreements are necessary. Why would they be? When there is complete trust, the absence of trust is an abstract and irrelevant proposition.

When love is lacking, then you want guarantees about love. When love is present, guarantees are not necessary.

Everything comes into being right now. All creation is happening now. The alpha and omega of existence are present in this moment. There will never be more love than is possible here and now.

Do you hear that? The greatest love that you can attain is attainable right now. It cannot be experienced in the past and future.

The attachment to form is about the past or the future. It is never about now. When love is present, form is irrelevant. If I love you now, it does not matter what you look like, what you are saying, or how you act. It just matters that I love you, that I accept you, that I feel connected to you. And if you feel my love and acceptance, then you have the freedom to be however you need to be in that moment. When you can be yourself without being concerned about losing my love, then your angelic nature can be realized.

When you and your partner hold on to the love, you become its embodiment. Forms may change, but you continue to love each other through all those changes.

Love and freedom are inseparable. You cannot love your partner if you do not have the choice. All forms of bondage are assaults not just on freedom, but on love itself, because love cannot exist when you lose the freedom to choose.

The great tragedy of love is not that you may choose not to be with your partner. That is sad perhaps, but not tragic. The real tragedy is that you and your partner may stay together or separate because you believe that you have no other choice.

If there is love, there must be the freedom to choose a form that works for both of you. And to do that you must hold on to your love for each other and let the form go when it no longer serves your highest good.

This takes courage. It takes heart. It takes patience. But that is the nature of love. And those who love each other through all the conditions, all the ups and downs of life, are patient and courageous beyond measure. (RTG)

Love Offers Freedom

You cannot love someone and seek to control her. Only by wanting what is best for her do you offer her freedom. And if you do not offer her freedom, you do not offer her love. (LWOC)

Letting Go of Interpretation and Control

Your experience of love will be diminished in direct proportion to your need to interpret or control it. Interpretation places conditions upon that which must be without conditions. When you establish conditions on love, you experience the conditions, not the love. You encounter the form, not the content. (LWOC)

Divorce

Relationships ultimately end themselves. The energy and interest is simply not there anymore. The road to divorce begins with the recognition that there is no longer a shared purpose and a mutual energetic attraction.

Not all relationships are meant to be marriages. Some are temporary learning experiences lasting a few months or a few years. Unfortunately, people marry before they know in their hearts they have found a lifetime partner. But, as long as the mistake is mutually ac-knowledged, no harm is done.

Shame about making a mistake in marriage does not serve anyone. Lots of people make these mistakes. Some people suffer with their mistakes, staying in relationships long after they have lost their sa-credness. Others bail out of their relationships too soon, before they have learned their lessons and come to completion with their partners. This is not a new story.

Divorce, like marriage, begins first in the hearts of the partners. It is an organic process of dis-entanglement. When people have gone as far together as they are capable of or willing to go, divorce is the only humane solution. It is unethical to try to hold another person against his or her will.

At best, the divorce happens in the context of gratitude toward the partner for the time shared. As such, it is not a separation, but a completion.

It would be dishonest to suggest that children are not wounded by the divorce of their parents. On the other hand, they are also wounded by the unwillingness of their parents to love and respect each other.

If the detachment of divorce helps the partners to come back into mutual respect, then it can be progressive for the children. Children benefit whenever they see adults acting in a loving and respectful manner to one another.

However, in a healing divorce situation, parents must focus in-tently on providing consistent attention to the children so that they do not feel abandoned or to blame. The importance of this cannot be overemphasized. (SOTH)

Detachment

True detachment comes from familiarity with others, not from es-trangement. Distancing others does not bring detachment, but its op-

posite. Only when you let others into your heart do you become capable of releasing them. (LWOC)

The Paradox

Relationships are a two-edged sword. They promise bliss, yet bring
up the most primitive, unintegrated emotions. They promise companionship, yet challenge you to deal with seemingly irreconcilable differences. They promise an end to loneliness, yet open the door to a
deeper aloneness.

The Purpose of Relationship

The beauty of every relationship is that it carries with it great potential for learning. When you realize that your partner has been a good
teacher for you, you can't be disappointed, even if the relationship
comes to an end.

No relationship lasts forever. People come together because they
have important things to learn together. When those lessons are
learned, they move on to other challenges with other teachers. That is
how it is.

The key is not to worry about how long a relationship lasts, but to
give it your best energy and attention. Experience as much joy as you
can with your partner. Learn as much as you can from the painful
times. Do your best to be honest and clear with each other. Stretch
your comfort zones a little. Be flexible and constructive. Be the first to
yield and to bless. Give without worrying about what you are going to
get back. And when you fall down, get back up and laugh at your own
stupidity.

You will never be perfect in your ability to give or receive love.
Don't try to be. Just try to be a little more open to give and receive love
than you were before.

No other area of your life offers you as many opportunities to
understand your wounds and heal them. Your partner is the mid-

wife to your birth into your full potential. Thanks to him or her, you learn to surrender the dysfunctional patterns that compromise your happiness. Through the mirror your partner holds up to you, you discover your wholeness and learn to give your gift to the world. (MOL)

7.

CREATING YOUR LIFE

THE KEY TO THE PRISON DOOR

The only prisons in the world are the ones of your own making. Remember, dear brother and sister: for every prison you create in your mind, there is a key that unlocks the door. If you can't erase the prison, at least claim the key to the door.

You are not a victim of the world, but the one who holds the key to freedom. In your eyes is the spark of divine light that leads all beings out of the darkness of fear and mistrust. And in your heart is the love that gives birth to all the myriad beings in the universe.

Your essence is unbroken, whole, dynamic and creative. It but awaits your trust. (SOTH)

Working with the Clay
If you want to discover your integrity, you need to stop pretending to be a victim. You need to stop pretending that you weren't given the right tools. You need to take the clay and work with it.

Once you know that wholeness has not been denied you, there are no more excuses. There can be no more procrastination. There is nothing that stands between you and your joy.

Your life is your work of art and you need to be busy about it even as a bee is busy pollinating flowers. And remember, work that is not joyful to you accomplishes nothing of value in the world. (SOTH)

The Potter and the Clay

It would be easy for the potter to reject the clay as inferior and unworthy of him. But were he to do so, his life would have no meaning. He is not defined by the clay, but by what he chooses to do with it.

The clay gets molded by your willingness to stay in your process. In your struggle and in your surrender, the clay gets molded. The work of art is offered, torn apart and offered once again. At some point, you know it is finished and you can work on it no more. And then you walk away from it and more clay is given into your hands. It has a different consistency, a different potential. It brings new challenges.

Just being in your life is the molding process. Even when it seems that you are resisting your life or denying what is happening, the clay is still being worked. You can't be alive and not be engaged in creating a work of art.

"What about the criminal?" you ask. "Has he created a work of art with his life?"

Yes, he has. His life is the record of his journey through his fears, just as your life is your record. Each of you has told your story. If you look into his heart, you will see that his story is not that different from your own.

There are no failures on this planet. Even the homeless, the prostitutes, the drug dealers are molding the clay that was given to them.

Because you do not like a particular piece of artwork does not mean that it ceases to be a work of art. There are no boring stories out there. Each tale is a gem. Each sculpture has genius.

Integrity is a universal gift. Everyone has it. It is part of the clay it-self. Whatever you build with your life will stand up. It will be there for you to reflect on and for others to see.

There is no right and wrong in this process. If there were, those of you who are "right" would be wearing permanent halos.

You cannot say that what one person builds with his life is less valuable than what another person builds. All you can say in truth is that you prefer what one person has built to what another has built. You have your preferences.

Fortunately God does not share them. Not yours or anyone else's. God listens to everyone's story. Her ear is to each person's heart. (SOTH)

The Myth of the Handicapped Creator

When you are not blaming others for your problems, you are blaming God. You think it's His fault that you are unhappy.

Like Job, you don't like being put to the test. It's not fun to have your bubble burst.

You need to realize that no magical incantation is going to open the door to the prison. It doesn't work that way. Freedom is much more simple and close at hand.

"Well," you say. "If I only had a helicopter or a 747 I could get out of this hole!" You don't realize how absurd that sounds.

Forget about that 747, brother. Just use the ladder.

"That crummy old thing? That can't possibly get me out of here!"

You know the dialogue. We've had this conversation before.

Others keep pointing to the ladder, but you keep looking away. You have a certain attachment to being an "innocent victim."

The problem is that you won't admit that you have the tools you need to extricate yourself from your suffering. For, as soon as you admit that you have these tools, you cease to be a victim. Nobody feels sorry for you anymore. The game of being a handicapped creator comes to an end. (SOTH)

Embracing the Gift

You cannot be compromised if you are in acceptance of your life. You cannot be resentful or racked by grievances. Whatever your life is becomes the vehicle. Whatever the body looks like is acceptable. Whatever gift you have to give is the perfect one. It does not matter if it is not the one you thought you would have or the one you wanted.

When you embrace the gift, the purpose of your life reveals itself. You see how every lesson, every problem, every moment of suffering was absolutely necessary for the gift to be given and received. (SOTH)

The Gifts of God

Whenever news comes that seems bad, consider this. Would God give you a questionable gift? Do not be misled by the wrapping on the box, but open it with trust. And if you still do not understand the meaning of the gift, be still and wait.

God does not give questionable gifts.

Often you will not know the meaning of the gift until the gift is put to work in your life. That can be frustrating, but it is inevitable.

The gifts of God do not feed your ego expectations. Their value is of a higher order. They help you open to your true nature and purpose here. Sometimes they seem to close a door and you don't understand why. Only when the right door opens do you understand why the wrong door was closed. (LWOC)

Not Working for Others

One artist does not work for another unless he is learning something of value to his craft. When he stops learning, he moves to another teacher, or begins working on his own. Nobody can keep him from his craft. No one can take him out of his life. For his life and his craft are one.

In a world where everyone is a genius, there are no bosses and no employees. There are only teachers and students in voluntary association. (SOTH)

What You Value

What you deeply value has your full, loving attention. It is nurtured, watered and brought into fullness and truth. It does not happen overnight. It does not happen exactly how or when you want it to. It flourishes through your commitment, your constancy, your devotion. What you love prospers. It unfolds. It gets roots and wings. This is the movement of grace in your life. (SOTH)

Moving Toward Your Joy Is Not Selfish

The gifts you have been given in this life do not belong to you alone. They belong to everyone. Do not be selfish and withhold them.

Don't imprison yourself in a lifestyle that holds your spirit hostage and provides no spontaneity or grace in your life. Risk being yourself fully.

Let go of the expectations others have for you and get in touch with what brings you the greatest joy and fulfillment. Live from the inside out, not from the outside in.

To move toward your joy is not selfish. It is in fact the most generous action you can take. That is because your gift is needed. The spirit of others cannot be lifted up unless you trust your gift and give it to the world.

Consider how empty life would be if others around you chose to abandon their gifts. All that you find wonderful in life—the music, the poetry, the films, the sports, the laughter—would vanish if others withheld their gifts from you.

Do not withhold your gift from others. Do not make the mistake of thinking that you have no gift to give. Everyone has a gift.

Your gift brings joy to yourself and joy to others. If there is no joy in your life, it is because you are withholding your gift. You are not trusting it. You are not actively bringing the gift forward into manifestation in your life.

Your gift is a creative expression that breaks down the barriers of

separation and allows others to know who you are. When others connect with you deeply, the Divine within you is made manifest.
(SOTH)

Appreciation Versus Approval

Only that which comes from your heart with great enthusiasm will
prosper on all levels. Only that which you love will touch others and
bring true appreciation your way.

Appreciation and approval are two entirely different things. Appreciation is the natural, spontaneous flow of energy back to you when
others feel connected to you and your story. There is nothing you can
do to precipitate appreciation other than to be yourself and tell the
truth.

When you have shared authentically, something essential always
comes back. It may not look like what you expect, because what your
ego is looking for is not appreciation, but approval. The search for approval is based on the consciousness that you are not enough. You
want others to give you the love that feels missing in your life.

You can't really give your gift if you are preoccupied with how
other people are going to receive it. Self-consciousness restricts the
flow of energy from you to others. People feel your discomfort and become skeptical or resistant.

When you don't receive the response from others you desire, you
may feel rejected. You may withdraw and refuse to give your gift, or
you may become even more self-conscious about giving it.

Energy cannot return to you unless and until you put energy out.
Putting out a demand is the opposite of offering your gift. Demands
and expectations drain other people's energy and announce to the
world "I need you to value me because I don't value myself."

If you value your gift, it won't matter so much how others respond
to it. Even if some people give you negative feedback, you won't be
dissuaded from offering your gift again.

Happiness and personal fulfillment flow—not from the reactions of others—but from the commitment you make to yourself. This commitment will be tested again and again. Over and over, you will be asked by the universe to offer your gift in the face of criticism, skepticism or apparent lack of appreciation.

If the gift is genuine, you will learn from apparent failure and rejection. You will learn to trust yourself more deeply and to be more authentic and loving in the way you offer your gift.

An authentic gift will prosper as you trust it. A pretentious gift will not. One is the gift of Spirit that has been entrusted to you to nurture and express. The other is the fantasy creation of your ego, which sooner or later must be surrendered if your true gifts are to emerge.

One is the bringer of appreciation, which deepens intimacy and connection with others. The other brings approval or rejection, both of which bring isolation and disconnection. (SOTH)

Nurturing the Gift

Many of your gifts go unacknowledged because they don't match your pictures of what a gift should be. Often, you devalue your gift by comparing it to that of others, or you place a condition on your willingness to offer the gift.

You say, "I will sing only if I have an audience of 1,000 people and I make at least $5,000!" Supposing not that many people have heard of you, how many offers to sing are going to come your way?

This is self-defeating. How is your lifework to evolve if you do not take the first step to bring it into existence?

Your gifts need to be nurtured before they can be fully expressed. When you first become aware of what your gift is, don't go around announcing it from the rooftops. Keep your own counsel. Begin singing in the shower. Find a teacher. Practice every day. Then when your gift is ready to be shared with others, find an informal venue that does not put a lot of pressure on you to perform or on others to respond.

Be easy with it, the way you would be if a child wanted to share a song. Be that child. No matter how anxious you are to grow up with your gift, you must take the time to be the child first. Learn, grow and let your gift be nurtured into manifestation. Take small risks, then bigger ones. Sing to small audiences and gain your confidence. Then, without doing anything, your audiences will grow.

Those who refuse to start small never accomplish anything. They shoot for the moon and never learn to stand on the earth.

Don't be afraid to be an apprentice. If you admire someone who has a gift that resembles yours, don't be afraid to ask for lessons. That is one of the ways you learn to trust the gift.

On the other hand, you can't be a student forever. There comes a time when the student is ready to leave the teacher. When that moment comes, step forward. Trust the gift. Trust all the hours you have practiced. Step forth. Have faith in yourself.

The way you relate to your gift says a lot about whether you are happy or not. Happy people are expressing their gifts on whatever level and in whatever arena life offers them. Unhappy people are holding on to their gifts until life gives them the perfect venue.

Part of trusting the gift is letting go of the way you think the gift should be received. That is not your affair. It is none of your business. No matter how great you become, you will never know who will be touched by your work and who will turn away.

To give the gift, you must release it. You must not be attached to who receives it and who doesn't.

You can't hold on to your gift and give it away at the same time. When you see the absurdity of trying to do this, you will give your gift the wings it deserves. (SOTH)

Creativity and Conformity

Original work breaks new ground. A true artist is ahead of her time. Her work does not conform to the demands and expectations of the marketplace. She claims a freedom that each of you must eventually claim: the freedom to be and express yourself fully.

However, self-expression without feedback is solipsistic. It is not a dialogue with anyone. It does not attempt to communicate. Without communication and dialogue, creative work does not grow. It turns in on itself. It becomes a private language.

The extremes of artistic license and artistic conformity are to be avoided. The former closes the audience out. The latter closes the artist in.

As an artist, you can't expect your creative endeavors to speak to others if you don't use a vernacular language. If you want to engage others and communicate, you must speak in a language that people understand.

This does not mean that you tailor your work to some abstract expectation you think others have of it. Rather, you speak plainly and directly, from the heart, the way you would like to be spoken to. As a result, there is no artifice or pretension in your work. Your work is genuine, heartfelt, authentic.

Will authentic work support you? Perhaps it will. Perhaps it won't.

In an enlightened society, all authentic work would be supported. But the world you live in has not reached that point of trust and investment in the creative process.

What you cannot afford to do is to deny the creative aspect of your being just because it does not support you financially. That is self-betrayal.

Find a way to make time and space for your creative self-expression. Give yourself an hour a day, or a day a week. Make a consistent commitment to your own creative process. Let there be a rhythm with it. Make it a ritual of self-honoring. Build it into the structure of your life.

Self-expression is essential to the honoring of Self. It is also an invitation to dialogue with others. As such, it is a gesture that builds community.

If you are true to yourself, you will neither conform to the expectations of others nor will you isolate yourself from their feedback. The desire for approval prevents honest self-expression. It is soft and apologetic. The need to shock or offend others prevents dialogue and intimacy. It pushes people away.

Authentic expression is neither offensive nor apologetic. It tells its truth and invites dialogue. It builds bridges of understanding between people.

Without the creative contribution of each person, social life becomes dull, humdrum, restrictive and boring. It caves in upon itself. There is no spark, no energy, no diversity or interchange.

A family or educational system that does not foster creativity and teamwork is not doing its job. In an enlightened society, children are encouraged to honor their creative process and respect that of others. Time and space are provided for individual self-directed work, as well as for sharing and cooperative group activities.

If you want to improve life for your children, start by honoring your own creative process. Do not become lost in the "busy-ness" of living. Set aside times to honor yourself and times to share the fruits of reflection and self-expression.

The more you trust your creative process and support that of others, the more you will be helping to create the conditions for a sane and loving world. Such a world is not built overnight, notwithstanding the promises of the prophets of abundance. It evolves over time as the commitment to Self takes root and reaches deeply into the ground of being. (SOTH)

Making the Commitment to Self

Your commitment to the expression of your gift will transform your life. The structures in your life which hold you in limitation begin to fall apart as soon as you make this inner commitment to yourself. Trying to change these structures from the outside in is futile. That is not how change occurs.

Change occurs from the inside out. As you embrace your gift and move through your fear of expressing it, old, outdated lifestyle structures are de-energized. Without receiving new energy from you, these structures crumble and fall apart. You don't have to tear them down.

Your work situation, your family life, your sleeping and eating patterns all begin to shift as you get about the business of honoring yourself and moving toward your joy. You unhook from roles and relationships that no longer serve your continued growth. This happens spontaneously, without forcing or violation.

When faced with your absolute, uncompromising commitment to yourself, others either join you or move swiftly out of your way. Gray spaces created by your ambivalence—your desire to have something and give it up at the same time—move toward yea or nay. Clarity emerges as the clouds of self-doubt and attachment are burned away by the committed, radiant Self.

When one person moves toward individuation, it gives everyone permission to do the same. Dysfunctional family structures are dismantled and new structures that honor the individuals involved are put in their place.

This is what commitment to Self does. It destroys sloppiness, co-dependency, neurotic bargaining for love, boredom, apathy and critical behavior. It empowers individuals to be authentic and responsible for their choices in life.

One person's fidelity to Self and willingness to live her dream explodes the entire edifice of fear that surrounds her. It is that simple. And it all happens as gently as the first "yes" said in the silence of the heart.

No one can be abandoned by your "yes" to yourself. In setting yourself free, you call others to their freedom. Whether they answer the call, of course, is up to them.

Your commitment to other people must be an extension of your commitment to yourself, not at odds with it. Somewhere there is a decision that honors you and others equally. Find that decision. Be committed to finding it.

Don't abandon yourself. Don't abandon others. Rest in your commitment to Self. Invite others into it.

Be who you are and be willing to share. Don't exclude others from your love. What else can you do?

Let the old form go. Let the new form of your life emerge at its own pace. Go willingly into the open space of "not knowing." Whenever you release the past, you must enter this space.

Don't be afraid. Don't be embarrassed. It is okay not to know. It is okay to let things evolve.

Be patient. Be gentle with yourself and others. Growing is a process. You can't always see what lies around the corner. (SOTH)

Right Livelihood: The Only Work There Is

If your work is not joyous, if it doesn't express your unique talents and abilities, and if it doesn't uplift others, it is not spiritual work. It is the world's work.

I have asked you to be in the world but not of it. What does this mean?

It means that you choose work that you can do joyfully in the spirit of love. That way your labor becomes a gift.

If there is sacrifice involved, there will be no joy. And so there will be no gift.

Do not cheat yourself by working out of sacrifice. Do not cheat others by working out of greed. Do not deny yourself what you need to live with dignity. Do not take more than you need. Material wealth will not bring you happiness.

Only work that is joyful will bring you happiness. Only work that is joyful will bring happiness to others. The means must be consistent with the ends.

Be wary of work motivated by guilt, fear or spiritual pride. Do not try to save yourself by helping others. Do not try to save others when it is you yourself who needs to be saved.

When you are authentically expressing who you are, your work naturally extends to those who will benefit from it. And they, in turn, support the work. This is God's plan. It requires no marketing.

Having found your lifework, the greatest obstacle to its fulfillment lies in your attempt to "direct" it. You cannot make your spiritual work happen. If you try, you will fail.

Spiritual work requires surrender. Worldly work requires the illusion of control.

As soon as you give up the need to control, any work can become spiritual. As soon as you try to take charge, the most spiritual projects begin to fall apart. (SOTH)

The Myth of Material Prosperity

There is no more truth in the religion of abundance than there is in the religion of sacrifice. God does not necessarily reward spiritual work with material success. All rewards are spiritual. Happiness, joy, compassion, peace, sensitivity: these are the rewards of a life lived in integrity.

You must learn, once and for all, to stop measuring spiritual riches with a worldly yardstick. If material success comes, it is often a test to see if you can transcend self-interest and greed. Material wealth, like all other gifts, is given so that it may be shared with others.

Don't make the mistake of thinking that your lifework must bring in a large paycheck. On the other hand, don't make the mistake of thinking that you must be poor to serve God. A rich person can serve God as well as one of humble means if he is willing to share his riches. It matters not how much you hold in your hands, but whether your hands are extended outward to your brother or sister. (SOTH)

You Bring In What You Allow

You bring into your life what you allow to come in. If you say "no" to what you don't want, you bring in what you do want. It is that simple.

The only factor that makes all this complicated is that you don't always know what you want or, if you do, you don't trust it and remain committed to it. When your unconscious desires are different from your conscious goals, what you bring into your life reflects a mixture of both.

You can want something on one level and not want it on another. When the spiritual adult and wounded child want different things, manifestation is always mixed. That is why the time you take to integrate and unify the different needs and wants of your psyche is time well spent. When there is un-conflicted desire in the heart and clarity on all levels of consciousness, the creative process flows easily. (MOL)

Three Steps for Creating Your Life

1. First, get clear on what you want. Take as long as you need to get clear. It might take a day, a month, a year. Don't ask for something you're not sure that you want.
2. Believe in what you want and move toward it steadily, no matter how implausible it seems or how many obstacles seem to be in your way. Unless you want something, heart and soul, and are committed to achieving it, your goal cannot be realized.
3. When you create what you want, celebrate it. Be grateful for it. Give up your pictures of the way you thought it would be. Embrace it just the way it is. Work with it. Use it. Love it and keep on loving it.

Your job is to be clear about the goal, committed to it, and grateful for its accomplishment in your life. You don't have to know "how" the goal is going to be realized in your life. Just do the best you can. Follow any strategy that feels right to you.

Remember, it is not the strategy that brings you toward your goal, but your desire to reach it and your commitment to accomplish it. When you know "what" you want and "why" you want it, "when, where and how" will be revealed to you.

All creation is really co-creation. You determine what you want, commit to it and move toward it, and the opportunities you need to realize your goal come your way. To be sure, you must keep your eyes open. You must keep surrendering your expectations and be willing to see the opportunities that arise, but you do not have to make them happen. They happen all by themselves.

One of the great "Ahahs" on the spiritual path is the recognition that you don't have to make your life happen. It happens by itself.

When you know what you want and are committed to it, it is spontaneously created in your life. Instead of trying to change "what is" to make it be what you want, you learn to accept it and dance with it. You don't have to sacrifice, beg, borrow or steal. You just have to be clear, committed, flexible and alert in the moment to the opportunities that emerge.

Of course, there is one more important thing. You must believe that you are worthy of having what you want. If you don't believe that you are worthy, it doesn't matter how good your process is. You will find a way to undermine it. (RTG)

Your Dream Doesn't Look Like Anyone Else's
If you are not doing what you want, then you must not want it enough. Maybe you are trying to live someone else's dream, instead of your own.

You can be sure that your dream doesn't look like anyone else's. It is unique to you. If you are not committed to your goal, question it. Having a goal means nothing if you are not committed to it. If you are not willing to put the full force of your being behind that goal, then your dreams are not going to become reality.

When you get really honest with yourself, you know that no one else is preventing you from realizing your goals. You are the only person who can sabotage your dreams.

People are ineffective for two reasons. Either they don't know what they want or, if they do know, they don't believe in it.

When you know what you want and you believe in it, nothing can stop you from bringing that into your life. Of course, when you bring it in, it might look a little different from what you expected it to look like. Your ego might object to it. But that's a different problem.

Your job is not to worry about how, when or where your dream is going to manifest. Your job is to get clear on what you want and be totally committed to it. Then, however it happens and however it looks, please accept it. Please celebrate the fruit of your labors. Then, you will gain confidence in yourself and learn to trust your life. That's how you learn to dance with the current. That's how grace manifests in your experience. (RTG)

8.

TEACHERS OF GOD

THE SHEPHERD RETURNS

There is no one who will refuse love when it is offered without conditions. And who will offer it but you, my brother or sister?

Today you will drink deeply from the fountain of my love. Tomorrow you will be the fountain. Tomorrow you will carry the gift you have been given into the world. You are the hands of God bringing comfort and healing. And as you give, so you will receive.

In the past, you have given and received through the lens of your fear. But that time is over. Now you know that your fear holds you apart from the love you want. It keeps you in exile from those who love you and need your love.

You can remain apart from the community of the faithful as long as you want. But the love of that community will not leave you, nor will it cease expecting your return. The family of faith never rejects anyone, no matter how scared or confused that person may be. For this family is the embodiment of love. It is the living example, the word made flesh as the heart opens to love and the mind opens to non-judgment.

Come. Lay your burdens down. Why hold on to your pain and suffering when love's promise can be fulfilled right here, right now? Why hold on to shame or blame when the breeze of forgiveness blows through the land, lifting hearts burdened by grievances and thoughts of retribution? Lay your burden down, my friend. Can't you see that your worries and fears and all the attachments they uphold will not fit through the doorway of truth?

The time of ambivalence and deliberation is over now. When the door opens, you will walk through it. For that is why you came. And no attachment to the affairs of the world can prevent you from fulfilling your spiritual destiny. Like all children, you will return home. And returning, you will go forth as I did and guide others to the source of joy and peace.

When the flock is lost, the shepherd appears. And you, my friend, are no less shepherd than I. In the times that come, many shepherds will be needed. Many witnesses to the power of love and forgiveness will be asked to stand. Through their example, my teaching will live and flower as it never has before. For when one person is certain of the kingdom and offers a loving hand, others follow easily. (MOL)

Who Are My Disciples?

My disciples help people feel connected to the loving God who watches compassionately over all of us. They live the love they talk about. They model the teaching.

They know that I did not come to die for their sins, but to recall them to the truth that they are sinless. Experiencing their own sinlessness, they can see the innocence of others, even when others feel unworthy and guilty.

My disciples see the light in each soul. They do not focus on the darkness, for they know that darkness is ultimately not real. They overlook apparent evil and injustice by focusing on the indwelling goodness of all beings. They understand that evil is but the perceived absence of something that can never be totally taken away.

By seeing the light in self and others, my disciples are constantly baptizing. They are always offering communion. Even as people are confessing their sins, my disciples are affirming the Christ within them. Their work is always healing. They are constantly recalling people to the truth about themselves.

My disciples do not focus on what is missing or what needs to be corrected. They focus on what is always there and can never be taken away. They focus on what is right and what is good. They do not look for weaknesses and thus they instill strength. They do not look for wounds, and so they help people find their gratitude.

My disciples know that every unkindness that one person does to another is done because there is an apparent lack of love in that person's life. One who attacks others cannot know that s/he is loved.

My disciples teach love by being loving. They teach love by accepting others as they are. In all their actions, they teach others that they are worthy of love. By teaching love, they are filled with peace. And the more peaceful they feel, the more loving they can be.

My disciples know that people often forget the truth about themselves. They become lost in their roles and responsibilities. They take each other for granted. People often feel threatened and build walls of self-protection. They forget to open their hearts.

My disciples do not chastise people for forgetting. They simply remind them gently, over and over again, that they are capable of giving and receiving love.

My disciples reinforce the good and the true, and let illusion and falsehood fall away by themselves. They do not berate people for making mistakes, but praise them for having the willingness to learn and grow from the mistakes they make. (MOL)

Ministering to Others

No one can force another to awaken. Each person clings to separation and control until the pain of it is unbearable. The pain threshold is different for each individual, but everyone crosses it in the end.

That is why I ask you not to preach to others, but merely to extend love to them. Those who are ready to receive love will receive it through you. Those who are not ready will continue on their journey without interfering with yours.

A minister attends to those in need. S/he extends love to those who ask for it, silently or in words. S/he does not browbeat unbelievers with words or concepts promising some future salvation.

Salvation is now for those who would be saved. Do not judge the others, for it is not for you to judge. Those who come later into the lap of God's love are not less worthy than those who come sooner.

Healing

Being a healer or miracle worker means accepting your inherent capacity to be free of conflict, free of guilt, free of judgment or blame. If you accept this capacity in yourself, you will demonstrate miracles in your life just as I did. (LWOC)

Ministering/Mentoring

When the truth is embodied, it is easily understood. Anyone who is authentic and compassionate becomes a model for others. S/he may be a teacher, a family friend or relative, a businessperson, or a big brother or sister. It is not what s/he does or says that is so important. It is how s/he does it or says it. A true mentor/minister expresses caring and love in his or her words and deeds.

Such people are magnetic and compelling, not necessarily because they have achieved important things in the world, but because they care and you can feel it. Love has risen up in them and it overflows them, anointing all who come their way.

When you learn to love yourself, you cannot help loving others. It is not hard to do. It's automatic.

You think that I am special because I loved so many people. But really I am one among many who moved into the lap of love and became its perpetual minister.

When you love, there is no limit on that love. It constantly recycles, flowing in and out of the heart. Like waves breaking and receding on a beach, the tides of love are steady and dependable. They touch every shoreline with their blessing.

Love is not something you do. Love is who you are. You are the embodiment of love in this moment. Nothing less.

But all this begins in your own heart. It begins with your willingness to love and accept yourself. That is where Christ is born.

Once born, S/He cannot be contained. There is no place where S/He cannot go. There is no place where this love cannot reach.

Wherever you go, the love of Christ goes with you. It moves with your legs, reaches with your hands, speaks with your voice and sees with your eyes.

Because of you, It is everywhere. Without you, It would be invisible. Is that not why you too must become a witness, a mentor, a minister of the love that abides in you and in all beings? No, not to preach or proselytize, but to listen, to comfort, to care. In your silence, love's presence is felt; in your acceptance, its compassion is experienced; in your smile, its delight is made manifest.

The love that expresses through you is the Christ Presence, the human vehicle ablaze with the divine light, the very embodiment of God's love. I am not the only Christ.

We are the Second Coming, you and I. We are the ones who have been asked to open our hearts, our minds and our arms so that the love of God can be experienced in this embodiment.

When I heard the call, I answered it. Now you hear it too. And you answer it by following this simple teaching which I gave to you once and give to you now again: "Whatever is not loving must be forgiven; and what is forgiven becomes love's patient blessing on an imperfect world." (RTG)

Awakened Ones

There is nothing glamorous about awakening. People who awaken do not become famous spiritual teachers. They do not build fancy organizations. They live for the most part unnoticed by all but a few students who recognize their freedom and inner authority.

Teachers who are valued by the world tend to teach at a very superficial level. For the world rewards tangible outcomes and effects, and spiritual accomplishments tend to be intangible.

One who masters the mind is not valued by society. He may be the most powerful being alive, but you will not find him in a position of power. In truth, even if such a position were offered to him, he would not take it. Such a person is not concerned with the manipulation of outer events.

For him there is only one question: "Are you happy right now?" If the answer is "yes," then you are already in heaven. If the answer is "no," then he simply asks, "Why not?"

You may give him thirty pages of testimony as to why you are unhappy, but he will simply ask again, "Why not?" And sooner or later, you will realize that all your reasons for not being happy are about the past.

All the master can do is ask, "Why not now?" He isn't interested in your past or future. He cannot tell you what to do, for the responsibility for doing belongs to you.

Teachers who tell you what to do are betraying their spiritual immaturity. A wise teacher asks good questions, but gives very little advice. (LWOC)

The Greatest Teachers Are the Most Humble

It is a rare person who can go about her work without calling attention to herself, without seeking publicity, without building an organization around herself. It is a rare person who inspires without taking credit, who heals without charging a fee and gives without asking anything in return.

The greatest teachers are the most humble, the most loving, the most empowering to others. If you wish to find such a teacher, you must look beyond appearances. Find the man or woman who promises you nothing, but loves you without hesitation. Find the teacher who makes no pretension to fix or to teach, yet who opens your heart when s/he looks into your eyes.

When you think of great teachers, you think of glitter, flowing robes and great crowds of people gathered together. But none of these trappings are required. Indeed, they often get in the way. The focus goes onto the guru, instead of onto the aspirant. But it is the aspirant who must wake up, not the guru.

Don't depend on some other authority to inspire or validate you. Pay attention to your own experience and guidance. Stop looking for fireworks and work with the warp and woof of your life. Learn to accept the unfolding tapestry, mistakes and all. (MOL)

Conversion

So much value is placed on words and concepts, yet this is not where the experience of conversion happens. Conversion happens primarily in the heart, and not so much in the mind.

People are not converted to some concept of God, but to an experience of love. One who does not believe in something beyond his small ego suddenly opens to a loving presence that exists both in him and in others. That is the experience that changes lives.

People do not surrender to love by adopting a set of beliefs and parroting them to others. They surrender to love when they experience it through you. It doesn't matter what they believe, how they dress, what songs they sing or how they bury their dead. All that is immaterial.

When you accept people as they are, then you become a true vehicle for love. You don't need to change people's beliefs or customs, or fix their lives. You just need to speak and act in a loving way toward them.

No one can resist a person who radiates love. Everyone comes to sit at his or her feet.

Can you imagine that? These people are not even invited, never mind proselytized, yet they come anyway. They come because love calls to them and they respond.

You do not have to go out aggressively to spread my message. You do not have to hit people over the head with it and drag them back to your churches or synagogues. Just love each other, and people will come. They will come and fill themselves to the brim, and they will return home with their cups running over. That is the way my teaching spreads.

Being a minister of love is effortless. You just keep loving, and people keep coming. You keep admitting your mistakes and confessing your worries and fears, and people hold you ever more deeply in their hearts. (MOL)

Who Needs Religion?

I hate to disappoint you, but the truth is that no one needs religion. You don't need to hold on to the husk. But you do need to break it open and plant the seed.

Whatever your religion is, know that it has dogmas and interpretations that disguise the truth. All religions are heavily burdened by the prejudices of followers who never opened to truth and beauty in their lives. What you have is a record of their fear, not an invitation to love.

But if you dig deeply enough in the garden of your faith, you will find the voices of truth that will help you open your heart to love's presence. And that is where you must focus. That is where you must plant the seed of faith that will take root in your life.

There are many beautiful trees that flower in the springtime. One is not better than another. Each has its special beauty. Seen together, they make an extraordinary garden. So it is with approaches to the divine. Each approach has its own beauty and integrity. It speaks to certain people and not to others. That is the way it should be. One tree is not better than another. One religion is not better than another.

Each religion has attached to it a climate of fear and rigidity that can destroy the tree before its seeds can be carried forth on the wind. This is true in every tradition.

If you belong to a tradition, you must find the seed, separate it from the husk, and see that it is planted in your lifetime. You must find the core teaching that connects you to love and pass that teaching on to your children. That is the only way that a tradition stays healthy. The form must change to better speak to the time and place. That way the essence of the teaching is preserved.

A barren tree will make no fruit. A religion that does not help its followers connect to love will not prosper. (MOL)

Answering the Call

You do not have to belong to a religion to awaken your spirituality. But it is easier to awaken to the truth and beauty of your life if you belong to a loving community of people. Such a community need not be religious. Many secular groups and communities provide their members with the same emotional support and empowerment that some people find in religious organizations. Even if you meet regularly with just two or three other people who are loving and supportive, you will find that it helps you transcend your personal drama and stay open to the purpose and meaning that are unfolding in your life.

That is why I have given you the *Affinity Group Process*.* It provides you with a very simple way of staying connected to love in your life. It is particularly helpful if you aren't comfortable with religion and don't have a secular support group in your life.

When the truth has been nurtured within you, it asserts itself clearly in your life. As you become more fully empowered, you may leave your support group, your church or your temple to follow your calling. Then, wherever you go, you give and receive support without hesitation. For when love is awakened within you, it is given freely to all who need it.

Each one of you is a minister of God in training. You will be called to serve your brothers and sisters when your connection to love is firmly established. When that call comes, you will have no choice but to answer it. For it is the reason for which you came, the purpose for which you are ideally suited in temperament and ability. (MOL)

---

*The Affinity Group Process is described in the book *Living in the Heart* by Paul Ferrini. See listing at the back of this book.

9.

SPIRITUAL COMMUNITY

HOLDING EACH OTHER'S INNOCENCE

The purpose of a spiritual community is to hold a vision of everyone's innocence. Members of the community love and accept each other here and now. Past mistakes, transgressions, misunderstandings, no matter how seemingly severe, are not held against anyone. Each person is seen as new, innocent, unstained.

The community holds a space in which the judgments members make about other people can be acknowledged and forgiven. Nobody tries to change, fix or heal anyone else. Healing is done by the Spirit in the instant the individual stops playing the role of victim and takes full responsibility for his or her life.

The community holds the space for self-forgiveness. It does not pretend to have the answer for any of its members. It simply extends to each individual again and again the recognition of her innocence.

The community sees the individual as acceptable as she is right now. No matter what else she seems to be asking for, all she wants is love and the community is willing to love her.

In a spiritual community, you learn to hold your innocence with absolute conviction and, as you do, you hold it not just for yourself, but for all of God's children. You realize that there is nothing beyond you for which you must seek, nor anything in the past which holds you back from living your truth. Because the light of Christ is established in your heart, it is reflected all around you. (SOTH)

A Spiritual Renaissance

Consciousness is shifting on the planet. The age of the individual is coming to an end. A spiritual renaissance has begun, characterized by the formation of small, decentralized communities guided through group consensus and the mutual practice of the forgiveness process.

These communities grow because there is a natural tendency for that which is loving and healing to attract that which needs healing and love. Since this happens magnetically, there is no need to go seeking outside.

You are all channels through which God's love can flow to others. There is no mystery in this. As soon as you make space for God in your heart, He brings the stranger to your doorstep. As soon as you make space for God in your community, He brings the outcasts and the disenfranchised into the sanctuary of your church.

That is the way of Spirit. When you offer love, those who are in need of that love will find you. They are brought to God through your loving presence.

There was a time when I offered to be the door for you. Now you too must become the door. (SOTH)

A Church Without Walls

The community I call you to is a church without walls, a place where people of all faiths come together to love, support and honor one another. My church has nothing to do with what you call Christianity, or with any dogma that separates people. It has nothing to do with any religious hierarchy or elaborate organizational structure.

All are welcome in my church. Both the poor and the rich, the sick and the healthy, those who call my name and those who call the name of another teacher. Each one is God's child and I accept all children of God as my brothers and sisters. I celebrate life in all its forms and in its quintessential formlessness.

I urge you to be broad-minded. When you enter my church, you do not need to take off your coat or your hat, but please leave your prejudices outside. They have no place in my church. Come to my altar not to hold on to your judgments, but to confess them, to release them to God before your brothers and sisters. You do not have to wear a special hat or robe to enter my sanctuary, but you do have to surround yourself with the awareness of your equality with all beings.

My church is a place of peace and reconciliation. It is a place where fears are acknowledged and trespass is forgiven. My church welcomes all those who admit their mistakes. It casts no one out who seeks the safety of its loving arms.

Many congregations purport to be mine, yet they hold on to their fears and institutionalize their judgments. The stranger and the outcast are not welcome in their sanctuaries. They have built a prison and called it a church. I would rather be worshiped by murderers and thieves than by those who pretend to do my will by judging and excluding others.

I do not now nor have I ever tolerated hypocrisy. Those who call themselves spiritual guides should set a sincere example for others. They do not have to be perfect, but they should have the courage to admit their mistakes and they should be compassionate about the mistakes of others.

My church provides a climate of understanding, safety and love. It is a place where each person can connect with her spiritual essence and the God of her understanding. (SOTH)

Undoing Religious Tyranny and Small-mindedness

People assume that they go to church or temple to be with others who believe the same thing they do. If this is true, then churches and temples simply legitimize narrow-mindedness and prejudice.

Anyone can find someone who agrees with his beliefs. Anyone can create a religion for insiders and exclude those who would challenge his beliefs. This has nothing to do with spirituality. It has more to do with the insecurities of the individual and his tendency to capitulate to the tyranny of the group mind.

Cults thrive on this kind of insecurity. They create a seductive environment that seems to be loving and then proceed to chop away at the ego structure of the individual until he is totally confused, self-doubting and helpless. In the name of spiritual surrender, initiates are asked to capitulate to the authority structure of the cult. In this way, brainwashing poses as enlightenment.

Hierarchical, closed belief systems promise Shangri-La and deliver Alcatraz. They offer freedom from suffering and deliver physical abuse and mind control. Those who are drawn into such situations have lessons around the abuse of power. You can't prevent them from enrolling in this classroom, but you can offer them a helping hand when they are ready to get out.

Fundamentalist groups offer a somewhat less dramatic experience of abuse, but still use the fear tactics of the group mind to control their members. Even traditional churches and temples do not tolerate diversity well. As a result, they lose members who are exploring their spirituality in an authentic way.

Dogmatic teachings and religious hierarchies no longer make people feel safe and secure. They must be replaced by compassionate teachings that respect the spiritual process of each individual and encourage respectful, heartfelt sharing.

Tolerance for differences is essential to the creation of a safe, loving space. It is not necessary for people to have the same beliefs to experience spiritual communion with one another. Communion happens in spite of the mind, not because of it. Communion happens through the extension of love and non-judgment. It can happen anywhere, with any group of people, if they are committed to loving and respecting one another.

The time has come for churches and temples to redefine themselves. They must cease to be places where minds cling to linear beliefs in fearful agreement, and become places of self-exploration, where differences are welcome. Love, not agreement, must become the bond that holds the community together. (SOTH)

Democracy and Respect for Differences

Democracy is not so much about agreement as it is about respect for different points of view. For democracy to work, people who have different ideas and values must be able to be heard.

A society that tolerates differences of perspective is a society that is based on the practical demonstration of love and equality. Those who seek agreement build totalitarian systems where individual freedoms are sacrificed and the whole never benefits from the wisdom of the parts. Such systems are doomed to failure.

It takes courage to disagree. It takes wisdom and foresight to maintain an environment of equality in which all perspectives can be considered. The path to truth has never been an easy one. It certainly has never been one based on expediency. (LWOC)

A Living Church

The church I call you to must embrace both the feminine and masculine sides. It must welcome everyone without conditions, yet be devoted to truth without compromise.

In a living church, each person is free to determine her own spiritual path. She is granted total freedom in this pursuit, and in return grants this freedom to others. She agrees not to try to convert or to fix anyone else. She asks for unconditional acceptance and support for her journey and gives the same to others in return.

Anyone who violates this agreement is asked to publicly discuss her motives and behavior and hear the non-blaming feedback of others. The goal is not to shame or embarrass, but to hear and to tell the truth, and ultimately to determine whether the individual embraces the spiritual guidelines that govern the community.

All violations of the public trust are dealt with in a loving and compassionate way. The desire is always for understanding and inclusion. But the guidelines that encourage truth and create emotional safety must never be watered down or compromised.

Mistakes are to be acknowledged and forgiven. Those acting in ways that hurt others are asked to look at their behavior and see how they impact others and themselves. Correction and forgiveness go hand in hand. Without forgiveness, correction is impossible. And without correction, forgiveness is incomplete.

The living church or temple must be faithful to its process. Since the process is loving, forgiving and supportive, many different types of people will be drawn in. The flexibility, tolerance and openness of the church/temple and its members will be continually tested. In all this, it must be firm within, and gentle without. All people must be treated fairly and with respect.

In the living church or temple, power always lies in the hands of the congregation. The role of the minister is to lead by example and to empower others to walk their own unique spiritual path. The more successful the minister is in empowering others, the more participatory the organization becomes. Then, it does not matter if the minister leaves, because the programs of the church or temple retain their energy and coherence.

By empowering others skillfully, a good minister makes himself dispensable. His job is quite simply to help transform old paradigm congregations into new paradigm ones. As a skillful facilitator, he invites others to take responsibility, to share their gifts and to co-create the organization with him. When the congregation is fully empowered, the minister's work in that place is complete and he will be drawn to a new environment that will challenge him further.

A fully empowered congregation does not need a minister, although it can certainly choose to have one if it wishes. A core group of church members that represent the diversity of the congregation can guide the church through intuitive consensus, going to the wider congregation to decide important issues. This group needs to help the congregation hold and continue to manifest the original vision of "a safe, loving, non-judgmental space in which people are empowered to share their gifts." If the safety of the space is compromised, the new paradigm energy of creative synergy will quickly revert to an old paradigm energy of polarization, separation and struggle for control.

I do not say this to make you into church builders, for frankly the only church you need to attend is the one that lies in your own heart. But if you attend an outer church or temple or wish to attend one, it will be helpful for you to understand the dynamics that can enable you to create a safe, loving space.

All social institutions can be transformed by following the *Affinity Group Guidelines.* Churches, schools, businesses, nursing homes, prisons, government agencies can all be called to a spiritual purpose through the implementation of these simple ideas.

Three things can be said about my teaching. First, it is simple. Second, it applies to all situations, circumstances and environments. Third, if you practice it, you will find peace in your heart and harmony in your relationships.

You would think these attributes would recommend the teaching, yet look around. Do you see anyone lining up at my doorstep?

Yet cults are springing up everywhere. Fundamentalist religion is booming. People continue to flock in great numbers for darshan with swamis and gurus.

Don't misunderstand me. I am not against swamis, gurus, fundamentalists or cult members. I'm just pointing out that my teaching— which absolutely works—is not very popular.

Somehow people intuitively understand that if they take up this path, their lives will never be the same. They aren't sure they really want a revolution happening in their lives.

I understand that. Many people like to play at surrender, while retaining their addiction to control. They want to love others who are like them while retaining their judgments about others who are different. That way, they appear to be spiritual, without having to risk becoming vulnerable. They talk about love, but keep a hard shell around themselves which pushes love away. They have the semblance of love, but not the real thing. Real love would crack their lives open. (SOTH)

A Healing Community

My church is a therapeutic, healing community, but without any therapists or healers. Each person is present for her own self-healing and all others are merely witnesses to that. They do not come to analyze her, fix her or enlighten her. They come simply to accept and bear witness to her process. In trusting her process to lead her exactly where she needs to go, they reinforce their trust in their own process.

My work is always about getting out of the way and trusting the Spirit to heal. When we try to become the healer, the minister, the teacher, the technician, we just add more confusion, fear and guilt to everybody's plate.

As a result, I do not offer techniques for fixing or salvation. I provide a safe space and offer you the opportunity to stand up and tell the truth about your experience. I offer you the challenge of co-creating that safe space and being a gentle witness to others. That is all.

That is enough for a lifetime.

You don't have to have all the answers to grow, to walk through your fears, to inhabit your life more completely. As you tell your story and witness to the stories of others, the alchemical process of transformation begins in your heart. And it, not you or I, is in charge of the journey.

I cannot tell you where that journey will take you. Indeed, it isn't important for you to know. But I can tell you to trust the process and know that it is bringing you home to yourself, home to the most profound intimacy, home to your eternal connection with the divine. (SOTH)

Walking Through the Fire Together

Genuine spiritual community happens only to the extent that it fosters an open mind and an open heart. You cannot foster an open mind if you teach any dogma. Giving people answers is manipulative and controlling. Instead, help people articulate their questions and begin the search for their own answers. Let them know that the community is a place where they can share ideas without being judged or preached to.

You cannot foster openheartedness if you exclude anyone from your community or give preferential treatment to any member. People open their hearts when they feel welcome and treated as equals. Nothing closes the heart down quicker than competition for love and attention. Most people are deeply wounded emotionally and react quickly and defensively to the slightest hint of unfairness, even if it is not intended.

This is why the primary focus of the community must be on setting clear boundaries and establishing a healthy group process. Each person must be given a chance to be heard and encouraged to communicate in a non-blaming way. Each member must be encouraged not to stuff feelings or hide them from others.

When a safe space is created in which feelings can be expressed without attacking others, misunderstandings, judgments and projections can be dissolved. People can return to their hearts. Trust can be re-established.

It is absurd to assume that this kind of physical, emotional and mental reconciliation can happen without a loving environment to foster it. Leaving a group together without teaching them guidelines and process skills is like leaving a toddler alone in a house. He may be okay for the first fifteen minutes, but after that he'll find the chemicals under the sink and the drawer where the knives are stored. You don't want to see the outcome.

And yet you know it. You see it over and over again. As soon as egos rise to attack and defend, it isn't long before the battlefield is strewn with corpses. And then, of course, you have the walking wounded, the ones who have been hit and don't know it yet. You assume that they are normal until you do something to trigger their repressed rage.

No, you don't want to leave a group of wounded people alone to fend for themselves. You want to teach them how to create and maintain a safe, loving, non-judgmental space. That's why the *Affinity Group Process* was developed.

A core group of community members must be skillful in practicing the *Affinity Group Guidelines*. Through their ability to model these guidelines, the entire community learns the process, and then even the most difficult situations can be resolved in a way that honors everyone.

Often, people's hearts and minds will close down. Sometimes, it may seem that all these "loving, spiritual" people are losing it, acting out their woundedness in unmistakable ways. And you will wonder: "Why did I come here? This is just as bad as my nuclear family experience, maybe even worse!"

You need to understand that everyone has a dark side. Everyone has un-integrated, traumatic material. It's time for you to drop your fantasy about what community is. It's not always a lovey-dovey experience. It's more like a furnace, fed by the coal everyone is digging up in the other person's backyard. And, unless process skills are learned early on, it's not very helpful or transformative.

Many people decide to eschew heart-centered, interactive spirituality for this reason. They go off on their separate journeys, meditating six hours a day, pursuing the elongated path of aloneness. But for many of them this is just retreat from the fire. It takes a lot longer to go around the fire than it does to go through it.

But don't attempt to go through the fire without the proper preparation. Don't enter community with others without understanding the depth of the ego's hold on your experience and that of others. Learn how to be with your ego and that of others in a compassionate way. Practice the guidelines. Develop good process skills. Then you can walk on hot coals. (SOTH)

A Community of Opening Hearts

When the mind is closed, the heart shuts down, and vice versa. When this happens, it is important to acknowledge it, to let others know that you are being triggered.

By confessing your judgments and fears to others, you release them more completely than you can by yourself. You help establish a group culture that is compassionate and forgiving of mistakes. Neither you nor others have to beat yourselves up when fear or judgment comes up.

When ego is held compassionately, it is no longer held by ego, but by something else more gentle and allowing, something merciful, accepting, forgiving. It doesn't matter what you call it.

Through the practice of voluntary confession, a community of equals is born. No one is more spiritual than another. Each person has judgments and wishes to release them. When one person acknowledges a mistake, the others think "there go I. I am no different from my brother." There is no pretension to spirituality here, no desire for perfection or shame about imperfection. There is just acceptance of the ego as it rises and falls. There is patience and compassion. This deepens the safety of the space.

When you establish a climate in which the ego is accepted and forgiven, life becomes much easier for everyone. Spirit holds the ego in its loving embrace and its ability to split the mind is arrested.

My church is a healing community, a community of unconditional blessing and forgiveness. It is a safe place where ego arises without judgment or condemnation, a sacred space where each contraction, each movement of fear, is gently acknowledged and released. It is a sanctuary where heart and mind close only to open more fully to the presence of love. (SOTH)

A Free and Loving Community

The great challenge before you today is to learn how to come together to create community based not on dogma or external authority, but on mutual equality and a deep respect for each person's experience. The question is "How do you accept and appreciate the differences between you while maintaining emotional connection and continuity? How do you experience freedom and love at the same time?"

Since most forms of love tend to be conditional, love is offered only when there is perceived agreement. Loving someone who disagrees with you is rare. Feeling emotionally connected to someone who has a very different set of experiences is unusual.

Real love is unconditional. It does not exclude anyone for any reason. It requires you to see beyond appearances, to see others from an inner conviction that all people carry the divine spark within them.

Real love does not seek to bind, control or enslave, but to liberate, to empower, to set others free to find their own truth. What church or temple has this for an agenda? What religious structure gives its members the freedom to self-actualize in the name of love?

What church extends love and inclusion to all? What society reaches out to those who live on the fringes and keeps inviting them back in? What community of human beings is dedicated to seeing beyond its fears and learning to love its enemies?

When I asked for a church, was this not the kind of church I asked for? Did I not ask for a community that would recognize the Christ Presence in all human beings, a community where no one would be ostracized or cast out? What is salvation, I ask you, if you do not offer it to everyone, regardless of his appearance or beliefs?

Love, my friends, means to give and receive freedom. It means to empower. There are never any guarantees in the act of loving. If you look for agreement or favorable response, you cannot love freely. And if love is not free, it is not love. It is bargaining, negotiation, commerce.

Perhaps you begin to see what a church like the one I call for would do for the world you live in. It would make no one wrong, but encourage each person to find out what is right for him or her. It would trust and support the love and the light that dwells in each human being. It would not foster a world divided into rich and poor, haves and have-nots, but a world in which each person has enough and is not afraid to share what s/he has.

A church and a society founded in my name would live by the principles I taught and teach. It would extend love and support freely to all. It would make no one wrong, condemn no woman or man, or ostracize any human being from the community of faith. It would not be defensive, greedy or proud, but open-minded, generous and humble.

These qualities lie within each one of you. You have only to cultivate them. There is not a single one of you who cannot love unconditionally. But you must be encouraged to do so. My church is a church of encouragement. It calls you to realize the highest truth about yourself. (MOL)

10.

ABUNDANCE

SCARCITY AND ABUNDANCE

Scarcity thinking results from your perception that you are not worthy of love. If you do not feel worthy of love, you will project lack outside you. You will see the glass as half empty, rather than half full.

If you see the glass as half empty, do not be surprised if before too long there is nothing left in the glass. Lack is the result of negative perception.

Of course, the same principle works in reverse. See the glass as half full and it won't be long before it is filled to the brim.

When you know that you are worthy of love, you tend to interpret the words and actions of others in a loving way. You do not easily take offense. If someone is rude to you, you consider the possibility that s/he may be having a bad day. You don't feel victimized or abused.

How you view life depends on whether you feel lovable or unlovable, worthy or unworthy. Either way, you will create an external situation that reinforces your opinion of yourself.

The experience of scarcity is not God punishing you. It is you showing yourself a belief that needs to be corrected.

Abundance comes into your life, not because you have learned to memorize some mumbo jumbo incantation, but because you have learned to bring love to the wounded aspects of your psyche. Love heals all perception of division and lack, restoring the original perception of wholeness, free of sin or guilt. (LWOC)

Your True Worth

Many of you study prosperity consciousness, yet what you do does not seem to prosper. Why is this? Because you do not know your true worth. If you knew your true worth, you would not feel that something was missing from your life. You would feel grateful for everything you have. (LWOC)

Trust

How can Divine Law support you when you are trying to fix yourself or others? Only when you stop trying to fix can that which is whole and unbroken reveal itself to you. (LWOC)

Needs

You can give and receive only what you have, not what you don't have. The attempt to give or receive what you do not have is futile. It can end only in disappointment and sorrow.

If you are loving, you receive love, because love always returns to itself. If you demand love, you receive demands for love. As you sow, so do you reap. The law of energy is circular. What goes out comes back and what comes back goes out. So how can you "get" something you do not have? It is impossible!

The truth is that you have everything that you need. Nothing that you need has been withheld from you. In this sense you can only "need" what you don't need.

Please stay with this paradox.

If you "need" something, then you believe that it is not yours to give. If it is not yours to give, then how can you receive it?

If, on the other hand, you know that it is yours to give, you will give and receive it simultaneously. And in this case you will not "need" it.

If you wish to demonstrate abundance, question every "need" you have. As long as you "need" something, you cannot have it. As soon as you no longer "need" it, it appears in front of you.

This is a simple law. You cannot receive what you are unable to give, and you can't give what you are unable to receive.

Giving and receiving are the same thing. Giving is receiving. Receiving is giving. When you know this, the whole chess game falls apart. The mystery is over. (SOTH)

The Economy of Love

People whose minds and hearts are open experience and extend love, gratitude and abundance as a matter of course. They don't have to do anything special. Being open, what they need comes to them. Being caring and compassionate, they give away what they don't need to others who need it. This is the economy of love. It is based on trust and faith.

By contrast, the economy of fear is rooted in the belief that there aren't enough resources for everyone. People who are fearful believe that their needs will not be met if they don't manipulate, control and hoard resources.

If you look around you will see both economies at work. The economy of fear seems to be more prevalent than the economy of love, but if you look carefully you will see that the tide is turning. That is because the more fearful people become, the more they must learn to rely on love to survive. While conditions seem to be getting worse, in fact they are getting better.

That is the good news. The bad news is that very few of you believe this. Most of you believe the doomsday prophets who say the world is condemned to unimaginable suffering and distress. This belief induces more fear and has the potential to become a self-fulfilling prophecy.

The real struggle before you today is not a struggle between good and evil, but a struggle between your belief in goodness and your belief in evil. Each of you must fight this battle in your own consciousness.

Believing in evil, you contract emotionally, become more defensive and cut yourself off from the energy of creation. Believing in good, you expand emotionally, open up to others and engage with the creative energy of the universe. That is the consciousness of abundance. (MOL)

The Meaning of Abundance

Contrary to popular opinion, abundance does not mean that you have a lot of money or material possessions. Abundance means that you have what you need, use it wisely and give what you don't need to others. Your life has poise, balance and integrity. You don't have too little. You don't have too much.

On the other hand, scarcity does not mean that you don't have enough money or material possessions. It means that you don't value what you have, don't use it wisely or don't share it with others. Scarcity may mean that you have too little. It may also mean that you have too much. Your life is out of balance. You want what you don't have, or you have what you don't want or need.

I assure you that you will not increase your happiness just by increasing your material possessions. You increase your happiness only by increasing your energy, your self-expression and your love. If that also increases your pocketbook, then so be it. You have more to enjoy and share with others.

The goal in life should not be to accumulate resources that you don't need and cannot possibly use. It should be to earn what you need, enjoy and can share joyfully with others.

The abundant person has no more or less than she can use responsibly and productively. She does not obsess on protecting what she has or in obtaining what she does not need. She is content with what she has, and is open to giving and receiving all the resources that God brings into her life. (MOL)

Fairness

To give what you have and take what you need keeps the flow of resources moving. To give less than you have or take more than you need creates an imbalance in the flow of resources.

When you give less than you have or take more than you need, someone else must take less than s/he needs. Then, it is only a matter of time before s/he feels resentful and tries to take back what s/he believes is hers.

No one but you can determine what you have and what you need. That is why no system of economics, no matter how pure, can create a fair distribution of the collective resources of human beings. Only fair people can create a fair economy.

Fairness happens voluntarily. It never happens by control. People have to be free to make mistakes and learn from them. Otherwise, the system is not open and growth is not possible. (SOTH)

No Sacrifice, No Free Lunch

When others try to please you at their expense, they do not offer love, but sacrifice. Most people who sacrifice do it because they are trying to buy your love and approval. Sacrifice is not a gift. It is a disguised bargain. It expects some kind of payment in return.

You have heard the expression "there is no free lunch." That is ultimately true. But there are lunches that appear to be free. You don't have to pay now, but you most definitely have to pay later. Eventually the bill collector will come and he will want interest too!

The devil's invitation comes in many guises. But his favorite one is some version of the free lunch. Watch out when food, money, sex or attention is offered to you "without strings attached." The longest strings are the ones that are invisible!

If you are responsible, if you have the ability to pay, a free lunch does not appeal to you. If you can go into an elegant restaurant, order a good bottle of cabernet savignon, and eat filet mignon and baked shrimp on the deck overlooking the water, why would you go to the local soup kitchen?

A responsible person doesn't steal from others. When someone has something you want, you pay your way up front. You support others by purchasing their services. You know that receiving without giving is out of harmony with nature and Divine Law. You don't seek that which is unfair, no matter how seductive it may appear. (SOTH)

The Dialogue Between Energy and Form

What you eat, what you think, how you breathe, and how you speak all determine how energy expresses through your body/mind vehicle. Every choice that you make in your life has an impact on how you give energy or receive it.

You are an animated form, an energy body. Your mind/body consciousness is a temporary container for the universal energy of creation. This energy expresses through you in a unique way, through your genes and chromosomes, as well as through your personality structure. As your mind/body consciousness expands with love, you become more open to giving and receiving the universal energy of creation. Conversely, when you contract in fear, you become less able to give or receive the energy of creation.

It is the nature of energy to expand. It is the nature of form to contract. This is one of the inevitable paradoxes you must live with.

The energy of creation wants to open you up and the structure of your mind and body resists that expansion. The important thing to realize is that all structure belongs to the past, while energy only exists in the moment. It is like water that flows by as you watch from the bank of a river. It is never the same water you are looking at. In the same manner, the energy inside you is never the same energy that it was five minutes ago. It is always new energy. That is fortunate indeed, because it means that you are never limited to the past. Every adjustment you make in consciousness in the present has an immediate effect on the energy that is able to move through you. As your physical body becomes more healthy and your personality structure becomes more flexible and integrated, you become increasingly able to give and receive energy, physically, emotionally, mentally and spiritually.

Love opens the mind/body consciousness to its maximum energetic potential, enabling others to "feel" the energy of acceptance, gratitude and kindness flowing directly to them. This opens their hearts and minds to their own potential and empowers them to share their creative gifts with others. This is how abundance is generated in the world.

Ego Blocks to Abundance

The energy of creation moves through you to others and through others to you. While this energy supports you in essential ways, there can be no personal ownership of it. As soon as you claim ownership of it, your connection to the energy is disturbed.

Your alignment with the energy of creation requires the relinquishment of your ego agenda. Your ego agenda operates from the belief that you can manipulate people and events to obtain the outcome you want. Your ego agenda is selfish and shortsighted. It does not consider the good of others, and therefore it does not consider your ultimate good.

When you cheat someone out of something s/he deserves, you lose not only what you thought you would gain; you also lose what you would have gained if you had acted in a less selfish way. Every attempt to gain in a selfish manner eventually leads to loss and defeat, because selfish actions are not supported by the universal energy.

Those who take advantage of others may seem to gain the upper hand through their great determination and skill, but they do not prevail in the long run. Their victory is a temporary one. Goliath reigns only until David rises up to defeat him. As I have said, "The meek will inherit the earth."

If you want to open to abundance in your life, you must give up the idea that you can gain through someone else's loss. That is the fearful thinking of the ego mind and it must be recognized and overruled if new patterns are to be set into motion in your life.

Fortunately, there is another way, a way that begins when you recognize that your good and that of your brother and sister are one and the same. When you accept your equality with others, you reconnect to the energy of creation, and that energy supports you. Because you are supported, you do not toil in vain. Results come spontaneously and on their own timetable. As long as you are able to relinquish your expectations and do your best to get along with others, life continues to cooperate with you.

The Divine Plan is essentially collaborative. It cannot be realized without the contribution of many people. Your piece needs to fit with other pieces, or the integrity of the whole will be compromised.

Those who are generous toward others find true happiness. Because they serve others, love serves them. Because they give without thought of return, the universe brings to them unexpected gifts. Because they live joyfully in the present, the future unfolds gracefully before them. (MOL)

11.

GRACE AND MIRACLES

GRACE VERSUS STRUGGLE

Grace happens when you abide with what is. Struggle happens when you push what is away or try to bring something else in. Grace happens when you accept. Struggle happens when you reject or try to fix. Grace is natural. Struggle is unnatural. Grace is effortless. Struggle takes great effort. Struggle means that you get in the way. Grace means that you stay out of the way. (RTG)

The Flow of Grace
When grace is in your life, there is harmony within and peace without. You honor yourself and others equally.

When you experience disharmony within or contention without, you know you are out of alignment with grace. Then, it is time to stop, breathe and re-center.

Grace is not continuous for anyone. New lessons emerge that must be learned. No matter how far the heart has opened, there will be times when it still contracts in fear. That is to be expected.

Grace comes and goes. Alignment happens and is lost. God appears and disappears. Self is forgotten and remembered.

The rhythm of the dance beats with each heart. It is a gentle, forgiving dance, not a rigid one. If you are looking for more than this, you search in vain.

Grace happens in the flow of life, not apart from it. And life is always moving, like a river, twisting and turning through the landscape. It begins as a mountain stream, rushing downward, impetuous and intent to reach its goal. Then it levels out and moves for what seems like an eternity through fields and plains, separating into different streams, joining with other bodies of water. By the time it reaches the ocean, it no longer has any urgency. Instead, it has a confidence born of experience. By the time it reaches the ocean, it no longer sees itself as anything other than ocean. It rests completely in itself, without beginning or end.

It will be that way with you too. When you enter fully into your life, all that held you separate will be gently washed away. Breathing in, you will open to embrace what comes. Breathing out, you will gently release it. (SOTH)

Resistance or Surrender

Life is either resistance or surrender. These are the only choices. Resistance leads to suffering. Surrender leads to bliss. Resistance is the decision to act alone. Surrender is the decision to act with God. (LWOC)

Christ Is a Being Not a Becoming

If you want to find peace, you must stop judging your experience and comparing it to that of others. Your experience, with all of its ups and downs, is perfect for you. It brings the lessons you need to learn to move beyond fear and guilt.

To live a surrendered life is to be present with your experience. It is to accept your experience without judging it or, if you judge it, to forgive yourself for doing so.

Increasingly, you become aware of when you dissociate from the moment and gently bring yourself back. You become aware of your fearful or anxious thoughts and see how they take you out of the silence.

In the present, you can just be. No strings attached. No judgments. No rules. Just be.

That is bliss. That is the flower of acceptance. (SOTH)

Gratitude: The Circle of Grace

You enter the circle of grace when you offer love to yourself or another. You enter the circle of fear when you withhold love from yourself or another.

When you stand inside of one circle, the reality of the other circle comes into question. This is why you often have the sense that there are two mutually exclusive worlds in your experience.

The grateful cannot imagine being unjustly treated. The resentful cannot imagine being loved by God. Which world would you inhabit? It is your choice.

Gratitude is the choice to see the love of God in all things. No being can be miserable who chooses thus. For the choice to appreciate leads to happiness as surely as the choice to depreciate leads to unhappiness and despair.

One gesture supports and uplifts. The other devalues and tears down.

How you choose to respond to life shapes your own continued perception. If you are living in despair, it is because you are choosing to depreciate the gifts that have been given you.

Each person who walks the earth reaps the results of the thoughts s/he has sown. And if s/he would change the nature of next year's harvest, s/he must change the thoughts s/he is thinking now.

Think a single grateful thought and you will see how true this statement is. The next time you are about to depreciate a gift that is given you, pause a moment and open your heart to receive that gift with gratitude. Then notice how your experience of the gift and relationship with the giver is transformed. (LWOC)

The Dance of Life

People who excel in the manifestation of their ideas learn to set realistic goals and implement them in a flexible way. If you want to understand what flexibility means watch the behavior of a young sapling in the wind. Its trunk is thin and fragile, yet it has awesome strength and endurance. That is because it moves with the wind, not against it.

When conditions are right for something to happen, it will happen without great effort. When conditions are not right, even great effort will not succeed. Moving with the wind requires sensitivity to the conditions at hand. There are times to rest and retreat, and times to move energetically forward.

Knowing when to move and when not to move is a matter of common sense and intuition. Abstract thinking needs to be combined with emotional sensitivity.

If you want to understand grace, look at the tree moving in the wind. That is the best metaphor you will find. The tree has deep roots and wide branches. It is fixed below, flexible above. It is a symbol of strength and surrender.

You can develop the same strength of character by moving flexibly with all the situations in your life. Stand tall and be rooted in the moment. Know your needs, but allow them to be met as life knows how. Do not insist that your needs be met in a certain way. If you do, you will offer unnecessary resistance. The trunk of the tree snaps when it tries to stand against the wind.

Move in the wind. Your life is a dance. It is neither good nor bad. It is a movement, a continuum.

Your choice is a simple one. You can dance or not. Deciding not to dance will not remove you from the dance floor. The dance will continue on around you.

All conditions open of themselves to the unconditional. Simply be open and present and you will fall into the arms of God. But resist even for a moment and you will get caught in a needless tangle of your own making. (LWOC)

The Search for Perfection

If you are trying to find the perfect job or the perfect relationship, you will be continually frustrated. The world does not offer perfection in this respect. It simply offers you an opportunity to learn to love yourself and others more deeply. Inevitably, growth involves change.

Ask yourself honestly: are you looking for a steady, predictable life? Is this what you want? If so, you must realize that the world cannot offer you this. Everything in the world is in the process of change. Nothing is steady. Nothing is predictable. Nothing will give you anything other than temporary security.

Thoughts come and go. Relationships begin and end. Bodies are born and pass away. This is all the world can offer you: impermanence, growth, change. (LWOC)

Love Is Without Form

Permanence cannot be found at the level of form. All form is in essence a distortion of the original formlessness of the universe. What is all-inclusive, all-accepting, all-loving cannot be limited to form.

Love extends to all at all times. Love is without conditions; that is to say it is without form. (LWOC)

Love Is a Gift

Love is a gift that must constantly be given as it is asked for in each moment. It takes no hostages, makes no bargains and cannot be compromised by fear. (LWOC)

Buddha's Window

The Buddha began in the same place where you begin. So did I. The nature of suffering does not change. You have not been given a special handicap, nor were you given fewer abilities.

There is no difference between you and Buddha, or between Buddha and I. You are pure being. The Buddha is pure being. You struggle with identification with form. So did the Buddha. So did I.

We are all tested. We all build on quicksand and get sucked down into the muck of conditioned existence. But we are not the conditioned.

We are the lotus swimming on the murky surface of the pond. We are the awareness, the profound discovery that grows out of the darkness of conditions. We are the white flower, nurtured by those murky waters.

If you are looking for beauty without sadness, you will not find it. If you are looking for celebration without the poignancy of pain, you will search in vain. All that is transcendent comes from the lowly, the light from the dark, the flower from the mud.

Give up your linear thinking, your rigid, left-brain expectations of what spirituality means. Life is not one-dimensional. If you are looking for the absolute, you must find it wherever you look. If the absolute is truly absolute, then there is no place where it is not found.

Don't choose one side of the argument. Learn to take both sides and work toward the middle. Both extremes reflect each other. Those who are in conflict share the same lesson.

There is only one way to freedom. Buddha called it the Middle Way, the way between all extremes. You can't get there by taking sides. You can't get there by choosing the good over the bad, or the light over the dark. Your path goes through the place where good and evil cross, where the light is obstructed, casting long shadows.

There are no maps that take you to this place. If you ask one person, he says, "Go to the right." If you ask another, he says, "Go to the left."

If you ask the pessimist where you can find truth, he will say, "It was here yesterday. You missed it." If you ask the optimist, he will reply: "It will be here tomorrow."

Who gives the correct answer? Is there, in fact, a correct answer? Or is the expectation of a correct answer itself the illusion?

When you can observe the argument without taking sides, when you can be in the middle of the battleground without attacking anyone, then you have arrived in the place where the lotus blooms. Few will notice you, but it will not matter. You have come home. You have slipped through the veil. You are no longer an object blocking the light, but the window through which it passes.

Can you imagine being a window that lets in the light, a window that shuts out the cold and opens to let in the fresh air? Can you imagine being so flexible and useful at the same time?

No longer imprisoned in a role, you are glad to be of help. No longer seeking, you are happy to point the way. When someone asks, "Which way to the divine?" you answer, "Any way will do."

You know that the outcome doesn't matter. Only being present on the journey, moment to moment matters. Between now and then, between this and that, the Buddha dwells.

"What a vague, dreamy man," you say. Yes, it is true, his existence spans centuries. Yet, there is no place where he has not been, no heart he has not touched.

If you will allow him, he will touch your heart too. If you will allow him, he will open the window in your mind that separates you from other sentient beings. (SOTH)

The Miracle of God's Love

When you are in touch with God's love for you, everything that happens in your life is miraculous. All you see are extraordinary opportunities to love, learn, create and be fully present in your life.

When you are not in touch with God's love for you, everything that happens in your life seems not to be good enough. You perpetually find fault with yourself and with others.

What is the secret to bringing miracles into your life? Your willingness to surrender to love's presence in each moment.

Miracles Come Spontaneously

Miracles do not come from linear, sequential thinking. They cannot be planned. You cannot learn to perform them or to receive them.

Miracles come spontaneously to the heart that has opened and the mind that has surrendered its need to control or to know. (LWOC)

Surrendering the Past

Learning to trust requires you to be neutral about what happens in your life. You don't have to see things in a positive light. Just stop seeing them in a negative light. Stop imposing your expectations and interpretations on what happens. Just let life unfold and see what develops.

God doesn't ask you to believe on faith. S/He makes a far more simple request: "Stop judging, stop finding fault, stop trying to make life conform to your pictures of reality. For a moment, set aside your knowledge and beliefs and experience your life free of the limitations you would place upon it."

When you do this, things go smoother. Problems resolve. Relationships move on course. Your life starts to work. After a while, you begin to realize that your job is just to show up, to be present, to let things happen.

You can't know God's plan as long as you insist on your own. God can't be in charge as long as you think you are the boss.

The main blocks to your relationship with God are your knowledge and your pride. Surrender these and you will make room for God's plan in your life.

What is God's agenda? It is healing, reconciliation, joyful self-expression and intimate communion. God's agenda is to allow the miraculous to happen at all times. Wherever your ego sees a problem or a limit, God sees an opportunity to love more deeply.

God says: "Let go of the past and make room for something new and more wonderful." You are afraid to do that because there is no guarantee that the new will be any better than the old.

You'd rather hold on to the old and invite the new in at the same time. That is the inevitable catch-22. The new cannot come in until the old is released. When you are attached to the past, you cannot move toward the future.

Letting go of the past is never easy. Yet it is the only choice that really works. When you let go of what used to be and accept what is, the universe instantly moves to support you.

It is the nature of the ego to become attached to the past, and to project the past forward into the future. The ego wants what is familiar, because it is basically uncomfortable with change. Its job is to create continuity.

And what is continuity but a projection of the old upon the new? If something is continuous, it is not miraculous. Miraculous events are not continuous with what happened before them. They represent a shift of energy, a movement out of past perception, past limitation. They are unpredictable, unexpected and in many cases inscrutable.

You call them miracles because God's hand is in them. But without your permission, they could not take place. Without your surrender of the past, miracles could not come into your life. You prepare the ground for them. You create the space in which the miraculous occurs. (SOTH)

What Is a Miracle?

There is a great deal of confusion regarding what a miracle is. Some people are cured of serious illnesses; others are delivered unexpectedly from dangerous situations or experience unanticipated good fortune. All of these situations are indeed miraculous. But what about the person who dies of an incurable illness, who is paralyzed in a serious accident or is the victim of some terrible crime? Are you to view these events as completely un-miraculous, as out of sync with God's laws? And, if so, can you say that those who experienced these events were people who were not spiritual or close to God?

Nothing could be further from the truth. All events cohere in a higher order, the meaning of which dawns on those who open their hearts and minds to their experience. No event, no matter how unfortunate, is devoid of purpose.

The cripple is no less holy than the man whose broken limbs are mysteriously healed. Don't make the mistake of thinking that you can have miracles on demand. Don't be foolish enough to believe that you are bad or unholy if you don't get the miracle you want.

Such thinking comes from looking only at the surface of life. And, if you want to understand the miraculous nature of life, you must look beneath the surface.

All events are miraculous in the sense that they have a higher purpose. Often, you don't see what that purpose is. You feel betrayed by God. You think you are being punished. But that is just a limitation on your part, an unwillingness to accept, to trust, to look more deeply for the meaning that eludes you.

The real miracle does not lie in the outer event. The real miracle lies in the spiritual purpose behind the event. The purpose may be to strengthen your faith or to challenge it. You cannot judge the meaning of an event until you know what its spiritual purpose is.

Miracles help you break through the limits of your own mind. They challenge your world view. They urge you to let go of your interpretation of life so that you can see the possibilities that lie beyond it.

It is odd, perhaps, but sometimes an apparent tragedy turns out to be an unanticipated blessing. You have heard people say, "Thank God for my cancer. Without it, I never would have transformed my life." Or, "Thank God for the lesson of my child's death. It helped me wake up to my purpose in this lifetime."

Sometimes what appears to be taken away is the greatest gift, because it calls you forward. It calls you forth out of your shell into the fulfillment of your life purpose. (SOTH)

Miracles and Physical Laws

The real miracle comes in your surrender to life as it is. When you come to peace and acceptance of your life, the miracle of God's love dawns in your heart.

Yet some people feel that a miracle has not taken place unless a physical law is transcended: the ocean parts and lets the people pass or the corpse is raised from the dead.

I hate to disappoint you, but these things don't happen. What happens on the physical plane happens according to physical laws.

That does not mean that spiritual laws are not in operation. They certainly are, but spiritual laws work with and through physical laws. There is no contradiction.

Spiritual law has nothing to do with how things work, but with the interpretation of your experience. It is the decision you make about what an event in your life means.

For example, I was crucified. If I had possessed superhuman powers, I could have stopped the crucifixion from happening. But my spiritual understanding did not make me a superman. It simply enabled me to see the truth of what was happening to me.

As a result, I did not interpret the crucifixion as an attack. I did not condemn my brothers, for I saw that their actions were motivated by fear. And I felt compassion for them.

Yes, I was crucified. But I did not close my heart. I did not cast blame on anyone. I surrendered to God's will in that moment, as I had done in every other moment of my life.

If you think your faith will stop the crucifixion, you are just as likely to be wrong as right. Perhaps your faith will help your executioners open their hearts and change their minds. Perhaps it will not.

Visualization can be powerful. It can alter perception and assist in healing. But I wouldn't suggest that you tie yourself to the train tracks and visualize the train disappearing as it approaches you at sixty miles per hour.

Miracle-mindedness is not demonstrated through the attempt to manipulate physical reality. That is an activity of the ego. The attempt to produce miracles on demand is the activity of a clown, not a spiritual man or woman.

You demonstrate your miracle-mindedness by surrendering to your experience and connecting with God's will for you in each moment. Your job is not to try to overcome physical reality but to be fully present with it. (SOTH)

Allowing Miracles

Sometimes you think you need a miracle, but all you need is a little common sense. Sometimes, you think you need a miracle, but all you need to do is walk through your fear.

I'm not trying to suggest that there is a shortage of miracles out there and that you must save them up for special occasions. On the contrary, there is no shortage of miracles happening in your life, but many of those miracles you don't see because you are expecting fireworks.

When you are doing the best that you can in your life, there are many little miracles taking place. When you are moving through your fear, seeing your projections, and reaching out lovingly to people who are dispirited or afraid, you are a miracle worker.

But, if you are smart, you don't call yourself a miracle worker. You don't call attention to yourself. You let others whom you empower and uplift take the credit. You help people build up their confidence so that they can learn to make their own miracles.

I did not take credit for the healings that happened in my presence. I was just the impetus that catalyzed these movements of healing and forgiveness. The faith that people had in me they learned to find in themselves. I gave people back to God. I did not ask for a following.

Nor do I want one now. Please don't go around saying "Jesus says this and Jesus says that." Forget Jesus. Just be a loving, accepting presence, and others will come home to the true Self through you.

You see, it does not matter who the door is. It could be me. It could be you. It could be another brother or sister. The door does not need to be celebrated.

When the door needs to be celebrated, it ceases to be a door. When people grasp the finger pointing to the moon, they can no longer tell where it is pointing. (MOL)

Through the Open Door

I never said that you should walk through brick walls or even that you should walk on water. I merely pointed to the open door and asked you if you were ready to enter. And that is all that you need to ask your brother and sister.

One who loves without conditions is never attached to the outcome. People come and go and you never know the whys and wherefores. You think that some people will easily pass through the gate, yet they turn suddenly away. You are convinced that others will never come within sight of the gate, yet they cross the threshold with unexpected grace.

Do not be concerned. It is none of your business who comes and who goes. The covenant is made in every heart and only God knows who is ready and who is not. (LWOC)

12.

SPIRITUAL PRACTICES

DEEDS NOT WORDS

If you know me in your heart, you know that I am not much for words. Words by themselves mean very little. Only when they are substantiated by actions do they have the power to demonstrate truth.

If you want to establish my teachings in your heart and in your life, you need to commit to a spiritual practice. Practice going into the silence each day. Practice keeping the Sabbath. Practice unceasing prayer and God-communion.

My life is the fruit of my practice. So is yours.

What good are lovely sermons if the one who gives them does not practice what s/he preaches? Actions always speak louder than words. People emulate what you do, not what you say.

I advise you to practice before you preach. Then, what you say will be consistent with your actions. Then, you will be living the word, not just speaking it. (MOL)

Practice, Practice, Practice

Mine is not an intellectual teaching. It is a practical one. "Love your neighbor" is not an abstract concept. It is a simple, compelling idea that invites you to practice. I did not invite you to an evening of discourse and argument. I did not ask you to profess or debate the Scriptures. I asked you to do what you find so difficult to do: to go beyond your limited concept of self. Any of the practices I gave to you will keep you busy for a lifetime. Although they are simple to understand, their challenge lies in the practice. (MOL)

Connecting to the Source of Love

Your heart is the place where love is born. It is the bottomless well from which you can draw as often as you need to. Every time you come to the well, you drink the waters of life. Your spiritual thirst is quenched. Your sins are forgiven. You are baptized, healed and renewed.

Whenever life feels difficult, there is only one place that offers you sanctuary. You must learn to make your pilgrimage there on a regular basis.

Don't look outside of yourself for answers. Don't seek refuge in the ideas, opinions and advice of other people. Don't go into your head and try to figure things out. Surrender all of that, and seek the place where love begins, in your own heart. It is your responsibility to reconnect with the Source of love when you need to. No one else can do it for you.

It doesn't matter what spiritual practice you do as long as it takes you into your heart and helps you connect with the Source of love. If it does that, then stay with it throughout all the twists and turns of your life. Hold to your practice. It is your lifeline. When storms come up unexpectedly, it keeps you afloat. Ever so gradually, it brings you home.

When the spark in your heart is attended to, it grows into a steady flame. When the flame is fed by acts of loving kindness to self and others, it becomes a blazing fire, a source of warmth and light for all who encounter it. (RTG)

Breathing

Silence is the essence of the heart. You cannot be in the heart unless you are in forgiveness of yourself and others. You cannot be in the heart if you are worried or angry. You cannot be in the heart if your breathing is shallow or labored.

When the breath is shallow, thinking is superficial. If you want to live a spiritual life, bring your awareness to your breath. Become aware of the times when you are breathing in a shallow way and bring your awareness to your thoughts. You will see that your mind is chattering. None of these thoughts has depth or significance. If you relax and breathe deeply, these thoughts will fly away like startled birds. And then you will abide in the heart.

When the breath is labored, thinking is driven by fear and anxiety. Become aware when your breathing is labored. Notice what you are thinking and feeling. Your mind-states will be rooted in the past or future. You will be focused on what other people are doing and how you can accommodate them or protect yourself from their actions. You are building a fortress of thought around your heart. Take a deep breath and relax. Now take another one. Breathe and return to the heart. Breathe and return to your essential Self.

Unless you return to the heart, you cannot see with compassion. And one who does not see with compassion does not see accurately. All that is perceived is a fabrication, hyperbole. It simply feeds your boredom or anxiety.

Breathing is the key to living a spiritual life in physical embodiment. Unless you breathe deeply and calmly, you cannot be in your heart.

If you do not know what I am talking about, put this book down and begin to breathe into your abdomen, counting to five on the inhalation and counting again to five on the exhalation. Breathe in this way for five minutes, gradually extending your count to seven, or eight, or nine. Do not force. Just expand gradually, as your lungs comfortably allow.

Now you are in your heart. Notice that you are deeply relaxed, yet surprisingly alert. Your consciousness extends to all the cells of your body. You are content where you are. You fully inhabit your body in the present moment. You feel warm and energetic. You feel safe and secure. Your thoughts have slowed down and become more integral. You are no longer focusing on the "shoulds" and "what ifs" of your life. Tension and anxiety are absent. Past and future have receded from your awareness. Your thinking is centered and dignified. You can stay with your thoughts because they are fewer and farther between.

Now bring your awareness to your heart, as you continue to breathe gently but deeply into your abdomen. Can you feel the presence of understanding and compassion in your heart center? Can you feel that you hold yourself and others in gentle acceptance?

Now you are in your heart. Now you are in the silence from which all sound comes. Like a boat on the ocean you feel the waves swell beneath you. You move with the waves, yet you know you are not the waves.

Thoughts come and go, yet you know you are not the thoughts. Some thoughts propel you farther out than others, yet you can still return to your center. Like a large wave, a particular thought may be charged with emotion, yet if you remain where you are, the emotion will subside. Now you know you can abide the ebb and flow of the tide, moving out and moving in, feeling the contraction and expansion of thought.

Beneath the thinking mind is a pure, non-judgmental awareness. As soon as you discover that awareness, the heart opens, and giving and receiving are effortless. (SOTH)

Going into the Silence

Take some time to be present. Breathe and be here now. Be in the silence of your heart. Let your thoughts come and go until the space between them opens. Let your feelings of anxiety, boredom, frustration come and go until a softness comes into your heart, a patience with yourself, a forgiveness that rides in and out on each breath.

Let peace come into your heart, all by itself. As you allow space to be there, feel the presence that comes in. That is the Spirit of God, call it what you will. Now there is only love; there are only blessings.

Once you have tasted the absolute joy of this communion, you will not want to be without it. You will find a few moments every day to breathe and be, to let the world spill out from your mind, to let peace come into your heart. You will do this not out of duty or the search for approval but because it is sheer bliss. You will make time for God in the same way that you make time to embrace your lover at night, because it feels so good, because it is such a deep blessing.

God is a living presence in your life, not an abstraction. S/He offers you a companionship that goes beyond the limits of form. When everything else dissolves, this loving presence remains with you, because you share one mind and the same bottomless heart. (SOTH)

Hearing Your Guidance

Once or twice each day, for at least ten minutes, make time to go into the silence. Put aside what preoccupies you, be still, and listen. You might find it helpful to do some yoga or deep breathing first to relax your body and calm your mind.

Sit or lie down in a comfortable position and just relax into the silence. As thoughts or feelings come up, just be aware of them and accept them. In the space between your thoughts, there will be a deep peace and stillness. Dwell there. Be completely alert and present there.

Sometimes when you rest in the silence, you may hear a voice, see an image or have some insight that has nothing to do with any of your everyday thoughts. When this happens, you feel an inner peace and rightness about what you have heard, seen or understood. That is a sign that you have heard your guidance.

Guidance comes from the place in you that is connected to God. Receive it gratefully. Learn to trust it and act on it. The more you do, the easier it will be for you to hear the truth as it unfolds within your consciousness.

By going into the silence on a regular basis, you will be cultivating a relationship with the indwelling God. The more you trust that relationship, the more it can begin to guide your actions in the world, bringing you step by step in line with your life purpose. (RTG)

Sabbath Is Sanctuary

Once per week, gather together with others in fellowship to remember the divine within each of you. In our tradition, the Sabbath has always been a holy time. It is a time when the whole community assembles to remember God.

On the Sabbath, you take a break from the ebb and flow of worldly affairs. You give thanks to God for all the joys in your life and you ask for God's help in meeting the challenges. Together you pray for understanding and peace. Together you create a safe space where people may open their hearts and move through their fears.

The safe space of the Sabbath encourages honesty and self-disclosure. People can share whatever is heavy on their hearts in an atmosphere of unconditional acceptance and non-judgment. Suffering can be acknowledged without anyone trying to fix anyone else. This is a place of confession and atonement. It is a place where the misfortunes and misunderstandings of your worldly experience can be righted in the forgiving light of unconditional acceptance and love.

Here the couple and the nuclear family find the extended family—the community—the microcosmic global village containing a diversity of human beings: black and white, old and young, male and female, rich and poor, educated and untaught. Here the individual's heart is open to all her brothers and sisters. Here she declares her equality and solidarity with other women and men.

This is a sanctuary, a safe, loving, non-judging space that is open to all. It is not a place where beliefs are espoused, but where the principles of love and equality are practiced. It is a place of forgiveness, a place where you are safe to leave the past behind and open up to the miracle of the present moment.

When you enter the door of this sanctuary, you leave your idols behind. You surrender your struggles for self-worth, approval, money or fame. Here recognition is given to you freely and without conditions. Here you are an equal child of God, a brother or a sister to each one who gathers with you.

Here, your children can learn how to take responsibility for their thoughts and feelings, how to communicate honestly without attacking others, and how to resolve conflicts peacefully. They can learn to express themselves creatively and to value the expressions of others. They can learn courtesy, respect and kindness. They can learn—not just from books—but from the living example of their mentors. (SOTH)

The Rhythm of the Sabbath

I do not ask you to meditate or pray for an hour a day, although there is nothing wrong with this. I simply ask you to remember your Divine Essence for five minutes out of each hour, or for one thought out of every ten. Nine thoughts may be about needing to fix yourself or someone else, but let the tenth thought be about that which does not need fixing. Let the tenth thought be about something which is totally acceptable, totally lovable.

This is the rhythm the Sabbath was meant to establish. For six days you could be absorbed in the drama of work and struggle, but on the seventh day you were to remember God. The seventh day was to be a day of rest, of turning inward.

Let the wisdom of the Sabbath be brought into your daily life. Then, when you eat, God will sit at your table. When you speak with your brother, you will remember to say something encouraging to him.

The Sabbath is a ritual of remembering. When you realize this, you can discard the outer shell and find a form of the ritual that helps you remember. (LWOC)

A Mantra That Works

Any place and any time in the course of your daily life, you can be doing spiritual practice. Whenever you find yourself getting confused, anxious, fearful, angry, etc., ask yourself "Am I loving myself right now?" This question helps you understand that beneath all fearful thoughts and behaviors lies the refusal to be gentle and loving toward yourself.

Even if your anger or upset feelings are directed toward someone else, you aren't being loving toward yourself. Indeed, the only way that you can be angry at anyone else is to forget to love yourself. When you are loving yourself, it is not possible to be angry at anyone else.

The mantra "Am I loving myself right now?" reminds you of your only responsibility while here in this embodiment: to love and take care of yourself. When love is established in your heart, it flows automatically to others.

This is anything but a selfish practice. It is a practice that takes you back to your heart, where love originates.

When you see that you aren't being loving toward yourself, you know what you need to do to return to peace. If you are having an argument with someone, you need to stop and say: "Excuse me, but I just realized that I'm not being loving either toward myself or toward you right now. I need to have some time to attune to love. Otherwise, I know I'll say things that I don't mean. Can we have a little break and come back to this conversation later?"

When you know that you are not being loving, you need to stop and find a way to connect with love. Take a walk, do some deep breathing. Be aware of the judgments you are carrying about others and see how they reflect your judgment of yourself. Work on accepting yourself right now in this moment. If there is a disagreement with someone, work on accepting the disagreement. Let this moment be okay just the way it is. It doesn't have to be perfect to be acceptable. Be aware that your inability to accept this moment extends it indefinitely. Most feelings shift when you accept them. Lack of acceptance just prolongs your pain.

If you are very angry, you may not be ready to have this conversation with yourself. First, you might need to run around the block, go to a deserted beach and yell or hit a pillow. Don't take your anger out on someone else. That will just create more pain for you. Find a harmless way to express your anger. Then look at how your anger crucifies you and holds you hostage to your pain. It may be provoked by someone else, but it is never anyone else's responsibility. (RTG)

Dropping Interpretation

Events occur with a certain rhythm and grace. But then you step in and try to give them meaning and the rhythm and grace are lost. As soon as you think you know what something means, you cease to be able to understand it.

Do not decide what something means. Just let it be. Live with it. Breathe with it. Then, you will begin to understand it. You may or may not be able to put your understanding into words, but it does not matter. Insight will come.

All the answers that you need can be found in the silence of your heart. You don't have to look to others for solutions or advice. When people come to you saying, "I have the answer," send them politely away. Their answer is just as toxic for you as your own judgment of the situation.

Admit "I do not know what this means." And trust the same intelligent force which brought this situation into your life to reveal its significance when it is time.

You don't need to practice elaborate systems of meditation or yoga. Simply cease judging, interpreting, conceptualizing, speculating. Let all that is not "being" fall away and "being" will flower of itself.

This is the most profound practice I can give you. In this simple practice, all the barriers to truth will come down. (LWOC)

Restoring Trust and Connection

When you and another person are not experiencing peace in your relationship, you are probably withholding feelings that need to be shared. The following steps will enable you to communicate your feelings to each other in a non-blaming way.

1. Identify your fear. Fear is at the root of all negative, stressful emotions, including anger and hurt. Be with your feelings long enough to identify the root fear. Exaggerate the fear if necessary.
2. Identify how you see yourself as a victim. Peace leaves your heart only when you think it is possible for someone else to do something to you against your will. How specifically do you feel powerless in this situation?
3. Own the fear and the feelings of powerlessness and state them to the other person in a way that takes total responsibility for your experience (e.g., When you didn't call, I felt abandoned and I got scared). Ask the person to listen to what you say without judging it or responding to it.
4. Thank the person for listening to you without interrupting and offer to do the same for him or her.
5. Listen without judgment or interpretation to what the person shares with you and acknowledge that you heard it.
6. Thank each other for making the space to listen. Don't try to resolve anything now. Just feel good about hearing each other.

This process works because it helps both of you take total responsibility for your feelings. It doesn't allow you to make the other person responsible for what you are feeling or vice versa. When you "own" what you are feeling and communicate it, the other person does not feel attacked, because you are disclosing information about yourself rather than blaming him or her for your experience. This keeps appropriate boundaries intact and does not invite mutual trespass.

The process also succeeds because it does not focus on "fixing" either the other person or yourself. The only outcome desired here is increased communication. Honest, heart-to-heart communication immediately restores the feeling of love and connection. When that happens, specific problems—which are merely symptoms of separation and disconnection—often disappear. (SOTH)

Not Fixing Others

When you try to fix or give advice to others, you are not being kind or generous. If you want to be kind to others, you need to accept them the way they are and stop trying to judge, analyze, interpret or change their lives.

You do this by realizing that they are okay just as they are in this moment. You hold the consciousness of their present perfection. If they want to share their problems with you, you listen with compassion, but you don't offer opinions or solutions.

Instead, you let them know that you have heard them. You might even share a time in your own life when you were feeling a similar way, but you don't pretend that your situation is the same as theirs or that what worked for you would work for them. Instead, you encourage them to stay in their own process and find their own guidance. You feel confident that the answers they need can be found within.

When you trust others to find their own answers, you treat them as spiritual equals. You don't pretend to know something they don't know. You grant people both respect and freedom. You trust the truth within them to light their way. That is love in action. That is the kind of unconditional love I ask you to offer one another.

Not fixing others means that you don't take inappropriate responsibility for the lives of other people. That gives you the time and energy you need to take appropriate responsibility for your own life. By taking good care of yourself on all levels—physically, emotionally, mentally and spiritually—you are able to respond to others in the most compassionate, patient and caring way. By contrast, if you neglect your responsibility to care for yourself in order to care for others, you get depleted energetically. Then you aren't in a position to be helpful to anyone.

It is a revelation to some of you to know that you are not here to rescue others from their pain, but merely to walk through your own. No one else can do that for you. It is your essential responsibility and will be throughout this embodiment. Even when you join your life with another person's life, this responsibility stays with you. Whenever you lose sight of it, or try to give it to someone else, you inevitably pay the price. (RTG)

Daily Rituals of Intimacy and Peace for Partners

If you are living with another person, you can create a safe, loving space for your relationship by engaging in simple rituals of mutual caring and affirmation. Each day celebrate your relationship by spending at least five minutes of quiet time looking into each other's eyes. Practice softening the hard shell of your life and letting your partner's love in. Remember why you chose to walk with this being at your side and reconfirm your commitment to his or her highest good. Start the day with the gift of your love for each other.

Each day remember each other and remember God. Pray for a day of learning, loving and self-disclosure. Pray to open your heart to each person who comes into your life. Pray to walk through your fears. Pray to be of help. Pray to listen for your guidance. In this way, the spiritual purpose of your partnership is renewed.

Each night before you go to bed repeat this ritual. Give thanks for all that happened that day and give any unresolved issues back to God with your willingness to do what is for the highest good of all concerned. Let any uneasiness with your partner be cleared verbally. Express your gratitude for each other. Looking into each other's eyes, let your heart be open. Rest in the safety of your partner's loving embrace. (SOTH)

Being with Your Fear in a Compassionate Way

When you are judging another or yourself, neither your mind nor your heart is open. When you are complaining, blaming, holding grievances, pushing love away or finding fault with your experience, you are contracted in heart and mind. Behind this contraction is a simple fear that you are somehow unworthy or not good enough.

Becoming aware of your fear is essential if you wish to reconnect to love. You cannot open your heart or your mind as long as your fear remains unconscious. You must bring your fear into conscious awareness.

When you see the fear that underlies your judgments, don't find fault with yourself. Just be with the fear and know that it is okay that you are afraid. Tell yourself, "I know I'm scared and feeling unworthy. That's why I'm blaming others."

Gently take the responsibility away from others: "It's not anyone else's fault that I don't feel good enough. I don't have to project my fear and unworthiness onto someone else. I can look at my fear directly and see that I need to bring some love and acceptance to myself. I can be with my fear in a compassionate way."

When you are able to hold your fear in a compassionate way, you reconnect to your heart. You open your mind. You feel energy as you release others from blame and open to your own love. Your consciousness expands. You stop seeing your situation in a limited way.

Love is the essence of who you are. Everything else that you think or feel about yourself or anyone else is just an illusion. Illusions are born when you stop loving yourself or another. The only way to dissolve illusions is to start loving someone—yourself or another person—right now. (RTG)

Four Steps to Working Through Fear

The key to everything is your recognition of your fear. Once you know that you are fearful, you know that any decision you make while in this state will be counterproductive. Your only constructive course of action is to recognize your fear and begin to work through it.

Here are four simple steps that can help you do this.

First, recognize your fear. Notice the signs that fear is coming up for you: rapid, shallow breathing, pounding heart, nervousness, anxiety, attack thoughts, anger, or hurt. Be aware of your physical, emotional and mental state without judging it or trying to change it. Acknowledge it to yourself and, if another person is involved, to the other person.

Second, recognize that the solution your ego offers you is motivated by this fear. When you listen to that solution, you don't feel any more peaceful. Indeed, you often feel more charged with anger, more victimized, more suspicious of other people and defensive toward them. Realize that your ego's solution cannot bring you peace.

Third, accept your fear. Get your arms around all of it. Say to yourself, "It is okay that I am afraid. Let me be with my fear and tune into where it is coming from." Don't be analytical about this. Don't go up into your head. Stay in your emotional body and listen to what's there. You will know when you have listened enough because you will begin to feel more peaceful, even though you don't have a solution to your dilemma.

Fourth, tell yourself, "I don't have to decide anything now. I can wait until my fear subsides to make any decisions that need to be made."

By doing these four steps, you will bring love and acceptance to yourself. Out of this compassionate place, a non-fearful solution to your dilemma can be found.

Do not put pressure on yourself. Pressure is just more fear coming up. Keep loving yourself and accepting your fear. Be patient and let the answer come from a non-fearful place in your psyche. (MOL)

Be Clear About Your Intention

In your interactions with other people, it is your intention that really matters. Do you intend to bless or to curse, to accept or to find fault?

It doesn't matter what happened yesterday or last year. It doesn't even matter what just happened. Right now you have a new choice to make.

What is your intention in this moment? Is it to bless or to curse? Were you so injured by what just happened or by what happened years ago that right now you insist on holding on to your grievances?

When your intention is to bless, you cannot hold on to the past. You must let the past go to be open to this moment.

If you have closed your heart or your mind, you cannot bless. You can only judge, blame, complain or condemn.

So ask yourself what your intention is. Are you here to bless or to judge? And if you want to judge, just be aware of it. Just be aware: "I am still carrying a past hurt, a past wound. I am not ready to bless."

Let the awareness "I am not ready to bless" be present. Realize that whatever you say or do in this moment will be a judgment or attack, because you are not ready to bless. In this moment, all you can do is be with your fear, your hurt, your anger, your judgment.

Admit "In this moment I can only be with my fear, because I am not ready to bless." That's the truth of what's happening and there's no harm done. There's no harm when you refrain from speaking or acting when you are upset. There is just the experience of being present for yourself in your pain and feelings of separation.

When you can be with yourself in this way, you bring love in. The more love you bring in, the more you begin to accept and to bless yourself and your experience. And before long, you are ready to extend that blessing to others.

Whose job is it to weather these moments of separation when you feel cut off from others or from God? Is it not your job? How can you make it any one else's responsibility? (RTG)

Not Reacting to the Fear of Others

Your goal is to know that everything you think, feel or do is coming from love. If it is coming from love, it will be a loving thought, a loving feeling, a loving action. You will be an instrument of love and understanding in the world. If it is not coming from love, then you will be sowing seeds of strife.

To refrain from speaking or acting when you are not ready to bless interrupts the reactive cycle of attack and defense. It helps you take responsibility for the contents of your own consciousness, instead of trying to blame others for how you think or feel.

In the same manner, when others project onto you, blaming you for their pain or discomfort, you must take care not to react to their accusations. They are not in their right mind. If you react, you too will not be in your right mind.

Instead, try to feel compassion for their cries for attention and for love. Tune into how much pain they feel and how difficult it is for them to face that pain. Then you won't feel attacked. Then, you won't feel that you have to defend yourself against the accusations of others.

Because you don't take offense when people inappropriately blame you, you don't engage their pain with your pain, their anger with your anger or their unworthiness with your own. You mirror back to them their innocence by refusing to make anyone guilty.

By speaking and acting only when you are able to bless, you stand free of the painful drama of mutual trespass and betrayal. You take care of yourself and others at the deepest level of being. Waves of illusion wash over you, but you stand simply and firmly in the truth that you are. (RTG)

The Dance of Acceptance

It is a radical act to accept what happens in your life exactly as it is. When you do that, you stop questioning the validity of your experience.

Instead, you begin to look at your resistance, your judgments, your negative interpretations of what happens.

When you see your resistance, don't judge it. Don't beat yourself up. Just notice your fear without judgment. When you identify fear, it no longer has the ability to run your life.

Acceptance is a lifelong dance. You get better at it the more you do it. But you never dance perfectly. Fear and resistance continue to come up and you do the best you can with them. Sometimes they slow you down, but slowing down might be exactly what is needed.

In the dance of acceptance, unconscious becomes conscious. Your fear becomes your partner.

You dance with what happens and with what you think and feel about it. The inner and outer dance are going on all the time. There is never a time when you can get off the dance floor and go and take a nap.

There is continual movement even in stillness. The stream never stops flowing. If it is not visible on the surface, then it continues underground.

You live in a dynamic universe . . . always moving, always changing. Sometimes you get tired and you want to get off the merry-go-round. "I shall dance no more," you self-righteously proclaim. But then, unexpectedly, you fall in love, or someone makes you a business offer you can't refuse. As soon as you really understand that the emperor has no clothes, his designer shows up with the latest fashions!

No matter how hard you try, you cannot get out of the drama. You can't stop the dance. It goes on with you or without you. That's why your only hope of having a harmonious experience is to learn to move with the flow instead of against it.

When you accept the eternal nature of the dance, it is easier to accept its specific content in the moment. That content may be that you are having a panic attack, yelling at your husband or kids, drinking too much or even contemplating suicide, but as long as you know that it's part of the dance you can come out of it. You never step into something you can't step out of, no matter how difficult it seems. That's one of the laws of the dance. When you take a false step, you take a breath and keep moving. When you lose the rhythm, you listen for a moment to the music and pick it up again.

Mistakes are part of the dance. But some people don't know this. Their business fails or their partner leaves them and they blow their brains out. They play for very high stakes. They think the dance is about success or failure.

Sometimes, people forget all the shades of gray and see only black or white. Yet black could not be black if white were not white. They are mutually dependent. You can't have one without the other.

It is paradoxical. It has always been paradoxical.

The greatest act of acceptance is to know that what happens is perfect for you. You are not given more than you can handle, nor is anything lacking in your life. To be sure, you can look at your neighbor's yard and think the grass is greener. Maybe he has a bigger house and a nicer car. But you can't see what they mean to him. You can't see if he's happy about his house or his car. You can only see if you are happy about them.

And, if you are not happy about them, then you can be sure you are feeling unworthy and unappreciated. And so that is what you must dance with. When you are not accepting your life as it is, you must dance with your lack of acceptance. You must learn to be with your resistance, your envy, your jealousy in a loving way. And that's quite an extraordinary dance.

The unhappier you are, the harder the dance becomes, because you must dance with your unhappiness. That's why acceptance is so important as a spiritual practice. The more you accept your life as it is, the easier the dance becomes. (RTG)

13.

THE INDWELLING GOD

ESSENCE

Essence is not born and does not die. It exists before physical birth and after physical death. Essence in you is not different from Essence in your brother or sister. Bodies seem to separate you from each other, but Essence unites you.

When you feel unloved, unworthy or cut off from others, you are forgetting your Essence. You think you are separate from other people and from God. You could not judge or attack otherwise.

When you remember your Essence, you remember your Spiritual connection to all beings. Attack is impossible when you remember who you are.

Essence within you is wholly lovable and loving. When you are in touch with your Essence, you know that each person including yourself is acceptable exactly as s/he is. You know that there is nothing about you or anyone else that needs to be improved or fixed. To know your Essence requires that you discard your judgments of yourself and others. (LWOC)

Lifting the Veil

Essence is not found in how life appears. That's just the veil. To find Essence, you must lift the veil.

Essence is the truth of who you are. It isn't the temporal, the changing, the inconstant. It is the eternal, the unchanging, the constant, because Essence is love and never stops being love.

If you aren't looking within, you can live your whole life and never know that Essence exists. You can think that life gave you a raw deal. You can be bitter, resentful, angry. There's nothing to be done about this if you insist on looking outside of yourself for validation or approval.

An about-face is necessary. You must turn to the place where Essence abides. You must look into your own heart. You must find the place in you that is unconditionally aligned with love.

You can't do this while you are blaming others or holding on to grievances. Nor can you do it when you are feeling guilty and are beating yourself up for making mistakes. All judgment of self and others must go. You must come to Essence empty, with open arms. (RTG)

Real Love

Real love does not change. It is formless, omnipresent, eternal. It does not exist apart from you. Once you know this in the depth of your heart and mind, you will no longer need to search for happiness outside of yourself. (LWOC)

Find What Is Real

Find what is real, what is true, what is consistent and dependable in yourself. Stop looking for solidity in others. If your life is anchored in the truth of your experience, then that truth can be shared. But if you are looking for truth, or love, or salvation outside yourself, you will be disappointed again and again.

Only by honoring yourself does the beloved come. Those who

twist themselves into pretzels in the search for love simply push the beloved away. (SOTH)

The Door to Essence

The door to the Essence opens through your heart. It opens through your gentle acceptance of yourself in this moment. It opens through your embrace of your experience.

The door to Essence opens through your gentle acceptance of others as they are in this moment. It opens through your willingness to be with them without judging them or trying to fix them. It opens through the attention and the blessings you freely extend toward others.

The door to Essence opens when you no longer need to make reality fit your picture of how it should be. It opens when you can surrender everything you think you know and come to each moment empty of expectations.

If you want to find Essence, stop looking for It in sacred books and religious practices. That is not where you will find It. If you want to find Essence, open your heart. Be gentle with yourself and others. See your judgments for what they are: the obstacle to peace within and peace without.

Essence is not some abstraction, but a living presence in your life. If you want to understand what Essence is, think of someone close to you who has died. That person is no longer in form, yet the Essence of that person remains with you. Essence is the breath that animates the human form. It is the original nature and the ultimate understanding. It is the blessing of love on all things.

How do you open to Essence? Stop resisting your experience. Stop withholding your love from others and pushing the love of others away. Stop blaming yourself for other people's problems. Stop blaming others for your grief or pain. Be with your joy without trying to prolong it and with your pain without trying to make it go away. Let yourself feel the joy of others without envying them; let yourself feel their pain without trying to fix them. Open to the truth of your life as it unfolds. (SOTH)

The Only Authority

Some of you are comfortable using the word God. Some of you are not.

The danger of using the word God is that you might think that God is apart from you. This is not the case. God does not live in the sky, or even in the ether.

The danger of using another word like Essence or Self is that you might think that God exists within your ego-structure. This is not the case either.

God is not present in your limited thinking nor is S/He a judge standing outside that thinking. S/He does not participate in the realm of illusion, nor does S/He punish those who do.

Realize that most of the concepts that you have of God come from other people. They are not based on your own experience.

Do not expect your relationship with God to look like anyone else's. God's presence in your life is totally unique.

Don't try to measure your spirituality by comparing what happens for you with what happens for others. Do not make the mistake of thinking that someone else has more spiritual knowledge than you do. That is preposterous. Anyone who is close to God knows that it is you who gives God permission to be present in your life, only you.

Forget the priests, psychics and shamans who would give you answers. They are the blind leading the blind.

Cultivate your relationship with God directly. Enter the silence of your own heart. Talk to God. Pray and ask for guidance. Open the dialogue and listen for God's answers within and in the signs that S/He sends into your life.

Get to know God in your own experience. Accept no substitutes. And know absolutely that any message of fear does not come from

God or from any of God's ministers. Any message that disempowers you or puts you down comes from a false prophet, a manipulator, an avenger. Turn away from such teachings, but send love and compassion to those who uphold them, for they are in great pain.

Neither take a teacher nor be one. Be a brother or a sister instead. Do not prescribe for others or let them prescribe for you.

Forget your physics and metaphysics, your exoteric and esoteric sciences. None of these systems can give you the answers you seek. None of them can lead you to peace.

Burn your Bibles, your channeled documents and your holy books. They are someone else's experience. Accept no teacher or teaching other than the one of your heart. That alone is God's teaching.

Do not take communion in a hall where fools preside and the flock is mentally asleep. Those who wish to be told what to do will find out soon enough that no one has the answers for them.

Do not give your power up to impostors. Accept only God's teaching into your life and take communion in the silence where you meet Her. You, my friend, are enough. You are sufficient. All the jewels of knowledge can be found within your own mind. All the joys of Spirit can be discovered in your own heart.

Gather with others in mutual appreciation and gratitude to God, but do not take direction from one another. Instead, honor each other's experience. It is sacred. It is holy. It is beyond comment or evaluation.

Celebrate your common experience. Meditate and pray together. Break bread together. Give, receive, serve together. But accept no other authority in your life but God's.

Each of you is guided in a unique way and has unique gifts to offer. Celebrate that guidance and those gifts. But do not try to give your guidance to another and do not accept another's guidance if he offers it to you. That is a false gift. For what works for one will not necessarily work for another.

When you understand that you have direct communion with

God at all times, you will stop looking for answers outside yourself. And you will stop giving answers when others come to you asking advice.

The only advice you can give to the seeker is this: seek for truth within your own heart, for there alone can you find it.

Share your experience? Yes, to be sure! Your story can be of immense help to others. But the boundaries of such an offering are clear. It is *your* experience you are offering, a story, not a prescription for others. Whatever truth someone else sees in it is the truth he is meant to receive. And this, of course, will be different for each person who hears your story.

Ultimately, you alone are responsible for the beliefs you accept. Someone can tell you terrible lies, but it will never be his responsibility that you believed them. So do not waste your time blaming the guru, the cult or the church. Thank them instead. Whether they realize it or not, they have done you a great service. They taught you clearly what to avoid.

Indeed, negative and positive teachings go hand in hand in building the character of the seeker. If you doubt this, think of the ones who sit in mesmerized bliss idolizing a teacher who takes their money, their sexual favors and their power and be thankful you have awakened from that kind of sleep.

Everybody at one time or another gives his power away, only to learn to take it back. That is an important and profound lesson on the spiritual path. Be grateful if you have learned this lesson. It means you are closer to your own truth, and if you are closer to your own truth, you are closer to God, the universal truth.

You come to oneness not through conformity, but through authenticity. When you have the courage to be yourself, you find the highest truth you are capable of receiving. Finding the highest truth in yourself, you recognize that truth when you see it manifest in others.

The man or woman of Spirit trusts others to find their own way. S/he seeks no students or disciples.

Those who seek followers must house and feed them. They will not find freedom, for they do not give it.

Freedom comes when you reject all forms of external authority and when you refuse to be an authority for anyone else. Paradoxically, that is also the moment in which the self becomes Self.

I urge you to claim what is yours. Empower yourself. Empower others. Be a brother, a sister, a friend, but accept no other teacher than the one who lives inside your heart. (SOTH)

Resting in the Truth

The true authority of your heart does not submit to the wants and needs of other people, however cleverly disguised. Nor does it submit to your own wants and needs, which are inevitably perceived in fear. The true authority of your heart blesses you and knows that you are completely loved and completely safe. It does not want. It does not need. It does not seek approval from others.

True authority is rock-solid and self-nurtured. It moves perpetually toward its greatest joy without harming others. It knows without hesitation that its joy is not at odds with the joy of others. It serves others not out of sacrifice but through the extension of an inner joy that is constantly bubbling up and spilling over. It is totally committed to its own truth and totally welcoming of others. It seeks not to convert others to its own experience, nor to push them away. It merely rests in its experience, content, full, willing to share.

The true authority of your heart does not desire to please others and obtain their approval, nor does it desire to please self at the expense of others. It is not drawn outward into other people's dramas, nor inward into the attempt to satisfy personal wants and needs.

Call it Essence, Self, Christ Mind or Buddha nature. Names do not matter. You access this Authority through your stillness, your quiet acceptance of yourself and others, your profound willingness to be present. You sink through the superficial dichotomies of mind into the depths of the heart. And there, not surprisingly, you meet God not as Other, but as Self. In the silence, there is just a single heartbeat. It cannot belong to anyone else, for there is no one else there.

Sit for a moment in profound forgiveness of yourself and the walls which appear to hold you apart from God's grace will dissolve. You will leave conflict behind. The world as you know it will disappear, along with your judgment of it. This is revelation. This is the parting of the veil.

Do not make the mistake of thinking that this experience happens only to the chosen few. It happens to everyone. It is your destiny. You will awaken, because you cannot sleep forever. You cannot be in resistance and pain forever.

Sooner or later there is a letting go of resistance. You stop reacting. You stop withholding your love or pushing the love of others away.

Then, there is nothing to defend and nowhere to hide. You become visible. You become vulnerable.

You can be in your experience without defending it. You can accept the experience of others without judging it or trying to change it.

What is this? It is the birth of the Christ Consciousness within you. It is your internalization of the divine, the indwelling Spirit of God come to rest in your heart. (SOTH)

The Divine Born of the Human

I will tell you this plainly. The human must die so that the divine can be born. Not because it is bad. But because it is the shell that holds the spirit, the cocoon that holds the wings of the butterfly.

But you do not have to wait until the moment of your physical death for the human to die. The human can die into the divine right now if you are willing to step into your divinity, if you are willing to stop playing the victim, if you are willing to stop resisting, defending, hiding, projecting shame and blame.

You cannot fly until you are willing to claim your wings. But once you do, you cannot remain in the dark shadows of your fear.

It is your choice. How would you choose? What would you be: victim or angel?

There is nothing in between! That which appears to exist in between is just the human shell: the being who has not yet chosen, the caterpillar dreaming of wings. (SOTH)

Light in the Darkness

You alone are Christ, Messiah, Savior. You are the one who brings the love you have sought from others, the one who brings release from self-violation and abusive relationships. You are the only one who can step into your experience and lift it up.

Only when you know that you are the light-bearer does the darkness disappear. But before you can become the light-bearer you must walk through your own darkness. The bearer of the light does not deny the darkness. S/he walks through it.

When there is nothing about yourself or anyone else that you are afraid to look at, the darkness has no more hold over you. Then you can walk through the darkness and be the light.

To pretend to be the light-bearer before you have faced your own fear is to be a pretender, an unhealed healer, a sham. All unhealed healers eventually come off their imaginary pedestals. Where there is only the pretension to light, the darkness still prevails.

To be the light you must embrace the darkness. You must come to terms with the ego mind and see its absolute futility. You must learn to look at fear with love in your heart: your fear, your sister's fear, the fear of the rapist or murderer.

You must know that all fear is alike and all fear is simply a lack of love. Love is the answer to your deepest sense of separation. Not someone else's love. Your love.

Once you take the torch of truth and bring love to the wounded parts of your mind, you take back your power. You surrender your victimhood. You can no longer be unfairly treated because you are the very source of love, acceptance, forgiveness.

Where does love come from? It comes from you. You are the way, the truth, and the life, just as I was. Don't look for the divine outside yourself. In your blessing of yourself, the entire world is forgiven. (SOTH)

Heaven Is Here and Now

When does the Kingdom of Heaven come to earth? As soon as you are willing to open your heart and walk through your fears.

When does the Messiah come? No, not later, but now. Now is the end of separation, the end of projection, the final death knell of fear. Now.

Do not place salvation in the future or it will never come. Ask for it now. Accept it now. God's kingdom manifests in this moment only, in this place only.

When does heaven come? When this moment is enough. When this place is enough. When this friend is enough. When these events and circumstances are acceptable. When you no longer crave something other than what stands before you. (SOTH)

Do Not Build on Shaky Ground

Do not construct your life on the changeable. Place your faith where it alone is safe, on the bedrock of your experience.

Act from a place of peace, not one of desire. For desires come and go, but peace is eternal.

Much of the psycho-emotional terrain you will encounter in this life is unsuitable for building. Some of it is harsh, unforgiving rock, some of it seductive quicksand. If you value yourself, do not build your nest in these places.

Be kind to yourself. No one else can bring to you a joy you don't already feel within your heart. Build on what you have, not on what you want. For want is an illusion. As soon as one desire is fulfilled, another desire replaces it. The chain of desire is endless. It always takes you away from yourself. (SOTH)

14.

THE NEW AGE

THREE STAGES OF CONSCIOUSNESS

There are three stages in the development of human consciousness. The first stage is subconscious knowledge. Driven by instinct and emotions, this is the state of ancient man/woman.

The second stage is self-conscious knowledge. It is characterized by the quest for information, which builds the intellect and the ego structure but does not establish lasting happiness or peace. This is the state of modern man/woman.

The third stage is God-conscious knowledge. It is characterized by the relinquishment of abstract, intellectual solutions driven by guilt and fear. It is rooted in a present-oriented acceptance of experience as it unfolds. This is the state of the divine human, or co-creator.

You are living at a time when stage two is coming to closure and stage three is being born. The entrance into stage three calls for a different way of living individually and collectively. It calls for a repudiation of the controlling mind. It calls for a thorough investigation of that mind, the fears on which it is based, and the utter futility of its creations.

The Old Testament is the teaching for the stage one human. It says: "Do this or God will punish you!" It is fear-based at the deepest emotional level. That is why God destroys whole cities in His wrath. The message to humans is "become aware of God outside of you."

In stage two, people are aware of God but still separate from Him. The New Testament as it has come down to you is the teaching for the stage two human. It says: "God is not vengeful. He loves you and asks you to come and embrace his teaching. Your life will be happier if you make room for God in your life." Stage two teachings focus on what you will miss if you keep God out of your life. It is the teaching of persuasion and is still based on fear and separation.

My teaching was and is a stage three teaching. I have always said to you: "You will find God in your own heart and in the hearts of your brothers and sisters. God cannot ever be separate from you, for the divine is your very essence." But when the stage three teaching is heard by stage two ears, the result is a stage two interpretation of that teaching.

Now this is changing. Many of you are hearing the teaching as it was originally intended. You are in communion with me and you are realizing that much of what you have been taught about me is false. You know that the only way you can verify truth is through its resonance in your heart and its revelation in your experience.

There are many apostles now, far more than there were when I was physically present in your experience. Now, together, you can move to stage three and experience the ending of the past and the establishment of grace as the guide in your lives. (SOTH)

Stage Three Teachers

Stage three (new paradigm) spiritual teachers claim no authority over others. They do not pretend to have the answers for others.

They do not preach. They do not try to fix. They simply accept people as they are and encourage them to find their own truth.

They don't deny the darkness, but they don't oppose it either. They just gently encourage the light. They know the light itself will heal all wounds.

New paradigm teachers encourage others to heal themselves through self-acceptance and self-love. They model unconditional love by listening deeply and compassionately, without judging or trying to fix.

New paradigm teachers don't encourage fear or guilt of any kind. They don't believe that people are evil or that the world is doomed. They understand the universal cry for acceptance and love. And that is what they give.

Do they give food and medical supplies if they are needed? Of course, but they also remember to whom they are giving them. They know that food is helpful, but it is not what is asked for.

Love is what is asked for. Love is the real food and love is what they give.

The new paradigm spiritual teacher is content to be a brother or a sister. S/he comes to you as an equal partner, as a friend. S/he treats you respectfully and s/he treats the person next to you in the same way. There is no hierarchy, no pecking order, no preference. (SOTH)

Being a Peacemaker

You are entering a time when the barriers of culture and religion will be transcended. With tolerance for diversity will come the perception of universal spiritual values that can be embraced by all. This is a time of great importance. Each one of you has a significant role to play in the dismantling of the barriers to peace.

Therefore I encourage you to find the place within where you are whole and complete. From that place, you will celebrate and accept all of the people who come into your life. From that place of peace within, you will be a peacemaker among women and men. This is my teaching. Throughout time, this has always been my teaching. (LWOC)

Equality: The Planetary Curriculum

In your classroom, the primary subject is equality. You are here to learn that all beings are equal regardless of their apparent circumstances. Men and women, black and white, Hindu or Catholic are all equal in their existential worth. All inequalities are of your own making and must be abolished.

Many of you have been working on this curriculum for a long time. You have developed many ingenious ways to distort your equality with other people. Some of you live in poverty conditions, while others have multiple estates. Some have too much food to eat; others do not have enough. Had you already mastered the curriculum here, these conditions of inequality would not exist. (LWOC)

The New Millennium and the Second Coming

The time that you now inhabit the physical classroom is a time of transition. Technologically, you have the ability to destroy the physical environment many times over. Yet there is more light available on the planet now than there has been in any other time in history.

Many of you expect me to come again in human form, but this will not be the case. My work here is almost over. And my physical presence with you now would only delay the transformation you are poised to make.

Why are you here? You are here to overcome your victimhood. You are here to accept your creative power to determine your reality and to help others do the same. Through your non-physical communion with me and other teachers in spirit, you are learning to let go of the conditions that reinforce your suffering.

I need the help of each one of you to fulfill my mission here. It is through you that my teaching is demonstrated in each moment. That is why the emphasis can no longer be on words, which separate people. The emphasis must shift to the active demonstration of the principles of love and forgiveness. (LWOC)

Beyond the New Age

As dogmatic, hierarchical religious teachings are appropriately rejected, a socio-spiritual gap is created. No longer willing to let outside authorities dictate to them what to believe, people try to find their own way of connecting with God, purpose and meaning in their lives. While this search may be liberating and fruitful for some, it is confusing and emotionally draining for others who may need more social participation and structure in their lives. It is not surprising, perhaps, to see some "recovering new-agers" gravitating toward conservative or even fundamentalist churches which offer a stable community where regular fellowship thrives and parents can raise their children in a safe, supportive environment.

The great gift of the New Age movement is the freedom it gives individuals to explore many different approaches to spirituality. This empowers them to make their own eclectic and creative synthesis of ideas. It helps people to ask their own questions and find their own answers. However, those religious structures that emphasize self-exploration and foster diversity often lack the kind of social and emotional cohesiveness found in more homogeneous religious communities which require individuals to conform to the group norms.

For many people, there is a clear choice between freedom and belonging. The more freedom one needs, the less chance one will find a community into which one can fit comfortably. What is empowering for the individual and what strengthens the group culture are by their very nature often at odds.

The weakness of the New Age movement is its lack of spiritual depth and emotional congruence. The plethora of self-help books, workshops and seminars synonymous with the phrase "new age" comes in response to a tremendous groundswell of interest in non-dogmatic, non-authoritarian approaches to spirituality. Unfortunately, the fervor of interest in new approaches leads to the development of heavily marketed, superficial tools that promise life-changing experiences without delivering them.

The down side of New Age consciousness is its "quick fix" mentality, its inference that the answer to all of your problems lies in something outside yourself. If one tool doesn't work, you can always find another one that promises bigger and better peak experiences. When there are a thousand approaches to truth, all of them touted by one persuasive person or another, it is hard for people to choose one of them and stick to it. Superficiality and dilettantism tend to be the rule.

As you know, not everyone who embarks on a journey of self-empowerment is capable of navigating the spiritual marketplace, sifting and shredding, and finally making an eclectic synthesis of tools and techniques that leads to the experience of inner awakening. While some have used this freedom to explore well, there are more casualties in the age of drive-in spirituality than there are success stories.

Confusion, contradictory beliefs, addiction to books, workshops and Madison Avenue promises of fulfillment lead to a spiritual cul-de-sac. Many new-agers do not know what they believe or where to turn. Many have not found connection to a loving community. Some have lived selfish lives that do not lead to deepening insight or compassion.

The wings that have been given to this generation grow tired now.

As many move into the second half of life, there is a need to settle down and grow roots. There is a need for friendship, eternal values, and beliefs that encompass and speak meaningfully to the pain and suffering of the past.

It is in this climate that my teachings can be understood and practiced at depth. This will result in the rebirth of small, supportive communities offering both freedom and belonging, individuation and solidarity, respect for each individual and devotion to the common good. (MOL)

Tending the Garden

Rapid technological development and social experimentation can leave an untidy mess. You don't have to apologize for the resulting chaos and confusion, because it was part of your learning process. However, you do have to clean up the mess you made.

Your collective garden needs tending. It has not been treated kindly or responsibly. It's time to plant some new flowers and pull out some old weeds. When you become responsible for your creations, they thrive. When you become aware of your mistakes, you can correct them.

This planet is a laboratory that helps you develop self-confidence, sensitivity and compassion. Every thought and feeling you have weighs in, so consider them well. Do not forge ahead blindly driven by doubt, anger or fear. You cannot afford to create out of that place anymore.

Earth has given you notice. Water and wind have risen up and spoken to you in your dreams. Fire has appeared to you as it did to Moses. There are no secrets here.

Forgive the past. You can address only what is happening now. Do what you can today. That will bring you the peace of mind you need to tend your garden lovingly and responsibly.

No, it is not too late. Don't give up on your garden just because the weeds have grown waist high. Put on your gloves and your old clothes and get to work. If you do that, you will model responsibility for others. And, before you know it, there will be a crew of volunteers helping you to pull the weeds and work the soil.

Some will call it a miracle. And that it will be. Yet this miracle would not have happened if you had not said yes.

Say yes, my friend. It is through you that the healing power of love is expressed in the world. (RTG)

15.

DEVILS AND SAVIORS

GUILT AND THE SAVIOR: A CREATION MYTH

In the beginning you shared in the omnipotent power of God's love. Nothing was impossible for you. But then you began to wonder what would happen if you acted apart from God. Doubt came in and you wondered, "What if something goes wrong?"

This doubt was just separation anxiety, but it gave rise to many other fearful thoughts. Among these thoughts was the thought, "If I make a mess of things, God might be mad at me and might not love me anymore." And that thought was the clincher.

It didn't take long to go from that thought to the experience of feeling guilty and cut off from God's loving presence. Now this separation was artificial and self-imposed, but it felt real to you. You believed it.

And so in your own mind you "fell from grace." You went from sharing in the omnipotent power of God's love to being afraid of that love. Another way of saying this is that you became afraid of your own creative power. So you hid it away where you couldn't see it. You stopped being a creator and became a victim. In other words, you turned reality inside out. You made love fearful.

When you are feeling separate, it's hard to remember what it was like before separation occurred. And that seems to be your peculiar dilemma. You asked, "What if I abused this power?" and then you proceeded to make a world in which your power was fearful. You did not stop and wait for God's answer to your doubt and fear.

Had you listened to God's answer, you would have heard something like this: "You are loved without conditions. I will never withdraw My love from you. Remembering that you are loved, you can act only in a loving way."

Had you listened to God's answer, your experience of separation would have come to an end. For God's answer derails your assumption that you are not loved.

Upon this neurotic idea, all "victim consciousness" is based. You cannot think hurtful thoughts or perform unkind acts unless you believe that you are unworthy of love.

Adam and Eve asked the same "What if?" question: "What if I ate the fruit of the tree of knowledge and became as powerful as God?" They too gave their own fearful answer, felt shame and hid themselves from God.

You are asking the same question right now. You are chewing the same apple. You too are playing hide-and-seek with God.

Indeed, it is the continual asking and answering of this question which keeps your experience of victimhood in place. In your self-created world, you are either a victim or a victimizer. As you explore these roles, you see that there is little difference between them. The victim needs the victimizer and vice versa.

You see, your spiritual life on earth does not begin until you decide to wait for God's answer to your question: "What if I make a mistake?" It does not matter what religion you are. It does not matter what your social or economic standing is. Each one of you will come to a point in your life when you are ready to challenge your own false assumptions.

You can't be a partner with God so long as you see yourself or anyone else as a hapless victim. The New Covenant asks you to recognize the Kingdom of God in your own heart, to reject the idea that God is separate from you, or that you or anyone else is unlovable. It asks you to reject the idea of evil as an idea created in fear, to reject the idea that God's power can be abused.

The New Covenant is your acceptance of God's answer to your question "What if?" It is the beginning of your personal salvation and the beginning of the human reception of the Kingdom of God on earth.

Once upon a time, you rejected your creative partnership with God. Now you are ready to reclaim it. Once upon a time you entertained the idea that you could be unlovable in God's eyes. Now you are ready to reclaim your eternal love communion with Her.

When you accept God back into your life, your whole experience of the world and everything in it changes. You are a father and a mother to every child who approaches you, a son or daughter to every elderly person. You are a friend to friend and friendless alike. You are a lover to the one who remembers s/he is loved and to the one who has forgotten.

Accepting your creative power is impossible without your reconciliation with God. For all power comes from Her. You share in that power as an equal partner, but you can never exercise that power apart from Her. Even in the "What if" dream, you could never separate yourself totally from God's love. In that dream, you crossed the threshold of pain and chose to return. So it is with everyone.

The power of God's love cannot be abused. It can be rejected, denied, hidden. But all rejection, denial and secret guilt have limits. Truth can be distorted but it can never be completely eradicated or denied. A tiny light always remains in the deepest darkness. And that light will always be found when the desire to find it arises.

You, my friend, are the hero of your own dream. You are the dreamer of the darkness and the one who brings the light. You are tempter and savior rolled in one. This you will come to know if you do not know it already. (LWOC)

Everything Is God

Everything is God, including that which tries to live without God. For what tries to live without God is simply a part of God that doesn't accept itself. It is God pretending not to be God.

People who do "evil" acts are not separate from God even though they feel separate. They feel unloved and act in unloving ways. But God has not stopped loving them. God is not able to stop loving anyone. For God is love, always love, in every moment.

Every sin is but a temporary moment of separation. It cannot be final. Every child who strays from God's love will return, because it is too painful to be separate from the Source of love. When the pain becomes too great, every wounded child turns back. There are no exceptions.

The world is a classroom for redemption. Everyone who comes here tries in one way or another to live apart from God's will. Each person experiences fear and listens to the ego's voice. Some simply realize more quickly than others that they can't find love in separation. (MOL)

Facing Your Fears: Forty Days in the Desert

If you ignore your fears, they can erupt unexpectedly, altering the emotional landscape around you. The people you love can be hurt; their trust in you can be eroded.

When I was in the desert for forty days, I experienced every voice of fear you can imagine. These were not devils outside of me that had come to tempt me. They were voices in my own mind that caused me to doubt myself or others.

You too have your time in the desert when you must face your own doubts and fears. This time of inner testing usually precedes your acceptance of your purpose here. For if you cannot move through your own fears, how can you begin to deal with the fears of others when they project them onto you?

The kind of strength and integration I am talking about here is not to be taken lightly. Can you meet your devils and learn to love them? Can you love when fear comes up? Before you begin your lifework, these questions must be answered. You must enter the darkness of your psyche carrying the light of awareness. Every fear that undermines your self-esteem must be faced.

If you are strong enough to face your fears and hold them compassionately, you take your appointed place in life. You emerge from the desert, having discovered the oasis. This bottomless well of love and compassion was never out of your reach. It merely rested beneath the shifting sands of your fear. (RTG)

Shame and the Perception of Evil

Peace will not come to the world until it comes into your own heart. And it cannot come into your heart as long as you see enemies or "evil" people outside of you. Every evil you perceive in the world points to an unforgiving place in your own heart that is calling out for healing.

Stop judging others. Stop the game of blame. See every judgment for what it is: an attack against yourself, an attack against God's daughter or son, a deepening of your own shame.

Apart from your judgments there is no hell. Yet you pretend there is a "devil" apart from your beliefs, or an "evil" not connected to your judgments. It is not true. Every evil comes from your judgments and every devil comes from the projection of your shame.

Do not see the drama happening outside of you or you will lose the key to the Kingdom. Those who see themselves as victims will not be empowered. Those who see themselves as weak will not overcome the obstacles in their lives.

The drama of shame and blame is happening only in your mind and that is where it must be dealt with. Believe for a moment "I am lovable; I am acceptable; I am worthy" and your victimhood comes to an end. Believe "I am capable of loving my brother regardless of how he acts toward me" and the invisible bonds of projection fall away.

You are the one who holds the key to the Kingdom. I invite you to use it. Give the love you have to give and the love you yearn for will find you, perhaps when you least expect it.

If you offer committed love, love that overlooks faults and soars above judgments, how can any less be returned to you? This is a circular world. What goes out comes back in and vice versa. It only appears to be linear. It only appears to exist in time and space.

In truth, thought and action are simultaneous. There is no "out there." Here and there dwell together. As soon as you have the thought "I am not worthy" an experience comes in to confirm that thought. This is not a punishment from God, but a testimony to the power of your mind.

Do not blame God for the apparent misfortune you receive. Do not blame your neighbor, or your spouse or your child. Do not even blame yourself. Simply ask to see it free of judgment, as it truly is. See how you called for it and it faithfully answered your call. See this without beating yourself. See this without beating the stranger who came to your door to deliver the message. Just see it in surrender, in reconciliation with your self and your experience.

God comes to you in many forms. Everything that happens in your life is part of your God experience. If your experience feels painful, ask, "What can I learn from this pain?" Do not ask the pain to go away. Do not reject the lesson. For every lesson turned away comes again in another guise. (SOTH)

Christ Cannot Be a Victim

Christ does not see himself as a victim. He does not blame others. He does not fight back. He does not resist evil.

The strongest power in the universe seems to be so weak, so easily overpowered, crucified and forgotten. But it is not so. All who attack the Christ must return to serve Him. That is the Law.

Christ cannot be a victim. He cannot make anyone else responsible for his experience. He knows that he is responsible for everything he thinks, says or does.

When you realize this too, you claim your Christhood. (SOTH)

False Prophets

I have said before and I will say again: "By their fruits, you will know them." Do not listen to the clever, persuasive words of those who claim spiritual authority. Look to their actions and see if what they do is consistent with what they say.

If you are wise, you will not follow anyone. Then you will not be misled. But if you must find a teacher or a leader, look for one who empowers you to hear the truth in your own heart. Look for one who loves you without seeking to control you. Find a teacher who honors you and treats you with dignity and respect.

Anyone who claims a special knowledge and sells it for a price is a false prophet. Anyone who needs you to bow down, agree with his opinions or carry out his agenda is a false prophet. Anyone who asks for money or sexual favors in return for spiritual guidance is a false prophet. Anyone who encourages you to give away your power, your self-respect or your dignity is a false prophet. Do not abide with such people. They do not have your good at heart. They do not even have their own good at heart.

Do not seek the company of one who smothers you and does not give you the freedom to be yourself. Do not accept a teacher who tries to make decisions for you. Do not accept the teachings or the friendship of one who criticizes you or blames you for his problems. Do not let anyone dictate to you or control your life.

On the other hand, do not dictate to others either. Any need you have to control others or to make decisions for them is abusive. Do not trespass on others or seek to take away their freedom to decide what they want. Any attempt to do so simply binds you to the wheel of suffering.

What you give to others is what you get back. Do not be a victimizer or a victim. Be yourself and allow others to be themselves. (SOTH)

The Antichrist

The Antichrist seeks salvation and peace by controlling others. His attempt to force reconciliation never works. What lives by the sword dies by the sword. Wrong means always lead to wrong ends.

However, even the Antichrist is not evil. He is simply starved for love. Being starved for love, he tries to buy it, demand it, control it. By so doing, he pushes love farther away. The more love eludes him, the more vicious he gets. His fear begets the fear of others.

Often the Antichrist impersonates Christ. The wolf appears in sheep's clothing. He seems to be gentle, compassionate and wise, but it is all an act. As soon as he has your allegiance, his true colors appear. That is why you must be very careful. You think you are worshiping Christ, but it is not Christ you are worshiping. It is the devil in disguise.

What is the devil? It is simply the ego mind: the scared, unhappy, angry little kid inside of you who feels unfairly treated and constantly manipulates others in his search for love. That's the only devil.

The devil is formidable only because you judge him and resist him. Don't push him away anymore. Take him in your arms and rock him. Hold him, speak gently to him. Love him as your own precious child.

When you have embraced the wounded child within, his angelic presence is revealed. Lucifer is, after all, a fallen angel. In your love, his fall is broken and he finds his wings. In his redemption, yours is guaranteed.

Lucifer means light-bearer. He is the wounded child transformed into the risen Christ, the angelic presence leading the human into God's eternal embrace.

The Antichrist impersonates Christ in his desperate search for man's allegiance and love. In the end, he gives up. He knows he cannot win. He awaits God's wrath. But, surprisingly, it does not come. Instead, God approaches him and lifts him up into his arms. "Welcome home, Lucifer," He says.

And so Lucifer regains his place in heaven. Through him, man is tested in the fire of perceived inequality and abuse. When Lucifer is redeemed, the light comes to man. Victim and victimizer meet face-to-face. Equality and justice are realized. (SOTH)

The Devil

If you keep looking for the devil in others, you will not find him. The devil is your own angelic presence defiled. It is all of your forgetting, all of your self-violation. It is the wounded one, the crucified one, the angel who has fallen from the sky into the muck, into the savage pull of worldly incarnation. (SOTH)

The Savior

God does not come from on high to free you from a world of your own making. Why would He take you from what you have chosen?

God comes through your gesture of acceptance toward your ego mind with all its fearful imaginings. He comes in the love and compassion you bring to the wounded one within you and outside of you. He comes when you reach down to embrace the dark wings that hover in front of the door of your fear.

These wings will not hurt you. They will not rob you of your innocence, no matter how much abuse has been given or received. See through the dark disguise and come into the warmth of these wings. There is a door here that leads straight to the heart.

You cannot come to God if you don't go through the dark night of the soul. All your fear and shame must be raised. All your feelings of separation must come up for healing. How can you rise from the ashes of your pain unless you will acknowledge the pain?

If you pretend the wound isn't there, you can't begin your spiritual journey. Don't deny that it hurts, brother or sister. Come into your pain. It is not what you think it is.

When you have the courage to approach the wall of your fear, it turns into a doorway. Come through this door. I am waiting for you on the other side. (SOTH)

16.

TRESPASS AND

ATONEMENT

ABUSE OR SELF-BETRAYAL?

If you are feeling insecure about your intelligence and someone comes along and calls you stupid, your buttons get pushed. The reaction comes from your insecurity. The trigger is incidental.

Every fear or insecurity you have about yourself is a button waiting to be pushed. The fact that people push these buttons is not at all remarkable. What is remarkable is that you blame them for pushing them.

When you wear a sign that says "hit me," are you surprised that a few people come along and take you literally? True, not everyone does. Some people just laugh and move along. But others stop and take you at your word.

Blaming the person who abused you won't solve your problem, because the problem is not abuse, but self-betrayal. As long as you are willing to betray yourself, there will always be someone around to abuse you. But stand up for yourself clearly and courageously, and abuse is impossible. (SOTH)

Equality and Mutual Respect

In order to experience equality with others, you must be willing to treat others with dignity and respect. Moreover, you must be clear that you expect to be treated in a respectful manner by all of the people in your life—spouse, parents, children, friends, people at work, even strangers.

If someone acts in a judgmental, critical or attacking way toward you, please tell that person immediately how you are feeling. Do so without blaming or attacking back, but ask clearly to be treated respectfully. That is your right. And that is the other person's responsibility.

Don't allow someone to treat you in an unkind or an unfair way without standing up for yourself. Mind you, I am not telling you to attack back or retaliate. I am simply telling you to stand up for yourself and insist that you be treated with respect.

The important thing is to oppose what is disrespectful when it happens. Otherwise you will feel resentful and entitled to make judgments of the person who criticized or attacked you. That kind of passive/aggressive behavior is no better than retaliating in the heat of the moment. The key is not to retaliate at all, but to stand up for yourself clearly and forcefully without impugning the dignity of the other person.

Unless you know in the core of your being that you deserve to be treated kindly, you will put up with unnecessary abuse. You will give your power away and allow yourself to become a victim. This is not spiritual. It is irresponsible to you and to the other person.

For a relationship between two people to work, each person must take responsibility for treating the other with dignity and respect. This creates a foundation of trust and mutual regard, on which genuine equality can be built. (MOL)

Permission to Betray

Don't be surprised if the person you accept as an authority figure in your life becomes controlling or abusive. By accepting an outside authority, you give your power away.

"But I didn't know he would take advantage of me," you say. And I say to you, brother or sister, "Wise up. Take responsibility for your life. Realize that you bought the farm. Stop trying to blame another for the choices you made."

You gave permission. Perhaps you did not know how bad it would be. The abuse came, as it frequently does, wrapped in sugarcoated promises. Financial security might have been offered. Or companionship. Or sex. You name it. It doesn't matter what the bait was. You swallowed it and you got hooked. Be wiser next time.

Don't accept anyone else's authority over you and don't accept authority over anyone else. Claim your freedom and offer freedom to others.

Those who try to bargain for love spend their lives in an emotional labyrinth with little hope of egress. Conditional love is an endless prison. The only escape is to tell the truth to yourself and others. Then you can walk free.

Do not seek approval from others or offer it when others seek it from you. Get out of the approval business.

Too many of you get caught in the horizontal journey. I have tried to tell you that, no matter how far you go in the exploration of "other," you will return to self.

There is only one person here who needs to give and receive love and that is you. Give love to yourself and include others in that love. If they do not wish to be included, let them go. It is no loss. You do not need another detour, another useless journey.

When someone makes you an offer you think you can't refuse, learn to refuse it. Don't betray yourself, regardless of the price.

The tempter will always come to you offering extraordinary gifts. Don't be fooled. He seems to have supernatural powers, but they are not real.

Don't say yes to his invitation to betray yourself. Remember, you are already whole. You lack nothing. Relax and breathe. This too will pass.

But the tempter shouts out: "No. You are not okay. You are lonely. You need companionship. You need a better job. You need a better relationship. You need more money, more sex, more notoriety; all of this will I give to you."

Surely, you have heard this pitch before! Some knight in shining armor or damsel in distress always appears when you are feeling low. Where has it gotten you in the past? How many knights or damsels have sped off on their steeds leaving a trail of blood and tears?

Yet this one seems better than the last. S/he is more sincere, more sensitive, more grounded, more _____. You fill in the blank. It is your drama, not mine.

If you look deeply enough, you will see that every pitch is the same. Every invitation to self-betrayal has the same sugarcoated promises and the same heart-wrenching core.

Those who seek salvation in another lose touch with self. They go off like Don Quixote on the great horizontal journey. And they always find damsels to rescue and windmills to fight.

But in the end, they return home tired, wounded and lacking in faith. The horizontal journey defeats everyone who takes it. There is no salvation to be found in the world.

Salvation is found at home, in your own heart. It is there that you learn to love the disowned, rejected parts of yourself. It is there that you discover your wholeness and become rooted in the integrity of your own experience. (SOTH)

Pain Is a Messenger

Pain is a messenger. It brings awareness. Many people push their pain away and ignore the message it brings. This is a delaying tactic. It is only a matter of time until the pain appears again.

Your pain tells you where and how you have betrayed yourself. That is important. Until you are aware of the self-violation, your journey to healing cannot begin.

Pain is not bad. It is not a punishment. It is a call to become conscious, to raise your hidden suffering into awareness. (SOTH)

Integrating the Dark Side

It isn't easy to face your pain, but this is how you heal. You become aware of the dark, disenfranchised aspects of self and bring them into conscious awareness. You bring your darkness to the light.

It is not an easy process, but it is a necessary one. You must redeem the parts of yourself you have abandoned or betrayed. If you have cut off your sexuality, you must reclaim it. If you have neglected your creativity or repressed your power, you must find a way to accept and express these important aspects of self.

Most of you project what you dislike or are afraid of in yourself onto others. If you are afraid of your power, you project it onto some powerful, charismatic figure through whom you try to live. When that person takes advantage of you or betrays you, you forget that it was you who gave your power away to this person.

Reclaiming all of yourself means facing the parts of yourself of which you are afraid or ashamed. Other people who embody these qualities merely help you discover them in yourself. That is why relationship is such an important tool in the work of inner integration. (RTG)

Responsibility, Not Blame

Blaming other people for your suffering just prevents you from healing. If you want to heal, don't focus on what the other person did. Look at your own actions and take responsibility for them. See what role you played in the scenario of mutual trespass. See what bargains for love you tried to make. Did you accept degrading conditions in exchange for attention and approval? Did you trade sex for financial security?

Perhaps now you understand that love cannot be bought or bargained for. If you accept love with conditions, you will experience the conditions, but not the love.

Real love doesn't establish conditions. It doesn't ask you to suffer or to sacrifice.

Remember, every abusive relationship offers you the opportunity to say no to what does not honor you. If you can say no now, you won't create suffering in the future.

Say no to self-betrayal and yes to honoring yourself. If you do not treat yourself in a respectful way, how can you expect others to respect you? It's time to face the truth: you cannot receive from others what you are unable or unwilling to give to yourself. (SOTH)

Healing from Trauma

Finding out what happened to you is the first step in the process of healing trauma. Secrets need to be disclosed or discovered.

If dissociation occurred, you may have repressed the memory of what happened. Yet invariably, the memory will surface as you become capable of looking at it. You cannot and should not rush the process.

Don't deny what happened. Don't make it up. Just acknowledge what happened and be with it. That is what starts the shift from untruth to truth, from secrets to revelation, from hidden discomfort to the conscious awareness of pain.

Pain is a door you walk through when you are ready. Until then, you are the doorkeeper, the sentinel who stands guard and decides whom to exclude and whom to let in.

It is okay not to be ready. It's okay to exclude people or situations that feel unsafe. You are in charge of your own healing process. You decide how fast to go. Don't let anyone else—including your therapist—dictate the pace of your healing process. It must be self-directed.

Others will always have ideas, suggestions, plans for you. Thank them for their concern, but be clear that you, not they, are making the decisions in your life. (SOTH)

The Great Equalizer

Pain is the great equalizer. It brings you to your knees. It makes you more humble and sensitive to the needs of others. It undermines all hierarchies.

If you have touched your own pain deeply, you know this. You feel compassion when you see others in pain. You do not need to push them away, nor do you need to try to fix them. You just hold them deeply in your heart. You offer them a hug and some words of encouragement. You know what they are going through.

For many people, it is easier to let others see the pasteboard mask than the contorted face behind it. They are proud of the spiritual adult, but ashamed of the wounded child.

However, those who have the courage to face their pain pull the mask away. They give themselves permission to be authentic and to grow. Their willingness to be emotionally present with what they are feeling opens a sacred passageway. Closed hearts start to pulsate, bodies begin to breathe and blocked energies are released. This is the first step in the healing process.

Other steps follow, for healing means movement. It doesn't mean falling in love with pain, holding on to it, or building an identity around it. It is not a stationary train, but a moving one. Once you get on it, it takes you where you need to go.

Pain is the great equalizer. It enables you to be honest and authentic. It empowers you to ask for unconditional love and support from others and to be willing to offer the same in return. It connects you with a healing community of human beings whose shells of denial are cracking. (SOTH)

Releasing the Attachment to Pain

The attachment to pain is just as dysfunctional as the denial of it. Yet some people see that their pain gets them lots of attention. They build a whole identity around being a victim.

However, the authentic person is not a professional storyteller. He is not a confession artist. He does not need to be the center of attention to feel good about himself.

The authentic person tells his story because the telling of it is an act of healing. As he tells it, he comes to a more profound understanding and acceptance of what happened. As he heals, others heal with him.

The moment he has integrated his experience, he no longer needs to tell his story. If he insists on telling it, it becomes a crutch that he leans on, even though his limbs have healed. He becomes more entertainer than witness, and his story—more polished than heartfelt—no longer empowers people.

The awareness of pain brings a shift away from dis-ease toward increased ease. It allows you to take the next step on your journey. When you share authentically, you empower yourself and others. You move on. They move on. A life of pain is no longer called for.

While pain and suffering are universal phenomena, they are temporary ones. They touch every life at one time or another, but they are not constant companions. They are messengers.

To say that the messenger is not present when he is standing at your door is utter foolishness. You need to answer the door and hear what he has to say. But when the message has been heard, the messenger can leave. His job is over. (SOTH)

Therapeutic Abuse

When suffering becomes a status symbol, a culture of unhealed healers is born. When it becomes "chic" to be a victim of childhood trauma or sexual abuse, therapists too easily get away with putting words in their clients' mouths. Memories of events that never happened are enshrined on the altar. Incidents of minor insensitivity or carelessness are exaggerated and painted with the language of guilt. Everyone imagines that the worst must have happened. This is hysteria, not healing. It is a new form of abuse.

Instead of inquiring into what happened and allowing the inner wounded one to speak, a professional label is placed on the wound. Instead of empowering the victim to find his voice and connect with his experience, his voice is squelched once again. He is given someone else's opinion of what happened to him and, in order to gain approval, he tells the story the authority figure asks him to tell.

The therapist projects her own unhealed wounds onto her client. Her subjectivity is taken for objectivity by the courts. Families are separated. More children are punished. The chain of abuse continues.

The attachment to pain is debilitating. The embellishment, exaggeration or fabrication of pain is insane.

Just as the creation of a priestly class of authority figures undermined the organic spirituality of the church, so the creation of a new class of therapist/healer authority figures undermines the ability of individuals to access the healing that is their birthright.

You can't make anyone heal any more than you can make people act in a moral way. Healing is a voluntary act. It happens as people are ready. Many people in therapy have no intention of healing. Many people dispensing therapeutic advice have no commitment to their own healing. For these people, therapists and clients alike, therapy is a form of denial.

Letting the wound heal by itself is just as important as ministering to the wound. You forget that the spiritual essence of the person does the healing, not the therapist or healer.

The compulsion to heal is just as vicious as the compulsion to wound. Indeed, they are different faces of the same coin.

The true healer respects the inner healing ability of her client. She helps her client make the connections that are ready to be made. She advocates integration, gentleness, patience. Thus, her clients get stronger. They heal and move on.

If you are working as a therapist, encourage your clients to avoid the extremes of denying their pain or embellishing it. Pain must be faced, not imagined. If it is there, it will express itself authentically. It will speak with its own voice. Your job is to invite the voice to speak, not to give it the words to say.

Scapegoating does little for anyone's healing. It is far better to encourage clients to overcome their shame about what happened than to find people to blame. Overcoming shame leads to healing and empowerment. Blaming others reinforces victimhood and powerlessness.

If you wish to help people heal, the question you must ask is not "How do you heal others?" But "How do you create a safe, loving space that supports healing?" If you can learn how to do that, then healing will happen by itself. (SOTH)

A Healing Community

The decision to heal is often a lonely one, yet no one ultimately needs to heal alone. Your healing is much quicker and much more profound when you are a witness to the healing of others.

A healing community is very different from a hospital, where people go to get fixed or die isolated and alone. In a healing community, people may die, but they do not die alone. They die surrounded by loved ones.

In a healing community, people learn to open their hearts and move through their fears. They learn to feel their anger and their grief. They learn to forgive themselves and others. They atone.

In a healing community, people bear witness to each other's joys and pains. They feel compassion for each other. They inspire each other. They help each other to become real, authentic, visible.

In a healing community, people gain the courage to be themselves and share honestly with others. They find true intimacy. They live and die having stepped more fully into their lives. (SOTH)

17.

LEARNING TO CARE FOR SELF

REPARENTING YOURSELF

From the time you were an infant, you were conditioned to value yourself only when people responded positively to you. You learned that your self-worth was established externally. That was the fundamental error, which has perpetuated itself throughout your life. Your parents' experience was no different from yours.

In the process of healing, you learn to value yourself as you are, here and now, without conditions. Thus, you are "born again," or "re-parented," not by other authority figures, but by the Source of love inside yourself.

No one else can do this for you. People can assist and encourage, but no one can teach you how to love yourself. That is the work of each individual soul. (LWOC)

Love Outside Self
The experience of unconditional love begins in your heart, not in someone else's. Don't make your ability to love yourself conditional on

someone else's ability to love you. Your attempt to find love outside yourself always fails, because you cannot receive from another something you haven't given to yourself. (LWOC)

Committing to Self

Most of you know what you want, but you do not wait for it. You compromise your values and priorities to fit the situations that present themselves to you. You take the job or the relationship not because it offers you what you want, but because you are afraid a better offer won't come. You live your life afraid to take risks because you do not want to give up the security you have.

In order to release these self-defeating patterns, you must put the needs and expectations of others aside and step fully into your life. Connect with your joy. Find the source of your energy and wisdom, and live out from that center.

You cannot reach out and take hold of life if you are always apologizing for yourself or seeking to win the approval of others. For a moment, stop looking for satisfaction outside yourself. Do what makes you happy. Do not question it or apologize for it.

Do it for one hour a day, every day without fail. Or do it one day per week every week without fail. Give this time to yourself as a gift.

Without a commitment to yourself, nothing worthwhile can be accomplished in life. If you have never committed to yourself, how can you commit to another?

You can't!

There are millions of people who think that they are in committed relationships, yet very few of them have committed to themselves. Most of them have used their "commitment" to another to avoid committing to themselves.

I have said before that until you meet the beloved within, you cannot meet him or her without. Others can give you only what you are willing to give yourself. And what you are unwilling to give—which of course is what you want—cannot be given by another.

Does this mean that all relationships constitute a betrayal of self and are doomed to failure? Not all perhaps, but far more than you think!

In the old relationship paradigm, the commitment to self is vitiated by the commitment to other. In seeking to please the other, self is abandoned. Since the abandoned self is incapable of love, this constitutes a vicious cycle of attraction and rejection. First the self is excluded, and then the other is excluded.

By contrast, all genuine relationship is built on the foundation of one's acceptance of and love for self. That is the primary spiritual gesture, the one that opens the door to the potential for intimacy.

When you know what you want, you can ask for it directly. When someone says, "I'm sorry. I can't offer you that," you say, "No problem. It will come in good time." You stay focused on what you want, regardless of what people offer you. You reject all the conditions with which love and attention are offered to you. You hold fast to the truth of your heart, accepting no less than you have promised to yourself.

And, in time, it comes, because you have been faithful to yourself. Because you have answered the call within your own heart, the Beloved appears unannounced at your doorstep. This is not a magical formula, but the fruit of a committed spiritual practice. (SOTH)

Discovering Self in the Great Drama

Love is omnipresent in the universe, yet you have a hard time staying connected to it. Perhaps that is because you believe that there is something wrong with you. You are afraid of being judged or rejected by others.

For most of your life, you have accepted other people's ideas and opinions as the truth about you. Yet what your mother, dad, teacher, or minister said about you is just their opinion. Unfortunately, you internalize the feedback you get from others and you develop your self-image based on it. In other words, your opinion of yourself is not based on what you know and find out about yourself, but on what other people tell you.

The "you" you know is a creation of other people's beliefs and judgments which you accept as true about yourself. Even your so-called personality is a set of behavior patterns you adopted to accommodate the behavior of significant others in your life.

Where then is the "real you" in the equation of self and other? The real you is the unknown factor, the essence that has been heavily clothed in the judgments and interpretations which you have accepted about yourself and your experience.

This is true for everyone, not just for you. People relate to one another not as authentic, self-realized beings, but as personae, masks, roles, identities. Often, people have more than one mask that they wear, depending on whom they are with and what is expected of them.

The true Self gets lost and forgotten among all these disguises. And its great gift of authenticity is not consciously acknowledged.

The true Self knows that you are inherently good, acceptable, capable of giving and receiving love. It knows that anything is possible if you believe deeply enough in yourself.

The true Self is not bound by the limitations, judgments and interpretations that the persona lives with. Indeed, it can be said that Self and persona live in different worlds. The world of Self is bright and self-fulfilling. The world of persona is dark and self-defeating. While Self finds light within and radiates it toward others, persona finds only darkness and seeks the light from others.

Self says "I am." Persona says "I am this" or "I am that." Self lives and expresses unconditionally. Persona lives and expresses conditionally. Self is motivated by love and says "I can." Persona lives in fear and says "I can't." Persona complains, apologizes and makes excuses. Self accepts, integrates and gives its gift.

You are Self, but believe yourself to be persona. As long as you operate as persona, you will have experiences that confirm your beliefs about yourself and others. When you realize that all personae are just masks you and others have agreed to wear, you will learn to see behind the masks.

When that happens, you will glimpse the radiance of the Self within and without. You will see a bright being, eminently worthy and capable of love, dynamically creative, generous and self-fulfilling. That is your inmost nature. And that is the nature of all beings in your experience.

When you accept who you really are, your arguments with others cease. For you no longer do battle with their personae. You see the light behind the mask. Your light and their light are all that matter.

When you contact the truth about you, you recognize that a great deal that you have come to accept about you is false. You are not better or worse than others. You are not stupid, or brilliant, or handsome, or ugly. Those are just judgments someone made that you accepted. None of them are true.

When you know the truth about you, you know that you are not your body, although you need to accept it and take care of it. You are not your thoughts and feelings, although you need to be aware of them and see how they are creating the drama of your life. You are not the roles that you are playing—husband or wife, mother or father, son or daughter, employee or boss, secretary or plumber—although you need to make peace with whatever role you choose to play. You are not anything external. You are not anything that can be defined by something or someone else.

The purpose of your journey here is to discover the Self and leave the persona behind. You are here to find out that the Source of love lies within your own consciousness.

You do not have to seek love outside of yourself. Indeed, the very act of seeking it in the world will prevent you from recognizing it within yourself.

You can't see the light in others until you see it in yourself. Once you see it in yourself, there is no one in whom you do not see the light. It does not matter if they see it or not. You know it's there. And it is the light you address when you speak to them.

The world of personae is a chaotic and reactive world. It is fueled by fear and judgment. It is real only because you and other believe in it and define yourselves by the conditions you find there. But those conditions are not ultimate reality. They are simply a collective drama of your making. Yes, the drama has its own rules, its costumes, its inter-relationships and its plan of action. But none of this matters when you take your costume off and step off the stage.

Mind you, the play will go on. It does not depend on you alone. But when you know it's just a play, you can choose to participate in it or not. If you participate, you will do so remembering who you are, understanding the part that you play without being attached to it.

Suffering ends when your attachment to all conditions dissolves. Then, you rest in the Self, the embodiment of love, the Source of creation itself. (MOL)

Solitude, Self-care and Integration

Solitude is a state of being. It is the result of caring for yourself and honoring who you are. It is a result of making room for activities that you enjoy and relationships that respect your boundaries.

When you live alone you can find a way to care for your body, feel your feelings and express your creativity. You can live in a place that inspires you. You can find quiet time to center yourself. You can walk in the woods or by the ocean. You can work at something you enjoy doing. You can be joyful, eat well, sleep well, refine the quality of your life. In short, you can care about yourself.

Solitude is necessary for your emotional health, whether you are living alone or living with another. Solitude gives you the time and space to integrate your experience.

Having lots of experiences means nothing if you do not take the time to learn from them. Jumping from activity to activity or relationship to relationship wreaks havoc on your emotional core. The time you take to integrate your experience is as important as the time you take to have the experience itself.

For example, if you eat a meal and then take a half-hour nap, you will wake up rejuvenated. You will have given your body uninterrupted time to work on digestion. Try to do the same thing with all of your experiences. Allow time for digestion and assimilation. Let your experience percolate within you. Be with it. Let it live inside you before you try to live out from it.

Every breath you take has three movements: an inhalation, a pause and an exhalation. The inhalation is for the taking in of experience. The pause is for its assimilation. And the exhalation is for the release of experience. While the pause is just a second or two, it is essential for the integrity of the breath.

Solitude allows you to pause. The quality of your life depends upon it. Your energy and enthusiasm arise from it.

If you drop out this part, your life will be an empty shell. A great deal may pass in and out of it. But nothing will stick. There will be no assimilation of experience or growth in consciousness. (SOTH)

Finding Love Within

No matter how spiritual you are, there will be times when you are not feeling love. At such times, ask yourself the question "How can I feel love right now?"

What you realize as you explore this question is that the only way you can "feel" love is to "think" a loving thought. Loving thoughts lead to the emotional state of feeling love. And out of this positive emotional state actions arise which connect you to others.

When fear and doubt arise in your psyche, you either entertain them or you don't. If you entertain them, you give your power away.

Don't do that. Just rest in your heart and love and accept the doubt and the fear. Then they won't have any power over you.

The reason that you are always looking for love from other people is that you do not realize that love comes only from your own consciousness. It has nothing to do with anyone else. Love comes from your willingness to think loving thoughts, experience loving feelings and act in trusting, love-inspired ways. If you are willing to do this, your cup will run over. You will constantly have the love that you need, and you will take delight in offering it to others.

The fountainhead of love is within your own heart. Don't look to others to provide the love you need. Don't blame others for withholding their love from you. You don't need their love. You need your love. Love is the only gift you can give yourself. Give it to yourself and the universe resounds with a big "Yes!" Withhold it and the game of hide-and-seek continues: "Looking for love in all the wrong places."

There is only one place you can look for love and find it. No one who has ever looked there has been disappointed. (MOL)

Alone, with Heart Open

When you finally realize that no one else can redeem you or betray you, your relationship to other people changes profoundly. They simply become friends, neighbors, fellow-travelers.

A new and healthy sense of boundaries is established in your relationships. You don't blame others for your pain. You don't try to make them responsible for your happiness.

You become capable of being a friend and receiving the fruits of friendship from others. Others no longer have to be perfect in your eyes. You see their shortcomings and mistakes without judging them harshly. You see their beauty and integrity without needing to possess them. (SOTH)

The Rhythm of Life

The simple beauty and majesty of life is to be found in its cyclical rhythms: the rising and setting of the sun, the phases of the moon, the changes of the seasons, the beating of the heart, the rhythmic unfolding of the breath.

Repetition provides continuity, familiarity and safety. Yet, many people are disconnected from the rhythms of nature and their own bodies. That is one of the tragedies of contemporary life.

Changes happen perpetually without the time to reflect on them and integrate them. Relationships begin and end before people can establish any kind of interpersonal flow. Emotional demands crater the landscape of the heart, tearing into the soft tissue. Trust is compromised, patience forgotten.

As telecommunications flourish, awareness and communion wane. More stimuli intrude. Life becomes busy-ness. The only quiet time is during sleep, and even that is prey to restless dreams.

This is what you call life, yet it is a travesty of life. It is life without breath, without energy, without intimacy. It is an attack on the senses, a violation of the spirit. It is life without heart, without rhythm.

The more unstable life seems, the more people gravitate toward the "security" promised by authority figures. People marry authority figures. They elect them. They go to their churches and join their cults. Yet, gradually, all these authority figures are discredited and their followers must pick up the pieces of their lives.

All who seek the sky without getting roots in the earth will be beat up by their experiences. In time they will return, shovels in hand, and begin the work of planting.

There are no wings without roots, except for birds. And they make sure to take shelter in trees with deep roots in the ground.

All that is spinning out to heaven will fall to earth, abused, shattered and forsaken. That which is rootless will learn to grow roots. That which has sought authority without will learn to find it within.

And then, with feet firmly planted in the earth, the eyes will notice the procession of sun and the moon. The senses will feel the rise of sap in the spring and the lifting of leaves in the fall. Blood and breath will be restored. Rhythm will return. Safety will be re-created where it authentically lies, in the heart of each person.

It is not just the reach of your hands toward the sky, but the rootedness of your feet in the ground that helps you bring heaven to earth. Spirituality is a living with, as well as a living for. It is the poetry of being, the rhythm of life unfolding in each person and each relationship, moment to moment. (SOTH)

The One and the Many

Because you inhabit separate bodies, it appears that there are many selves and that each has its own destiny. However, in truth, there is only One Self and one destiny. To discover the One Self in yourself, you must surrender to the uniqueness of your life experience. You must claim your own authentic process and journey. The more you individuate, the closer you come to touching the universal experience.

All who touch the universal experience by walking through the door of Self fall directly into the heart. They no longer have to talk about love or forgiveness. They are the essence of love and forgiveness.

This should indicate to you the utter futility of following someone else's ideas or using their experiences to validate your own. Only by accepting what comes directly and experientially to you will you find the door to the universal.

It is paradoxical perhaps: to encounter the universal, you must fully individuate. The teachings of self-abnegation are false. To go beyond the small self, you must become it fully. You must inhabit it and break through it. (SOTH)

18.

INTOLERANCE AND
SPIRITUAL PRIDE

INTOLERANCE

Love is the only door to a spiritual life. Without love, there are just dogmas and rigid, fearful beliefs. Without love, there is no compassion or charity.

Those who judge others, preach to them and seek to redeem them are just projecting their own fear and inadequacy. They use the words of religion as a substitute for the love they are unable to give or receive.

Many of those who are most forlorn and cut off from love live in the shadow of the pulpit and mount the steps of judgment every Sunday to spread the message of their own fear. Do not judge them, for they are in their own painful way crying out for love. But do not accept the guilt they would lay at your feet. It is not yours.

Those who live a genuinely spiritual life—regardless of the tradition they follow—are centered in their love for God and their fellow beings. When they meet, they have only good wishes and praises for one another. For them, labels mean nothing.

For those who practice their faith, God is the only authority, and men and women, no matter what they believe, are absolute, unconditional equals. All are equally loved and valued by God. There are no outcasts, no heathens.

I have said it before and I will say it again: Religious dogma, self-righteousness and spiritual pride create division, ostracism and alienation. They are the tools of judgment, not of love.

Those who find fault with others are not following my teaching. My disciples learn to look upon all that happens with an open heart and an open mind. They grow increasingly willing to surrender their narrow beliefs and prejudices. Their life is their teaching, and it is lived with loving deeds, not with harsh, unforgiving words.

How many people who profess to be Christians live in this way? And so I ask you, "How can you be a Christian and not practice giving and receiving love without conditions?" Better to throw away all your other beliefs and hold to this practice than to study Scripture and practice judgment. (MOL)

All Are Called, but Few Answer the Call

The path I have laid out for you is an open one. Anyone who wants to can follow it. No prerequisites are necessary: no baptisms, confessions or communions. Nothing external can prevent you from embracing my teaching.

But this does not mean that you will be ready to walk this path. If you are still holding on to your dogma or creeds, you will not be able to take the first step. If you are convinced that you or anyone else is evil or guilty, you cannot step forth. If you think you already have the answers, you may begin to walk, but you will be on a different path.

My path is open to all, yet few will follow it. Few are willing to give up what they think they know to learn what they know not yet. This is how it was when I first walked the path, and it is how it is today. All are called, but few answer the call. (MOL)

I Recall You to the Truth About Yourself

You live in a world where everyone is made guilty. Everyone is made wrong. And most teachings come down on you like a sledgehammer, offering correction at best, condemnation at worst.

My teaching is not like that. I tell you that you are not evil, no matter how many mistakes you have made. I recall you to the truth about yourself. Your challenge is to open your heart to that truth.

How do you do this? You do this by refusing to condemn others, by not judging, not complaining, not finding fault. You do this by celebrating your relationships and feeling grateful for the love and nurturing that you have in your life. You focus on what is there, not on what is not there. By finding the good in your life, you reinforce it and extend it to others. (MOL)

Religious Righteousness

Only those who are full of pride think that they have exclusive understanding of the truth and the right to judge others. The Christian religion—the religion that purports to be inspired by me—is riddled with countless cases of spiritual pride.

I am not one to condemn adultery, or divorce, or abortion. For if I were to condemn these situations, those involved in them would be crucified. You would have yet another inquisition, another holy war pitting good against evil, just against unjust.

My job is not to condemn, but to understand and to bless. My job is to see the fear in people's eyes and remind them that they are loved.

If that is my job, why would I have you beat and burn and excommunicate those who are most in need of your love? You would bring me to the level of your fear, put your words in my mouth and attribute them to me. My friend, stop and behold yourself. You have misunderstood. You are mistaken. My teaching is about love, not about judgment, condemnation or punishment.

I have given you only two rules: to love God and to love each other. Those are the only rules you need. Do not ask me for more. Do not ask me to take sides in your soap opera battles. Am I pro-life or pro-choice? How could I be one without also being the other? It is not possible.

When the truth comes to you, you will no longer need to attack your brother. Even if you think you are right and he is wrong, you will not attack him with "the truth," but offer him your understanding and your support. And together you will move closer to the truth because of the love and gentleness you share.

Every time I give a teaching, someone makes it into a stick to beat people with. Please, my friends, words that are used to beat people up cannot come from me.

I have offered you the key to the door within. Please use it, and do not worry about the thoughts and actions of others. Work on yourself. If you would serve this teaching, learn it first. Do not be a mouthpiece for words and beliefs you have not brought fully into the rhythms of your life.

All who extend my teaching do so from the same level of consciousness as me. Otherwise what they extend cannot be my teaching. (SOTH)

Honoring Mother and Father

If you follow my teaching, you must know that I call upon you to become the embodiment of unconditional love, non-judgment and compassion. I challenge you to accept each person who comes before you as a Child of God, no less perfect than you or I am. I challenge you to give to each other the love and freedom Mother and Father have given you. I call you to love and let go, to nurture and empower, to comfort and inspire.

Love is peaceful, but not static. It is dynamic, but not overwhelming or controlling. It gives the gift you need to receive and receives the gift you need to give. It is both feminine/receptive and masculine/active.

If you want to be a vehicle for love, you must practice both giving and receiving, leading and following, speaking and listening, acting and refraining from action. Love flows to and from you naturally as you accept the polarities of your experience, integrate them and realize your wholeness.

You are a child of the Father and the Mother, as am I. As a man, you must emulate the Father and embrace the qualities of the Mother. As a woman, you must emulate the Mother and embrace the qualities of the Father. Just as God is neither male nor female, but both together, so are you a synthesis of male and female qualities within a particular body/mind vehicle. (MOL)

Moving Beyond Prejudice

Women have an equal place in my teaching. Those who have denied women their rightful place in church or synagogue are not following my teaching.

Gays and lesbians, blacks, Asians, Hispanics, fundamentalists, Buddhists, Jews, lawyers and politicians all have a place in the community of faith. Everyone is welcome. No one should be excluded. And all who participate in the community should have the opportunity to serve in leadership positions.

My teaching has never been exclusive or hierarchical. You have imposed your prejudices and your judgments on the pure truth I have taught. You have taken the house of worship and made it into a prison of fear and guilt. My friends, you are mistaken in your beliefs.

But it is not too late for you to learn from your mistakes. Repent from your unkind actions and make amends to those whom you have injured or judged unfairly. Your mistakes do not condemn you unless you insist on holding on to them. Let them go. You can grow. You can change. You can be wiser than you once were. You can stop being a mouthpiece for fear and ignorance and become a spokesperson for forgiveness and love.

No ship has ever been refused refuge in the harbor of forgiveness. No matter what you have said or done, you can acknowledge your mistakes and learn from them. That is the meaning of atonement.

The past cannot condemn you if you are willing to open your heart and mind right here and now. Your willingness to change is the power of God working within you. And It, not I, will bring you home. I will simply welcome you when you arrive here. (MOL)

Prescription for Peace

Don't try to save the world. Don't try to save others. All that just adds to your job description.

You have sufficient challenge in your life just learning to embrace your own experience. Life has given you plenty to chew on.

Nobody comes into embodiment with an empty plate. Everyone has at least a scrap or two to digest. (Some have seven-course meals! But I'm not going to point any fingers!)

Don't be discouraged by this. Since each person must deal with what's on his plate, let him deal with it as happily as he can.

Don't interfere in the lives of others or you will have a second or a third helping to dispose of. Stay detached from what someone else does or does not do. Don't even have an opinion about it. Just let it be.

Don't borrow someone else's experience. Don't try to give someone else your experience.

Sleep in your own bed. Prepare your own food. Clean up after yourself. Practice taking care of yourself and let others do the same for themselves.

That is your job. You are not here to do for others what they must do for themselves. Your job is simply to be present in your experience as fully and as magnificently as you can. (SOTH)

19.

TRUSTING YOUR GUIDANCE

THE PEARL OF GREAT PRICE

I ask you to remember that no one knows more than you do. No one has anything to give you that you do not already have.

Forget your gurus, cults, dogmas, metaphysics. None of this will bring you freedom from suffering and pain. It will only add to the burden you carry.

Be realistic about your experience here. There is only one person who needs to wake up and that is you. Those who have a gift to give you will not withhold it. Those who withhold information or love from you have no gift to give.

Beware of those who would make you jump through hoops or stand in line. They are just lining their pockets at your expense. Do not tolerate the idea that salvation lies somewhere else. It doesn't.

Don't buy the idea that there is something out there to achieve if only you were better behaved, more worthy, more spiritual, more intelligent . . . you fill in the blank. If you allow it, people will be only too glad to prescribe for you or take your freedom away.

Don't line the pockets of those who make empty promises to you. It doesn't matter what they promise: more security, more money, more peace of mind, more enlightenment.

You already have everything you need. You already have absolute security. You already have peace of mind and all of the resources you need to fulfill your creative purpose. There is only one thing that you do not have. And that is the awareness that all this is true.

And nobody can give you that awareness. Not me, not some used-car salesman, not some swami peddling samadhi. If someone tells you he can, it's time for a belly laugh. Put your arm around him and tell him that's the best joke you've heard in fifty years.

Do you hear me? Nobody can give you that awareness! Awareness is not a gift, but a gesture of the self, an energetic movement to be present and embrace life. Simply desire to be aware and awareness is. It comes and goes with the breath. If you want to be aware, breathe! Breathe in to embrace this moment. Breathe out to release it. Breathe, breathe, breathe. Each breath is an act of awareness.

If I came to your doorstep and told you I was selling breaths for $5 million a piece, you would think that was pretty funny, would you not? You would tell me, "That's very nice, brother, but I already have all the breaths I need." Of course you do.

But you keep forgetting that you have them. You keep buying the insurance policy, falling in love with Prince or Princess Charming, chasing doctor-I-can-make-you-feel-good or swami-I've-got-it-all-come-and-get-it-for-five-bucks. You know, they all have such long names, it's a wonder you can pronounce them!

Take a breath, my friend. That's right, a deep breath. Nobody has what you need. Did you hear me? Nobody!

You see, you really are all alone here. But it's not as problematic as you think. Because there is no part of you that's missing. If you just hang around yourself long enough without giving your power away to others, you will retrieve all the fragmented and dissociated aspects of yourself, for no other reason than they never went away. They just got covered over in your race for the exit.

"Just hang around and you'll get it." Great advice from a holy man, right? "I guess we better send this guy to entrepreneurship training or to a spirituality and business workshop or he won't make a living."

I have news for you, friends. I don't need to make a living. I *am* a living. And so are you. Just hang around and you'll get it. Because you never lost it. You just pretended to lose it.

One moment you were fully present, and then the next moment your body was there, but your mind was on vacation in the Bahamas. Now, after thirty years or however long it's been, you can bring yourself back, claim your body, and be present in the moment.

Can you believe that thirty years passed between one breath and another? It may seem strange, but I'm telling you it is a common experience. You needn't be embarrassed.

The next time someone asks how old you are, just tell the truth: "People say I'm forty-five, but I've only taken four breaths!"

I'm just kidding you. Or am I? How many breaths have you taken with complete awareness?

Don't worry about the past. Just begin now. Breathe and claim your life. Breathe and let go of all the mental and emotional crutches you have carried. Breathe and release all the words ever said to you by authority figures.

Breathe and soften. Breathe and strengthen. Breathe and be. You are authentic. You are intact. You are a child of the great Spirit that animates us all. (SOTH)

Let Others Find Their Own Truth

One of the greatest black holes on the spiritual path is the need to prescribe to others. Even if you know what is good for you, the truth is that you do not know what is good for other people.

So stop waving your Bibles, your Sutras, your holy books. Don't insist that others live the way you think they should live. If you are concerned about others, love them. Be a beacon of compassion. That is how you get people to take notice. Not by preaching.

Let others find their own way. Encourage them. Cheer them on. But don't think you know what's good for them. You don't know. Nor will you ever know. A co-dependent preoccupation with the lives of others keeps you from taking responsibility for your own life. (RTG)

Don't Play by Other People's Rules

If you look carefully, you will notice that those who have the greatest need to tell others what to do have the least faith in themselves. They haven't even begun to hear the voice in their own hearts; yet they are up on a soapbox telling others what to do.

I have told you many times to be careful. Things are not always as they seem. Wolves are disguised in sheep's clothing. Prisons of fear and judgment masquerade as temples of love and forgiveness. It helps to keep your eyes open. Don't join the crusade until you see the fruits of people's actions.

Your job is not to follow others, but to find the truth of your heart. You alone know what course of action is best for the fulfillment of your purpose here. But that knowledge is often buried deeply in the heart. Sometimes, it takes a lot of listening to connect with your own wisdom. In some cases, connecting to yourself is not possible until you stop listening to what other people think you should do.

When you are used to living by other people's rules, it can seem overwhelming to set your own priorities and make your own decisions. You don't know whether you can handle the responsibility. But if you don't take responsibility for your life, who will?

Nobody else can take responsibility for living your life. Not your boss, your parents, your partner, or your children. Not your church, your friends, or your support network. You alone must do it.

If each of you would nurture the truth within your hearts, you would collectively give birth to a very different world. It would be a world of realization, not sacrifice, a world of equality not prejudice, a world of insight and respect, not collusion and despair.

So stay in your life. Stay in your heart. Everything that you need to fulfill your destiny will be found within. Listen to your guidance, honor it, act on it, be committed to it and it will unfold. When you are joined with your true nature, the doors you need to walk through will open to you. (RTG)

Maps and Signs

When you are embarking on a journey it is helpful to look at a road map. A road map is an intellectual construction that helps you get a general sense of how to proceed. Yet it is not, and can never be, an actual description of the road. No one can tell you what the road will be like. Only your experience can do that.

The best that linear, sequential thinking can give you is a map of your potential experience. But it cannot guide you through that experience. When you are in the midst of the experience, there are signs that help you out.

The detour sign tells you when there is a need for a change of direction. Highway signs tell you to get in the right lane or the left. There are signs telling you where there are places to eat, to sleep or to get gas. Without reading these signs you could not have a successful experience.

Signs come from the interface between outer and inner reality. They are created through your intuitive connection with life. Signs happen only in the present moment. You don't get a sign that says "Go right tomorrow or sometime next month." The sign says go right now or very soon. Signs show you how to navigate in the here and now. They are extremely useful and important.

When you go on a journey, a map can be very helpful. Left-brain information can help you to prepare. But once you embark, signs are a necessity. Are you paying attention to the signs that arise in your life? Or are you trying to live your life with a map alone?

Each of you has access to guidance at a deep emotional level. A sign may simply tell you "this feels right" or "this doesn't feel good," but that is often the only information you need. You don't need to have a vision of a saint in order to receive guidance.

Guidance is your greatest ally in life. When you rely on your guidance, you can get by with a minimum of planning. But when you ignore your guidance, no amount of planning can guide you home.

By all means look at your map to find the place where you want to go. However, once you embark on your journey, learn to rely on your guidance to help you get there. Trying to figure out "exactly how" you will get there is an exercise in futility. You simply can't know in advance. But when you are in the midst of your journey, signs will appear to guide you through the twists and turns. Seeing these signs and learning to trust them can save you a lot of aggravation. (SOTH)

Prayer

Prayer is the ongoing dialogue with God. It is the process by which you continually empty out what you think you know and surrender to the mystery in the moment.

Petitioning God for certain outcomes is not true prayer. Petitioning is exactly what it sounds like. Why approach God as a nagging child? It is neither dignified nor effective.

If you want your prayers to be effective, admit your fears and judgments and ask to see beyond your preconceptions and prejudices. Ask to learn the lesson the situation brings. Ask for guidance, support, help, relief from suffering. Ask for the highest good of all concerned.

And then be quiet and listen for God's answer. Let your mind be joined with Her mind. Let your heart open to Her love. Let yourself open to a greater reality than the one you have yet been able to perceive.

God's answer will always uplift your heart. Listen to the answer and energy and optimism will return to your life.

Prayer is your gesture of opening, confiding, asking for help.

Guidance is God's response. It brings comfort, clarity and peace to you.

If you already know what the answer is or "should be," then you can't really pray. Prayer comes from the place of not knowing.

If you seek validation of your ego perceptions or expectations through prayer, you will be disappointed. God will tell you the truth, even if this is not what you want to hear.

Successful prayer takes you into an expanded sense of reality in which your heart and mind are more open than they were before. It helps you to see things more generously and compassionately.

Prayer is an opening to God's unconditional love for you. It is an opening to God's unconditional acceptance of you as you are.

When you enter the temple of prayer, you are blessed beyond measure. You cannot emerge from the temple bearing ill feelings toward others or toward yourself. For, in entering, you surrender, and, in surrendering, you are washed clean of all judgments you make about yourself or others. (SOTH)

Hearing God's Answer

You cannot be aware of God's presence until you have addressed your fear in a loving way. You attract the divine presence through your love and acceptance of all aspects of yourself. You prepare the inner temple for God to come.

When problems arise and fear comes up for you, remember, "It's okay to be afraid. It's okay not to know the answer." That is the beginning of your surrender to the divinity within. That which knows cannot take charge until you realize that you don't know and ask for help.

And who, my friends, is God but the One in you who knows and understands, the One who loves and accepts you without conditions, under all circumstances, now and for all time? That being is not outside of you, but in your heart of hearts. When you ask sincerely, this is the One who answers. When you knock, this is the One who opens the door. (MOL)

Your Unique Path

Your path has its own simple beauty and mystery. It is never what you think it is. Yet it is never beyond your ability to intuit the next step.

Authentic spirituality is not linear, mechanistic or prescriptive. It cannot tell you, "Do this and do that, and such and such will happen." It can only invite you to keep your heart and mind open. It can only invite you to listen to your guidance and trust it. Action that comes from this place is a living prayer. It cannot be anticipated or repeated. (LWOC)

The Call to Awaken

Deeply embedded in your psyche is the call to awaken. It does not sound like the call that anyone else hears. If you are listening to others, you will not hear the call.

But once you hear it, you will recognize that others hear it too, in their own way. And you will be able to join with them in simple support. Blessing them, you bless yourself. Setting them free to travel their own path, you will set yourself free to travel yours. (LWOC)

20.

TELLING THE TRUTH

RE-NEGOTIATING COMMITMENTS

Often, in the course of living, commitments need to be revised. A plan is made for the future that is not materializing. No matter how hard you try to follow the plan, it just won't come together.

Re-negotiating commitments is not a sign of weakness or inconstancy unless it happens chronically. When something doesn't seem to be working for you, the best thing you can do is tell the truth to the other people involved. More often than not, you will find that others have their own reservations about the plan. Revising the plan is therefore in the interest of all parties.

Abuse and betrayal happen when plans are held rigidly or agreements are broken in fear. If you make a commitment and don't feel comfortable keeping it, it is your responsibility to communicate this to the people involved. At all times, you best honor others by telling the truth about your experience. (SOTH)

The Conditions for Abuse

To say "yes" or "no" to another person is a clear communication. But to say "no" and mean yes or to say "yes" and mean no creates the conditions for abuse. (SOTH)

Saying "No" in a Loving Way

Some of you believe that if you do not say "yes" to another's demands you are not acting in a loving way. That is not true.

Never say "yes" to another's demands. That is not loving yourself. Do not place another's needs before your own. Love has nothing to do with sacrifice.

Some of you believe that you must say "no" to the love of others to protect yourself from their demands. That is not true. By saying "no" to love, you push opportunities for intimacy and sharing away.

Please see how you reject others to try to keep yourself and how you reject yourself in order to try to keep others. Both gestures are a denial of authenticity and intimacy.

Only one who honors his truth is capable of intimacy with another. Only one who honors the other person's truth can be completely authentic.

Say "no" when you feel trespassed upon, and then forgive the trespass. Do not let the "no" to the person's behavior become a "no" to his/her call for love and support. (LWOC)

Commitment to the Truth

Need I remind you that commitment to the truth is not popular? Often it means saying "yes" when others would say "no," or saying "no" when others would say "yes."

Many of you cannot imagine that saying "no" can be a loving act. Yet it is very easy to say "no" in a loving way. If your child is putting his hand on a hot stove, you say "no" quickly and firmly. You do not want him to hurt himself. And then you put your arm around him and reassure him that you love him.

How many times does your brother come to you with his hand on the stove? You cannot support behavior that you know will be hurtful to another person. And you don't want your friends to support that kind of behavior in you. (LWOC)

Honesty and True Friendship

A friend is one who is free to agree or disagree. A friend will speak to you truthfully. She may or may not perceive the situation accurately, but she is not afraid to tell you what she thinks. A friend speaks her truth and then reminds you that you are free to make your own choice. This is love in action. A friend loves you equally whether she is saying yes or no. She is willing to share her experience, but she doesn't try to impose her opinion on you.

You can't be a friend if you are not willing to tell the truth. But honesty alone is not enough. Honesty and humility must go hand in hand. Your humility says to your brother "This is the way that I see it. I may be right or I may be wrong. How do you see it? After all, you are the one who must make the choice." (LWOC)

Standing for Truth

My crucifixion was an act of civil disobedience. I accepted torture and death, because I refused to speak anything but the truth that I knew in my heart.

To stand for the truth in the face of opposition is not an easy thing to do. If one values one's body too much, one cannot do it. Only one who values the truth above all else can put himself in harm's way for the sake of what he believes in.

Surely, I am not the only one you know who has done that. There are many you know who have risen above their fear to stand up for what they believe in. (MOL)

Non-violence

Standing up for truth is a forceful act, but it is not a violent one. One who stands for truth must do so in a loving way or it is not truth s/he stands for.

There will be times when you must stand up for yourself and for others who are being mistreated. You cannot live your life in a state of fear, cowering in a corner while others make decisions for you. You must stand up and be counted.

But please do so lovingly, compassionately, respectfully. Do it knowing that there is no enemy out there. Each brother or sister, no matter how angry, fearful or distraught, deserves your support and your respect. And how you act means as much, if not more, than what you do or what you say. (MOL)

Standing Alone with the Truth

Learn to stand alone with the truth. Do not rely on psychics, teachers, therapists or gurus to discern or intuit what is good and true for you.

Trust in your connection to the Source of all things. You have everything you need to be guided wisely in your life. You are no farther away from God than I am. You don't need me to bring you to the feet of the Divine. You don't need your partner or your teacher to bring you there. You are already there.

God is incapable of moving away from you. When you do not feel the presence, it is because you have moved away. You have given your power to some earthly authority. You have left the place of the indwelling God in search of something special in the world. That search always comes up empty, but that doesn't mean that you won't keep trying to find the answer somewhere outside of yourself.

Many of you think that I want your exclusive allegiance. Nothing could be further from the truth. I am not necessary to your salvation. You are the lamb of God. You are the one who has come to forgive yourself and release your world from its chains of envy and regret.

If you have a teacher who empowers you, I am happy. It does not matter to me if that teacher is a Buddhist or a Jew, a Christian or a Muslim, a shaman or a businessman. If you are learning to trust yourself, if you are becoming more open in your mind and your heart, then I am happy for you. It does not matter what specific path you are on, what symbols you believe in, or what scrolls you consider sacred. I look to the fruit of those beliefs to see if you are stepping into your divinity or giving that power away to someone else.

No, I do not want your exclusive allegiance. I simply ask you to choose a teacher and a teaching that empowers you to discover truth within your own heart, for there alone will you find it. When you give your power away, to me or to anyone else, I know that you have not heard me.

You and I are God's children. We carry divine love and wisdom within us. All the answers to our problems lie within us.

I stand before you as a model of one who realized his divinity while living in a body in this world. I demonstrate to you the power that manifests when one listens to one's inner voice and follows it, even when other people judge or object. I stand for the inner authority of the universal heart-mind that holds everyone in equal reverence. I know that when you trust the divine within, you cannot help but become authentic.

I have tried to show you a way of cutting yourself loose from parental authority, cultural authority and religious authority. I have told you that the laws and customs of men and women are limited by the conditions of their experience. They cannot see beyond them. However, there is a reality beyond their narrow, and subjective experience. It dwells in the core of their being. It is who they are when all the false beliefs they have accepted from parents, family, culture and church or synagogue have been stripped away.

I have asked you to have the courage to stand alone so you can shed the narrow identifications that prevent you from knowing who you are. I have asked you to leave your homes and your work, so that you could stand back and look at your life from a distance, seeing the self-limiting, fear-based patterns of relating. I have asked you to stand back so that you would realize that you do not have to sell yourself short.

A man and a woman must leave the home of their parents and open to new experiences if they are to create a home of their own. For the same reason, you must leave your school, your career, your religion and your relationship so that you can discover who you are apart from the conditions of your life.

You are not just a son or a daughter, a husband or a wife, a carpenter or a plumber, a black person or a white person, a Christian or a Jew. Yet if you identify with these roles, you will not discover the essence within you that goes beyond them. Nor will you find a way to transcend the inevitable division these external definitions will create in your life.

I have asked you to listen to others with respect, but never to accept their ideas and opinions as an authority in your life. I have asked you to find that authority within, even though no one else in your life agrees with it. And I have asked you to follow that inner authority even in the face of outright criticism from your friends, your family, your church, your race, your political party and your country.

I have asked you to stand alone, not because I wish to isolate you, but so you can know the truth and anchor in it. For there will be times when you will have to stand in that truth in the midst of a crowd of people who would ignore it, scapegoating and condemning their brothers and sisters, as they once condemned me. There will be times, my friend, when you will be the voice in the wilderness that helps people find their way back home. And you could not become that voice if you did not leave home and learn to stand alone with the truth.
(MOL)

Truth, Essence and Love

Truth lies in the heart along with essence and love. They can be embodied and expressed only when you do not need to be right, loved back or approved of.

To reach truth, love and essence, you must refuse to be satisfied with their imitations. If you accept conditional love, you will not experience love without conditions. If you accept any form of dogma, judgment or prejudice as truth, you will not know the pure truth of the heart. If you seek the approval of other men and women and are attached to the way they receive you, you will not express your essential Self even when it is called for.

If you mistake the false for the true, you cannot affirm what is true or deny what is false. That, my friends, is the difficulty of words and concepts. To penetrate to the core, you must go beyond words and concepts.

When you speak of love, please ask yourself, "Is my love free of conditions?" When you speak of truth, please ask yourself, "Is my truth free of judgment or opinion?" When you speak of essence, ask, "Am I attached to the way people perceive or receive me?"

Freedom to be yourself requires more detachment than you think. As long as you want something from anyone, you cannot be yourself. Only when you want nothing in particular from anyone are you free to be yourself and to interact honestly and authentically with others.

I do not say this to discourage you, but to prepare you for the depth and breadth of the journey you are on. To be a self-realized person requires that you disconnect from all expectations and conditions whether they come from you or from another.

Your goal is to accept every person you meet just the way s/he is and to be yourself regardless of how other people receive you or react to you. When you meet someone who revolts you or pushes your buttons, you are not seeing truth or essence in that person. If you feel expansive when people love you and depressed when people dislike you, you are not established in the truth of your own essence.

Love is both difficult and easy. It is difficult because you have so many attachments and expectations that block its flow toward you and from you. It is easy because, when you drop those attachments and expectations even for a moment, love comes to you and emanates from you spontaneously and without effort. (MOL)

21.

THE BODY:
A MEANS NOT
AN END

BLESSING THE BODY

Whenever I point out the inherent limitations of the physical body, someone inevitably interprets my statements to mean "the body is bad, inferior or evil." This need to reject the body is a form of attachment to it. Where there is resistance to desire, desire itself is made stronger.

The body is not bad or inferior in any way. It is simply temporal. You will never find ultimate meaning by satisfying its needs. Nor might I add will you find ultimate meaning by denying its needs. Taking care of the body is an act of grace. Preoccupation with bodily pleasures or pains is anything but graceful.

If you wish to follow the path I have laid out for you, accept your body fully and care for it diligently. When the body is loved, it does its work with efficiency and grace. (SOTH)

The Body Is a Means

Being in the body is both a privilege and a challenge. Many lessons are learned thanks to the opportunity the body provides.

Yet you must remember that everything the body can do for you will one day be undone. The pleasures of food, drink, sex, sleep, entertainment, what will these mean when the body is no longer? To worship the body is as unhelpful as it is to demean it.

The body is a means. It is a vehicle for gathering experience. It has a purpose. I used my body to complete my mission here, just as you must use yours. I experienced physical joy and physical suffering, just as you no doubt have. Each person who comes into the body experiences ecstasy and pain, love and death.

The body is a vehicle. It is a means for learning. Please do not disrespect or demean it. Please do not make it into a god that you worship. Don't make it more or less important than it is.

When you enjoy and care for your body, it can serve you better. But no body is perfect. All bodies eventually break down. Bodies are not meant to last forever. Those who speak of physical immortality have missed the point entirely.

Your challenge is not to stay in your physical body forever. It is to surrender to your experience that it may be lifted up and guided by grace. Then, you will be an instrument of salvation for yourself and others.

I once asked you to be in the world but not of it. I suggested that you be in the body, honor it, use it as a vehicle for spreading love and acceptance, without being attached to it.

I also asked you not to build your house on sand, where every storm takes its devastating toll. Some things are temporary and temporal, and some are eternal. The body is not eternal. The best it can be is a temporary servant. (MOL)

Sex: Bodily Communion or Addiction?

The enjoyment of your sensuality is essential for the full unfolding of your life. Having a partner who loves you, cherishes you and touches you with gratitude is nothing other than a divine gift.

Some people oppose healthy sexuality because they have trouble accepting their own sexuality. These people—including many clergy—would poison the waters for others. Pay them no mind. They have their own difficult lessons in this life.

The only sexual expression that is reprehensible is sex without love. Some people are addicted to this kind of object-oriented sex. They try to find their satisfaction through the pleasure of orgasm. This never works, because after the peak of every orgasm is the trough of existential contact with the partner. If you love the person you are with, the trough will be a peaceful, comforting space. If you do not love the person, the trough will feel hollow and uncomfortable.

Sex without love is ultimately unsatisfactory and addictive. More will always be needed: more sex, more partners, more stimulation. But more is never enough. When you engage in sexual activity with someone you do not love, you dishonor yourself and the other person.

Sex without love lays the foundation for abuse. If you wish to save yourself much grief, do not engage in sexual behavior with someone you don't love. Even if you are in a loving partnership, do not engage in sexual behavior when your heart is not open to your partner. Sex without love, under any guise, fragments the energy of your union and exacerbates your emotional wounds. (SOTH)

Making Love

Let your lovemaking be a joyful act, an act of surrender to the Christ in yourself and your partner. Physical love is no less beautiful than other forms of love, nor can it be separated from them. Those who view physical love as unholy will experience it that way, not because it is, but because they perceive it that way. (SOTH)

Fidelity and Betrayal

When you are truly committed to your partner, it is impossible to betray him or her, for to betray the partner is like betraying yourself. You just can't do it. You may experience an attraction to another person, but you don't consider taking that person to bed.

The urge to sexual union is an important part of the sacrament of marriage. A spiritual relationship is meant to be a full-chakra embrace. Sexual passion is part of a greater attraction to be with the person.

Whenever it splits off, sex becomes an attack.

Some married people engage in non-loving, non-surrendered and non-devotional sex. This behavior is often the beginning of a process of fragmentation that often culminates in infidelity.

When love is mutual and the partners are surrendered to one another emotionally, sexuality is completely uplifting and sacred. But when communication in the relationship becomes careless and shoddy, when time is not taken for one-to-one intimacy, the relationship becomes an empty shell. Energy and commitment disappear from the relationship, and sex becomes an act of physical betrayal.

Communion can be restored if there is mutual willingness and trust. For the goal of a full-chakra union is realized entirely through love, energy and attention. (SOTH)

Marriage and Children

Once a child has entered your life, s/he becomes part of the fabric of your embodiment. There is no way to escape responsibility for this relationship. It will continue throughout your lifetime. And you will use this relationship, as you use all your intimate relationships, to lessen your guilt or to intensify it.

Dogmatic rules about marriage and children are not helpful if you would walk this path. I have asked you to "love all equally." That includes your spouse and your children. If you walk away from your spouse and children without full forgiveness and completion, you are simply postponing what must inevitably happen if you are to find peace.

Does it matter how long it takes? No, not to me, but I would not be honest with you if I did not tell you that the longer you wait, the more pain you will experience. (SOTH)

Abortion

"Is it ever right," you ask, "to take the life of an unborn child?" I must tell you that it is never right to take a life, under any circumstances. Does that mean that it will not happen? No, that is for sure. And when it does happen, one needs to have compassion for all those involved.

You do not live in a perfect world. To expect others to be perfect is to attack them. That is not my teaching. Even perceiving others as wrong is a form of attack. Do not attack your brother or sister. Nothing good can come of it. (SOTH)

Marriage Versus Celibacy

The inner meaning of celibacy is abstaining from marriage, not from sexual intercourse. A celibate person is one who is committed to living a solitary life in communion with God. That might mean not having sex with anyone or it might mean having sex with a consenting partner who also chooses to live alone.

Celibate people are honest and clear with other people about their decision not to marry or live with anyone. They choose to live alone because their creative pursuits and/or spiritual practices require the majority of their time and attention and make living full time with another person an unwise and unwieldy proposition.

There is nothing wrong or right with celibacy. It is one spiritual path. Marriage is another. Both paths have their challenges and their rewards. Moreover, during the course of one's lifetime, one may choose to be married first, then celibate, or celibate first, then married. Such choices are progressive. Society would do well to acknowledge the importance of different interpersonal models as people go through inevitable life cycle changes.

Of all the choices available, abstinence is the least likely to suc-ceed. It is tragic that some religious organizations have demanded this sacrifice from their clergy. Very few people are capable of sexual absti-nence. Those who try and fail often engage in secretive, abusive be-havior in order to satisfy themselves and maintain their positions of authority. Witness the many cases of pedophilia that have under-mined the authority of the clergy in your time. When confronted by this kind of unfortunate behavior, an enlightened church understands that it is time to rethink its position on both celibacy and abstinence.

People who are attracted to the solitary way of life should be given as many options as possible. An honest but unconventional life is to be greatly preferred to a traditional life twisted by secrets and lies.

When form does not express the Spirit that inhabits it, it becomes a prison. Many of your institutions, both religious and secular, have ceased to embody the ideals with which they were created. It is far better to let the form go or revise it than to let Spirit die out because of lack of vision. (SOTH)

22.

LEAVING THE PAST BEHIND

SALVATION EXISTS ONLY NOW

You practice forgiveness not to buy future salvation, but because the practice of forgiveness allows you to experience salvation right here, right now. You practice acceptance not to score brownie points with God, but because acceptance reminds you that everything is perfect right here, right now.

Your entire spirituality is lived in this moment only. It has nothing to do with anything you have ever thought or felt in the past. It is happening right now, with the circumstance that lies before you. (LWOC)

Bliss

You experience darkness and scarcity only when you find fault with the situation you are presented with in the moment. When you see the situation and feel gratitude for it, you experience only bliss. (LWOC)

Finding the Center

Do not try to move out of darkness. Do not try to move into bliss. Just be where you are and be willing to love and accept what's there. (LWOC)

Surrender

Right now, you are either happy or you are finding fault with the circumstances of your life. Try for a moment accepting your life exactly as it is. The appearance may seem perplexing, but do not judge it. Do not find fault with yourself or with others. Rest in the strength of your surrender. Entrust the outcome to God. (LWOC)

Mistaken Identity

You may think that somewhere along the line something in you got broken, or perhaps you are just missing some parts. But you have no missing or broken parts. All of your wholeness is fully present right now. (LWOC)

Who Made Those Chains?

Your entire physical experience is an awakening to self-responsibility. You have come here to betray yourself at your brother's hands. He is simply the instrument of your self-betrayal. When you realize this, you forgive yourself and him. You release the past. You enter the present authentic and free.

I have told you that you are free to live whatever life you choose to live. "Fat chance!" you say, pointing to the chains on your feet.

"Who made those chains?" I ask.

"God did!" you angrily exclaim.

"No. It is not true. God did not make the chains. If He made them, you would never escape from the prison of your own beliefs." (SOTH)

Leave Your Nets

Until you can bless the past, you won't be free to leave it. You cannot "leave your nets" and take the fish with you. In time, the fish will rot and leave a terrible stench. For miles around, people will anticipate your arrival.

"The fisherman is coming," they will say. Your past walks in front of you. This is not the way to freedom.

Throw the fish away. Give them their freedom so that you can claim your own.

Be strong in your conviction about your own life, but gentle with others. Do not judge their needs just because you cannot meet them. Just be honest about what you can and cannot do, and wish them well.

Remember, the one whom you reject follows you. Only acceptance brings completion. (SOTH)

The Ego's Terror

Your ego is terrified of the unknown. No matter how terrible the known past is, your ego prefers it to the unknown present. All of its energy goes into trying to make the present into the past. Although it tries to create safety, in truth it creates continued terror. Outwardly, life seems safe and predictable. Inwardly, the dynamite has been lit. No matter how many times your fear pushes you out of the present moment, it inevitably brings you into it full force, because the price of denial is pain. (SOTH)

Watch Your Plans

Watch your plans consciously. See if the external structure you create for your life continues to match the internal reality as it unfolds. See how you compromise yourself by taking what is true in one moment and legislating the next with it.

Your goal in watching is to recognize the temporality of your thought/feeling states. What feels very important in one moment is not necessarily significant in the next.

Be with the ebb and flow of your thought/feeling experience without judgment and it will take you beyond the very limits it seems to present. Only the attachment to mind-states creates suffering, not the mind-states themselves. (SOTH)

Letting Go of the Past

Most external changes follow internal shifts of allegiance and attention. When someone ceases to be committed to a relationship, a shift takes place. Energy is withdrawn from one direction and placed in a new direction.

You can argue until you are blue in the face about whether it is right or wrong that someone's commitment has changed, but it won't do you any good. You cannot prevent other people from going forward in their growth, even if you don't agree with their decisions.

If you look deeply enough, you will see that every apparent "loss" you experience brings an unexpected gain. When one person leaves a relationship that is not growing into deeper intimacy, the other person is set free too.

In the same manner, when you cease to be committed to your career, it falls apart. It is no longer as challenging and fun as it used to be. You can blame this change on your boss, but you will be missing the whole point. The job no longer works because you are no longer giving it your love, your support, your commitment.

Holding on to the job or the relationship will not help you get on with your life. But don't be surprised if it takes a while to let go.

When something in your life is not working, you often try to fix it. Then, if that doesn't work, you may pretend for a while that it's fixed even though you know it isn't. Finally, you realize that your heart just isn't in the job or the relationship. That's when you are ready to let go of it.

Letting go is an act of substantial courage. There is always some degree of pain in the release of someone or something that once brought you joy and happiness. You will have to be patient and mourn the loss. But when your mourning is over, you will see things differently. Opportunities you never could have dreamed of will come into your life.

As the old dies, the new is born. The phoenix rises from the ashes of destruction.

The fire of change is never easy to weather. But if you surrender, the conflagration is quickly over. In the enriched soil, the seeds of tomorrow can be sown.

I have told you that unless you die and are reborn you cannot enter the Kingdom of Heaven. No one comes here to earth without suffering the pain of loss. Every identity you assume will be taken from you when it is time. Every person you love will die. It is just a matter of time. And it is just a matter of time before you too leave your body and the world behind.

All sacred teachings exhort you not to be attached to the things of this world, because they are not permanent. Yet you get attached nonetheless. That is part of the process of your awakening: getting attached and letting go, embracing and releasing. In this way, love is deepened and wisdom is born.

You will experience many small deaths in the course of your life, many times when you must let go of the arms that once comforted you and walk alone into an uncertain future. Every time you do so your fears will rise up and you will have to walk through them.

Don't be impatient. No one is reborn instantaneously. It takes time. It is a process. The tide goes out and comes back in. People let go of one attachment only to form another one that challenges them more. Life is rhythmic, but progressive. As earth and water breathe together, the shape of the beach changes. Storms come and go.

In the end, a profound peace comes and pervades the heart and mind. Finally, the ground of being has been reached. Here the changing waters come and go, and the earth delights in them as a lover delights in the playful touch of his beloved.

A deep acceptance is felt and, with it, a quiet recognition that all things are perfect as they are. This is grace, the presence of God come to dwell in your heart and in your life. (MOL)

Happiness Happens Now

Happiness happens only in the present moment. If you become concerned about whether you will be happy tomorrow or even five minutes from now, you won't be able to be happy now. Your scheming and dreaming take you away from your present happiness.

Many of you have important jobs serving others. Yet you are not happy right now in this moment. I must ask you: "Do you really believe that you can help others find happiness when you are worried and stressed?"

I must ask you, "Are you willing to give up your lofty goals for the sake of your present happiness?" All of the chaos and confusion in your mind can be transcended through your simple decision to be wholly present and attentive right now. That is the miraculous truth. (LWOC)

The Kingdom of Heaven

If you could be without time for a single instant, you would understand your salvation. In that timeless moment, nothing you have said or done means anything. In that moment, there is nothing to own: no past, no future, no identity. There is just the moment of pure being, the moment you inhabit all the time without knowing it. Imagine that: you are already in heaven and do not know it!

You are in heaven, but heaven is not acceptable to you. Heaven does not support your ego, your schemes and your dreams. Heaven does not support your power struggles, your lessons or even your forgiveness process.

Heaven does not support your soap opera of crime and punishment, sin and salvation. In heaven, there is nothing that needs to be fixed.

In this moment also, there is nothing that needs to be fixed. Remember this, and you are in the Kingdom. (LWOC)

Walking the Tightrope

The more attached you are to the past, or the more invested you are in a future outcome, the harder it is for you to accept "what is" and work with it.

What happened in the past can prejudice you toward what is happening now. It can prevent you from opening fully to the present. For example, if you were hurt by someone in the past, you might be afraid to be in a relationship with someone else now.

Some things belong to the future, not to the present. For example, you might want to get married sometime in the future. But if you are always seeing your present relationship as a potential marriage, you may not give it a chance to unfold naturally.

The truth is that you don't know specifically what will happen in the future. You may have a general sense of the future, based on the way the present is unfolding. You may know what the next step is. But that's about all you can know right now.

To be in the present, you need to stay centered in what you know and put the past and the future aside. If you keep bringing the past in or trying to plan for the future, you will start getting behind or ahead of yourself. You will sow the seeds of conflict within and without.

So this is a balancing act. You need to walk the tightrope between the past and the future. And you can't expect to walk without tipping to one side or the other. But when you do, you must lean the other way, so that you can come back to center.

Centering means being present. It means staying with what you know and dropping what you don't know. You don't know that the past is going to repeat itself. You don't know that your present experience is going to extend into the future. Things may change or they may stay the same. Old patterns may dissolve or they may reappear. You don't know these things. All you know is how you feel about what's happening right now.

If you can stay with this, then you can be honest with yourself and with others about your experience. You can say what you are able to commit to and what you cannot commit to right now.

Things may change in the future, but you can't live right now hoping they are going to change. You must be where you are, not where you want to be.

This is difficult work. The past is saying "Don't open. It's too scary. Don't you remember what happened when . . . ?" and the future is saying "This is taking so long, why don't you just jump in and do it?" The past is trying to hold you back and the future is trying to rush you, an interesting dilemma don't you think?

The truth is that you need to listen to both voices and reassure them that they have been heard. Then, you can rebalance and come back to center. Then, you can try to find a pace that feels good for right now.

That is what the tightrope walker must do. She can't worry about losing her balance in the past. She can't dream about a perfect performance in the future. She needs to focus on what's happening right now. She needs to put one foot in front of the other. Every step is an act of balance. Every step is a spiritual act. (RTG)

Trusting the Christ Within

When you act out of fear, you don't solve any problems. You just add to the imbalance and the hysteria.

Don't act out of fear. Let the fear come up. Ride it as a wave and return to your center. Then it will be time to act.

Realize that you have just the amount of time that you need to complete your journey. So don't rush. But don't hesitate either. Proceed forward with faith, confidence and enthusiasm. Take no thought for yesterday or tomorrow. What you say and do today will be enough.

Move in the direction of your greatest joy. Choose something to do that expresses your love, your gratitude, your appreciation.

Don't beat yourself because you suffered in the past. Forgive the past and move on.

Do what you have always wanted to do. If nobody wants to pay you to do it, do it for free. If nobody encourages you, redouble your efforts. Do not withhold your gift. The salvation of the world depends on all people expressing the gifts they have.

Don't worry about the future. You are the one creating it. Don't tie it down to the past. Release it to do its work. Have faith. Don't be attached to the results. Trust.

The one you are trusting is God incarnate, the Christ Him or Herself. How can you fear the future when Christ is with you? Put your trust in that One. (RTG)

Fortune-telling

Many people want to know what is going to happen to them in the future. They go to psychics, astrologers, tarot-card readers and so forth, hoping to hear something that will make them feel better.

The absurdity of this can only be appreciated when you know that the future cannot be predicted. True, there are lines of force emanating from a person's consciousness. There are patterns that are set in motion. But every moment offers you a new choice and that choice alters your destiny. Unfortunately, the more preoccupied you are in finding out what will happen to you in the future, the less attention you can give to the choices you need to make now. That is why a fascination with fortune-telling is discouraged in many spiritual traditions.

The obsession some of you have with the past can be just as dysfunctional as this preoccupation with the future. Many people go to therapists or psychics looking for knowledge of the past which could explain problems in the present. They engage in a variety of forms of psychoanalysis, dream therapy, inner-child work, hypnotherapy, past-life regression and so forth. While this work may help some people move on in their lives, it becomes a quagmire for others. A tool meant to help becomes a dogma. A technique meant to assist you in discovering the source of your pain becomes an invitation to wallow in it and become its perpetual victim.

When you emerge from such therapies with stories about child-hood trauma or abuse, or memories of previous lifetimes, you would do well to ask yourself if these stories help you to stay focused and em-powered in the present moment. A preoccupation with the wounds of the past can prevent you from taking responsibility for your present experience.

Very little is gained on the spiritual path as a result of these excur-sions into yesterday or tomorrow. The projected dramas of past or fu-ture are distractions that take you away from the real challenges facing you right now.

It is important to watch how your mind continues to grasp for ex-ternal answers to your problems and how fascinated you get in the im-agery of change. What does not change is far less interesting to you. You don't like being told "there's nothing out there to get!" When the guru tells you to go home, you are disappointed. You had hoped that s/he would send you on another retreat, another crusade or mission of mercy.

There are enough windy, circuitous roads out there to keep you traveling for a long time. There are enough detours on the spiritual path to keep you spinning your wheels ad infinitum. After taking enough of them, you realize that none of them are going anywhere in particular. They all eventually bring you back to the place where you started. (RTG)

Dropping Your Stories

You don't have to be concerned about what happened in the past or what will happen in the future. You don't need any more stories to put you to sleep.

Your stories of the past reinforce your fears and justify your rituals of self-protection. Whenever you connect with what you want, you also connect with all the reasons why you can't have it. You want to leave your job, but you can't. You want to commit to this relationship, but you can't. On and on it goes: the perpetual catch-22. You want to bring new energy into your life and hold on to your old habits at the same time. You want change, but you are afraid of it.

Your pain is a known quantity. You don't want to trade it for an unknown pain. You prefer a familiar suffering to an unfamiliar one. That's why your spiritual adult's heroic plan for the transformation of your life is inevitably undermined by the fears of your wounded child, who doesn't think s/he is lovable, and therefore cannot have a vision of a life without pain. To the wounded kid within, any promise of release from pain is a trick that entices you to let your defenses down and become vulnerable to attack.

Into this duplicitous environment of the psyche at war with itself then come a variety of professional fixers: psychiatrists, counselors, preachers, self-help gurus. Each claims to have the answer, but each solution offered and taken just compounds the problem.

Professional fixers believe your stories of brokenness and try to heal you. If your story isn't juicy enough, they help you make it more compelling. It's all about high drama, about sin and salvation. It never occurs to them or to you that maybe nothing is broken, that maybe there is nothing in you that needs to be fixed.

The external problems you perceive in your life are projections of the internal conflict: "I want but I cannot have." If you would allow yourself to have what you want, or if you would stop wanting it because you know you can't have it, this conflict would cease. Having what you want or accepting that you can't have it ends your conflict. It also ends your story.

There's no more drama of seeking once you have found love, joy, and happiness . . . "And they lived happily ever after. . . ." Story over. Drama complete. Now, what's next?

The truth is you are not ready to give up your dramas. Your story has become part of your identity. Your pain is part of your personality. You do not know who you are without it.

Letting your drama go means letting the past dissolve right here, right now. If you can do that, it doesn't matter what happened in the past. It has no power. It doesn't exist anymore. You are writing on a clean slate.

That means that you are totally responsible for what you choose. There are no more excuses. You can't blame what happens on the past or on your karma, because there is no more past, no more karma.

When you no longer interpret your life based on what happened yesterday or last year, what happens is neutral. It is what it is. There is no charge on it.

The freedom to be fully present and responsible right now is awesome. Very few people want it.

Most of you wear your past like a badge of honor. You stay in the drama because you love it. And so you have to heal all the make-believe wounds you think that you have. It doesn't matter that those wounds are not real. They are real enough to you.

And so the drama continues: "Seek but do not find. I want, but I can't have. I want to be free, but I want my security too."

You can't tell a person who is in prison getting three meals a day that freedom is its own security. S/he wants those three meals a day no matter what. Then s/he will talk about freedom.

When you are attached to what you already have, how can you bring in anything new in? To bring in something new, something fresh, something unpredictable, you must surrender something old, stale and habitual.

If you want the creative to manifest within you, you must surrender all that is not creative. Then, in the space made by that surrender, creativity rushes in.

If the cup is full of old, cold tea, you cannot pour new, hot tea into it. First you have to empty the cup. Then you can fill it.

If you want to give up your drama, first find out what your investment is in it. What is your payoff for not finding, not healing, not living happily ever after?

And then be honest. If you don't want to move through your pain, tell the truth. Say "I'm not ready to move through my pain yet." Don't say "I wish I could be done with my pain, but I can't be." That is a lie. You could be done with it, but you don't choose to be done. Perhaps you enjoy the attention you get from being a victim.

You can't be on a spiritual path until you are done being a victim. When you learn to accept responsibility, there are no excuses. When you are not ready, you say "I am not ready." When you are ready, your actions flow from that readiness, and actions always speak louder than words. (RTG)

The Open Door

Life has its own rhythm. If you are surrendered, you will find it. But surrendering is not so easy.

Surrendering means meeting each moment as new. And to do that, you cannot be attached to what just happened. You can appreciate it. You can savor it. But you must let it go where it will.

You can't control what happens. Resisting is an attempt to control. Don't resist. Don't control. Don't have attachments to the past or expectations of the future.

Just be where you are. Bring everything into the now. Bring the attachment, the expectations into the present. Be aware of your resistance. See the drama of your disappointment. See that you did not get what you wanted. See how it makes you feel. Watch it. Experience it. But don't lose yourself in the drama.

When you can see the drama without reacting to it, you can stay anchored in the here and now. You can remain present. You can see which doors are closed and which ones are open.

Please, don't try to walk through closed doors. You will hurt yourself unnecessarily. Even if you don't know why a door is closed, at least respect the fact that it is. And don't struggle with the doorknob. If the door was open, you would know it. Wanting it to be open does not make it open.

Much of the pain in your life happens when you attempt to walk through closed doors or try to put square pegs in round holes. You try to hold on to someone who is ready to go, or you try to get somebody to do something before s/he is ready. Instead of accepting what is and working with it, you interfere with it and try to manipulate it to meet your perceived needs.

Obviously, this doesn't work. When you interfere with what is, you create strife for yourself and others. You trespass. You get in the way.

That is why awareness is necessary. When you know that things are not flowing, you need to step back and realize that your actions are not helpful. You need to stop, pause and consider. You need to cease what you are doing because it is not working and you don't want to make the situation worse than it is.

Stopping the offensive action is the first step in the process of At-One-ment for your trespasses. Unless you stop, violation continues. The door stays shut.

After stopping, acknowledge your mistake, first to yourself and then to others. Then vow not to repeat your mistake again.

This is the forgiveness process in its most simple terms. You become aware of your mistake and learn from it so that you do not have to repeat it.

When you interfere in the natural order of things, there is suffering. As soon as you stop interfering, suffering stops.

It is a simple movement from dis-ease to ease, from discomfort to comfort, from disharmony to harmony. You don't need to make the forgiveness process difficult or esoteric. It is a natural, organic process.

When the door is closed, you cannot enter. You must wait patiently or move along and see if another door will open. As long as you are forgiving yourself and others, there is a good chance that the right door will open. Only when you refuse to learn from your mistakes or when you hold on to your grievances does it seem that the doors are repeatedly closed to you.

Fortunately, God does not hold grievances. Nor does S/He punish you for your mistakes. God keeps saying to you: "That didn't work too well, did it? Next time, perhaps, you can make a different choice."

It isn't helpful to obsess about your mistakes and feel bad about them. Guilt doesn't help you act more responsibly toward others. But learning from your mistakes does help you take greater responsibility and move on in your life with more harmony and integrity. That's what it means to atone.

Guilt does not contribute to atonement. If anything, it impedes it.

When something does not work, a correction must be made. Adjustments of this kind are a natural part of living in a harmonious way. You can't be right all of the time. You are going to make mistakes, but if you can acknowledge and correct these mistakes, then you can stay on track. The doors will keep opening to you.

Grace comes when correction is constant. Fulfillment happens when you don't just talk about forgiveness, but live it moment to moment. Then, it does not matter how many times you stray from the path or put your foot in your mouth. You can laugh at your errors and put them behind you.

You cannot fit through the door if you are carrying the past around. Don't feel guilty. Instead, take responsibility for correcting your mistakes. That way you don't carry around a lot of excess baggage. The more responsibility you take for your thoughts, feelings and experiences, the lighter you travel and the easier it is to correct for your mistakes.

Guilt is not constructive. If there is nothing you can do to make the situation better, then just accept it as it is. Sometimes, there's nothing to be done. It's no one's fault. Life is just as it is. And that's okay.

In knowing that life is okay, no matter how ragged and unfinished it seems, there is room for movement. A shift can happen. A door can open.

The most important door is the one to your heart. Is it open or closed? If it is open, then the whole universe abides in you. If it is closed, you stand alone, holding the world off. Trust and the river flows through your heart. Distrust and a dam holds the river back.

A heart in resistance gets tired quickly. Life wears heavily upon it. But a heart that is open is filled with energy. It dances and sings.

When the door in your heart is open, all the important doors open in the world. You go where you need to go. Nothing interferes with your purpose or your destiny. Everything that you are unfolds naturally in its own time, without struggle or restraint. The unexpected happens without difficulty. Miracles are everyday occurrences. (RTG)

23.

DEATH, DYING
AND BEYOND

THE DEATH OF THE EGO

You cannot avoid the death of the ego, nor can you avoid the death of
the body. But these are not necessarily the same. Do not make the mistake of believing that your ego dies when your body does, or that your
body dies when your ego does. (LWOC)

Ego
Your ego is the part of you that doesn't know that you are loved. It
can't give love, because it doesn't know it has love to give.

When you love and accept your ego, it recognizes that it has love.
The contracted aspects of consciousness relax. Resistance ceases to be.
As soon as ego recognizes it has love, it ceases to be ego.

Ego must die as ego to be reborn as love.

Now you know why most people resist enlightenment. The idea
of waking up is scary to anyone who is still asleep.

Your fear of death and your fear of waking up are the same fear.

The unlimited, universal Self is not born until the limited, temporal self dies. (LWOC)

Dying

Dying is one of the best ways to learn to be present. If you want to wake up quickly, try dying. When you are dying, you are aware of things in a way you never were before. You notice every breath, every nuance, every flower, every word or gesture of love.

Dying is like a crash course in waking up. Now that doesn't mean that everyone who dies wakes up. It just means they've taken the course.

Disengaging from meaningless identity is an inevitable aspect of the path back home. The less you have to protect, the more blissful your experience becomes.

While I would not go so far as to say dying is fun, I would say that dying is "not fun" only because you are still hanging on to some shred of self-definition. (LWOC)

Change and the Changeless

Although some things change, other things never do. Thoughts change, emotions change, houses and jobs change, bodies change, the world changes. But the core of you does not change.

On the surface, each one of you looks different. Differences in physical appearance, personality, temperament, culture, religion, national heritage, all contribute to your uniqueness. But all of you need air to breathe, food to eat and water to drink. All of you need acceptance and love to flower. When you are nurtured physically, emotionally, intellectually and spiritually you are happy and joyful. For this is your natural condition.

When you look at two people who live in their natural condition, you know them to be the same, even though they look different. The same light shines in their eyes, even though one has brown eyes and the other green eyes. Both have an easy and relaxed smile, and you feel equally safe being in their presence.

Human nature may be different, but divine nature is the same. When divine nature and human nature blend together in a person's heart/mind, you have all of the strengths of the individual's authentic gifts and temperament without the insecurity, anxiety and divisiveness of ego consciousness. Each person can be unique without threatening or undermining the uniqueness of anyone else. People can be themselves without trespassing on others.

This blending of the personal and universal reflects psychological integration and interpersonal harmony. It demonstrates congruence within and without. In this state of consciousness, that which changes and that which does not change come together. Individual differences survive without being divisive.

And so when the moment of death comes and one is asked to surrender the personal, it is not difficult. One prefers the stillness of the absolute to the chatter of the conditional. One would gladly trade this breath for the breath that does not come and go.

That which changes arises out of the changeless and returns to it. You cannot imagine the point of origin or the point of return, but you have known moments in your life free of self-consciousness or fear, moments when you felt connected to everyone and everything without trying. And those moments give you a clue of what the deathless state is like.

The closer you get to this state when you are in the body, the less you will fear the moment of death. For you have brought the universal into the personal, the divine into the human, the unconditional into the conditional. (MOL)

Incarnation into the Physical Dimension

While you may have great spiritual insight after you have detached from physical experience, you can't necessarily access this insight once you have incarnated in the physical dimension. Why is this?

Science teaches you that when you leave the gravity of earth's magnetic field, you become practically weightless and capable of performing athletic feats you would be unable to perform on earth. An athlete in a zero-gravity environment has no trouble jumping fifteen feet high. He can even fly through the air. But bring him to earth and he is hard-pressed to jump seven or eight feet high. And he wouldn't seriously entertain the thought of flying.

The dense conditions of physical experience are difficult to master. It takes time to develop physically. You start in your mother's womb totally dependent on her. When you are born, you are physically helpless. You have to learn to feed yourself, to walk, talk and manipulate your environment. Let's face it, for someone who has recently experienced a non-physical environment where the effects of thought are instantaneous, this is pure torture. In time, consciousness contracts, and moves to more fully inhabit the physical body, thus shutting off awareness of other dimensions with their creative possibilities.

Put simply, consciousness gets absorbed into the density of the physical environment. There it feels trapped and victimized. It does not remember its less limited state. It does not remember that it is not a body. (LWOC)

Angels

If you want to experience your angelic nature, you must learn to be completely human, completely authentic, completely present and open to your experience. Angels are not seven-foot tall creatures with wings. They are beings who have learned to honor themselves. Because they have walked through the door, they can hold the door open for you.

Your presence as an angelic being manifests as you wake from the dream of self-abuse. Don't see angels outside of yourself. That is not where they will be found. They live in a dimension that you can touch only through your heart. (SOTH)

Reincarnation and Past-life Memories

Reincarnation, as it commonly is understood, does not exist. All incarnations are simultaneous. All dreams of self are present in this dream. That is why it is not helpful to concern yourself with who you were in some past life. There are no past lives, any more than there are past experiences.

Do not go in search of memories from the past. If they come up, acknowledge them, be with them and integrate them. Do this not to empower the past, but to complete it, so that you can be present now.

Once the past is released, it no longer exists in consciousness. You don't even remember that it happened.

Remember the question: If a tree falls in the forest and nobody hears it, did it make a sound? The answer is no. Without an experiencer, there is no experience.

That is why self-forgiveness works. When the experiencer ceases to relive the experience, the experience ceases to exist and the experiencer returns to the present innocent and unabused.

Are there past lives? Only if you remember them. And if you remember them, you will continue to live them until you come to forgiveness of yourself.

The key to all of this is simple: Do not gather wood unless you want to make a fire. Do not stir the pot unless you want to smell the stew. Do not solicit the past unless you want to dance with it.

But if there is a fire in your house, you must pick up your things and leave. If the stew is boiling, you can't help but smell it. If the past is dancing in your mirror, you can't pretend to be in samadhi.

Resistance of experience creates endless detours. But so does seeking.

Do not resist. Do not seek. Just deal with what comes up as it arises. (SOTH)

Ascension

When you act in a loving way and speak loving words, the Spirit dwells in you and is awakened in others. Then you are the light of the world, and physical reality does not seem as dense as it was before. This is the correct meaning of the word "ascension."

When love is present, the body and the world are lifted up. They are infused with light, possibility and celebration of goodness. The world you see when Spirit is present in your heart and your life is not the same world that you see when you are preoccupied with your ego needs. The world that you see when you are giving love is not the same world that you see when you are demanding it.

If you want to go beyond the body, learn to use it in a loving way. Think and speak well of yourself and others. Be positive, constructive, helpful. Don't look for problems. Don't dwell on what seems to be missing. Give love at every opportunity. Bring it to yourself when you are sad. Bring it to others when they are complaining or being ungrateful.

Be the presence of love in the world. That is what you are. Everything else is an illusion. (MOL)

Transcendence/Serving Others

As soon as you begin to see that your needs are the same as the needs of others, the veil begins to lift. You stop needing special treatment. You stop giving others special treatment. What you want for one, you want for all. You do not make one person more important than others.

The perception of equality is the beginning of the transcendence of the body and the physical world. All bodies are essentially the same. All bodily needs are essentially the same. All emotional needs are essentially the same. All beliefs in separation are essentially the same.

When you no longer need to hold yourself separate from others, you can serve others without being attached. You can give without needing to know how the gift is being received.

Service is an opportunity, not a job description. You cannot serve and have an identity or an agenda. You can't serve and be attached to the outcome.

When you help another person, you help yourself. You help your mother and father. You help your third cousin. You help the drunk on the street corner. Your help goes to those who need it.

Help has nothing to do with you as helper or helpee, other than your simple willingness to give and receive in the moment. Help is for one and for all. You cannot offer it to one without offering it to all. Nor can you offer it to all unless you offer it to one. (SOTH)

A Game of Hide-and-Seek: The Unity Teaching

It seems that there are two worlds, but truly there is only one. Fear is but the lack of love. Scarcity is but the lack of abundance. Resentment is but the lack of gratitude.

Something cannot be lacking unless it was first present in abundance. Without presence, absence has no meaning.

This is like a game of hide-and-seek. Someone has to hide first. Who will it be? Will it be you or me?

In truth, it matters not. When it is your turn, you will hide, and your brother will find you, as I found him. Every one gets a turn to hide and everyone eventually is found.

The world of duality emanates from wholeness and to wholeness returns. What is joined separates and comes together again. This is the nature of the human/divine dance. (LWOC)

24.

FORGIVENESS

SURRENDERING YOUR BELIEFS

Nothing will crucify you faster than your own thoughts. Better not to think at all, if you can do it. And if you can't, if you must think, think about simple things. Think about washing the dishes or doing the laundry. Think about things that must be done. And then let the mind be free of thought.

Everything you believe about the nature of your existence keeps you limited to the past. If you want to experience the present moment, give up all your concepts of it. Just be present in your life as it unfolds.

Watch the tendency of your mind to try to figure everything out. Watch how it tries to structure and plan, revising, plotting and replotting. Watch how it tries to hold on to mutually exclusive possibilities. Watch how easily it goes into opposition and conflict.

Your mind is always looking for the thread of the story so it can continue to weave the plot, or at least maintain the illusion of control. But the interesting thing is that there is no plot. Or, if there is a plot, you are part of it so you can't possibly see what the plot is. That is the inevitable limitation of manifest existence.

If you could see the plot, you might give it away. You might tell all of your friends, "It's all a sham. There is no world, no heaven, no birth, no death, no self, no other, no ego, no God, no nothing."

If everything you see is a reflection of a belief that you have, then are you the observer, the observed, or both at the same time? It is like a rock skipping over the surface of the pond. You see it skipping, but you don't know who threw it. You see the ripples, but you don't know who caused them.

Are you the dreamer or the dream? If you don't know, just stay with the question. Stay face-to-face with the unknown. That is as close to truth as you can come. (SOTH)

Two Paths of Liberation

Much of the frustration you feel on your spiritual path comes from the fact that you cannot experience something and study it at the same time. If you stand back and observe, you will not have the experience the participant does. And if you participate, you will not have the same experience as the observer.

One spiritual method asks you to become an observer. Another asks you to be a participant. Either method works, but you cannot practice both at the same time. If you want to "know," you must learn to stand back and observe. If you want to "be," you must dive into the experience.

My own teaching is oriented to those who would dive in. It is an experiential journey into the roots of abuse. You learn by making mistakes and learning from them. That is the atonement process. (SOTH)

The Gift of Forgiveness

Forgiveness is the only gift that asks nothing in return. And so it is the only gift that can be given and received without guilt.

God gave you one gift for your journey and one gift alone. He said: "My son, remember, you can change your mind at any time."

He did not say: "Do not leave, son." He did not say, "Son, you will be miserable until you return to Me." He just said: "Remember, you can change your mind at any time."

You can change your mind about every painful and unforgiving thought that you think. You can question each unhappy thought and think another thought that releases you and brings joy into your heart.

God did not say: "I will not let My son make mistakes." He said: "I trust in your return and I give you a gift to see you home."

All your mistakes mean nothing to God. To Him, you are but a child exploring your world and, through trial and error, learning the rules that govern it.

God did not make those rules. You made them. You forgot only one thing, and God gave that to you with His blessing. He said: "No matter where your journey takes you, son, remember, you can change your mind at any time."

With a single loving thought, He made temporal what you would make final. He made unreal what you would make real.

You created the ashes of death. He created the wings of the phoenix. To every unhappy thought you would think, God gave a single answer: "Remember, son, you can change your mind at any time."

Like Prometheus, you tried to steal the fire of the gods. But He did not punish you for this. He did not chain you to the rock where you would live throughout all eternity with vultures as your only playmates. He said: "Take the sacred fire, son, but be careful, and remember you can change your mind at any time."

Like Adam and Eve, you stood in the Garden and became curious about good and evil. When he knew your desire for knowledge would not pass, he sent the sacred snake to you with an apple and invited you to eat. Contrary to popular opinion, He did not trick you into sin and then banish you from the Garden. He just said: "Be careful, my son. When you eat this fruit, your perception of the world will change. This Garden may suddenly seem a dry desert where nothing grows at all. Your body with all its innocent grace may seem to be a home for dark desires of which you are ashamed. Your mind, which now shares my every thought, may seem to think thoughts opposed to mine. Duality and feelings of separation may seem to enter your consciousness and experience. All this and more may arise from this tiny bite you would eat, but remember, son, you can change your mind at any time."

Not only does God not condemn you for your mistakes, He is not concerned about them. He knows the child will burn himself with an open flame. But He also knows the child will learn to keep the flame carefully and use it to warm himself and light his way.

He understands that your decision "to know" will bring you into dangerous situations, situations when you think your happiness depends on the way another treats you. He knows that you will forget your origin, and that there will be times when the Garden seems but a distant memory. He understands that there will be times when you blame Him for all of your troubles and forget that you were the one who chose "to know." But all this does not concern Him, because, before you left hell-bent on your journey of separation, He said: "Just a minute, son. It may be a long time before we meet again. Won't you please accept this simple gift from me, and keep it wherever you go in remembrance of me?"

Most of you do not remember answering, "Yes, Father." But I assure you that you did. And so the voice of God went with you as you went into exile. And it is still with you now.

So, when you feel forlorn and lost, when you forget that you chose this journey, remember: "You can change your mind at any time." I am here to help you remember that.

This is not my gift, but God's gift to you. Because I received the gift from Him, I can give it to you. And if you receive it of me, you can give it to your brother.

But I caution you, do not be concerned with the identity of the giver. I am not important. I am not the gift, but the one who extends it, as indeed are you. Let us remember the origin of the gift so that we can give it and receive it freely.

God gave you the gift of forgiveness. This gift travels with you wherever you go. When you do not trust it, He sends His Son to you to remind you of the gift. And His Son tells you that you must give the gift if you would keep it.

Many beings of light have come as the Christ, bringing that simple reminder. All have the same purpose, for Christ is not a person, but a keeper of the flame, a giver of the gift and a messenger of love. Light comes from him, because he has remembered light in the darkness of the world. Love comes from Him, because he has received the gift and learned to give it unconditionally to all who would receive it.

Together, let us give thanks to God for His gift of love and forgiveness, for His eternal trust in us to find our way back home. Father, we remember that your voice is with us in every circumstance and we rely on It to guide our thoughts and our footsteps. Thanks to you, we are not alone. Thanks to you, we have our brothers. You did not let us leave comfortless, but gave us mighty companions to light our way.

In your name, we celebrate our journey here, and pray without ceasing for the end of guilt, the single cause of suffering. And toward that end, we embrace the gift you gave us, the only gift that we can receive or give without guilt. Thank you, Father, for the gift of forgiveness. We will use it wisely. We will use it in every circumstance. With it, we will bring Your light to all the dark places of our souls. (LWOC)

Mirror of Innocence

When the snow falls, it covers ground, plants, trees, houses and roads with a white mantle. Everything looks fresh, new, innocent. Forgiveness comes in the same way, undoing the grievances of the past, replacing judgments with acceptance. In the light of forgiveness, you see your problems and challenges differently. You feel capable of meeting your life just the way it is.

Walking out into the new snow, you leave fresh footprints behind you. No more hiding or pretending to hold back. You have ventured forth boldly and anyone can follow you.

Forgiveness is as far-reaching as the snow. It touches everything in your life, everything in your heart and your mind.

For forgiveness to bless you, you must be willing to receive it, as the ground receives the snowfall. You must be willing to be occupied and cleansed by something greater than you.

In every successful relationship, forgiveness is an ongoing practice. Without forgiveness, there can be no communion between people. Instead, old wounds are aggravated by hidden resentments.

This will not do. Negative thoughts and feeling states must be cleared on no less than a daily basis. Do not go to sleep angry with each other. Do not let the sun rise or set without making peace. Nurture your relationship. Give it the time it deserves. Be ready to let go of thoughts and feelings that can only injure and separate.

In your dance together, find a way to soften and come together when you feel angry or hurt. Come to each other as equals and admit your fear. Surrender your need to be right or to make the other person wrong. You are both right in your desire to be loved and respected. You are both wrong in your attempt to blame the other person for your unhappiness.

Relationship is a dance in a theater of wounds. As hard as you try to avoid hurting your brother, he continues to cry out in pain. Your fear is triggered by his fear and vice versa. It's no one's fault. That's just the way it is.

After you have danced enough, you no longer take the drama so personally. You just get better at dancing out of your pain toward your joy. When you do that, the whole atmosphere onstage changes. An option arises that was not seen before.

To some, the earthly journey seems to be an arduous trek through a veil of tears. But even to these travelers, there are moments when the sun comes out and rainbows arch across the sky, moments when the pain slips away and the heart is filled with unexpected joy. Even when the dance is difficult, one feels grateful for the opportunity to participate and to learn.

Life is essentially dignified. It is true that you resist and sometimes even refuse to learn your lessons. But learn them you do. You move onward and upward and, as you do, body and mind become imbued with Spirit. Once identified with a specific mind-set and a specific body, you are eventually set free to love without conditions and to receive the love that is offered you without resisting or defending.

That is the nature of your journey here. It is a good journey. May you take the time to appreciate and enjoy it. May you open your eyes and see the sun peeking through the clouds. May you see the light reflected by the snow-covered ground and the white boughs of the pine trees: light sparkling in all directions, embracing all of you, right here, right now. (MOL)

Namaste

I accept your humanity and I bow to the divinity within you. I accept your equality with me and I also accept the fact that you sometimes forget who you are.

I acknowledge the absolute and the relative. The gentle voice of God and the passionate cries of the wounded child commingle here, in this mind, in this world. Joy and sadness commingle. Strength and tears, beauty and betrayal, silence and cacophony interpenetrate.

It is a simple world, breathing in and breathing out, approaching the divine and moving away. And it is also complex in its near infinite variety of forms.

Each self is the unqualified presence, yet each must approach God in its own unique way. Within oneness, paradox abounds.

Here we dwell together, my brother and sister: here in the silence, each of us with our unique dance, our unique call for love and truth. Yet every heart that beats here belongs to one great Heartbeat.

My wish for you is a simple one. May you find that Heart in your heart. May you find your voice in that silence. May you awaken to your true identity. (SOTH)

BENEDICTION

There is only one son of God
and you are s/he.

From that one, you receive.
To that one, you give.

When you look at yourself,
may you remember.

When you look at your brother or sister,
may you also remember.

When you look away in fear,
remember only this:

Subject and object,
lover and beloved,

are not two,
but one and the same.

What you give
and what you receive

are reflections
of each other. (LWOC)

APPENDIX

MY ENCOUNTER
WITH JESUS

HEARING THE VOICE

Born into an atheist family, I had little use for religion or spirituality until I was twenty-three years old. I was living then in East Cambridge, Massachusetts. I had just completed graduate school and had been searching in vain for a teaching position. Needing to put bread on the table, I took a job driving a truck.

Each day I got up at 4:00 A.M. and rode my bicycle to work through the cold, windy streets of Cambridge, loaded up my truck and began my deliveries in downtown Boston. As I drove over the bridge by the Museum of Science, the pale muted rays of dawn struggled to penetrate the clouds. It felt gruesome to me.

Light was having a hard time making it into the darkness of this world. When I looked around me, all I saw was exploitation and suffering. When I looked within, all I felt was sadness and pain. I saw no reason for being here.

My life was solitary. I had ended a long-term relationship earlier that year. I was in mourning for that connection and unable to reach out to others. I had not been able to find work in my chosen field. And I had just moved from the quiet and beauty of Vermont back to the city. I was having trouble adjusting to the noises of police and fire sirens screeching in the middle of the night. I could not understand the gangs of kids that roamed the streets at 3 A.M. throwing barrels full of trash out onto Cambridge Street.

Everyone in the city seemed angry or sad. I wasn't much different, except that I lived for the poems I wrote when I got home from work. They supplied the only meaning in my life. If my life did not shift somehow by the time I completed the collection of poems I was writing, there would be no reason to continue it.

I was depressed, suicidal. When I drove across the bridge into Boston, dawn continued to announce to me its anguish. I appropriately entitled my collection of poems *The Thorns of Dawn*.

I did not know at the time that I was experiencing my own crucifixion. I did not know that life was bringing me to the edge of death so that I could be reborn in Spirit. I did not know that I had to experience the utter meaninglessness of life to recover its original meaning.

When I finished that collection of poems, I talked to God for the second time in my life. I talked to God, even though I doubted His existence, even though He had refused to answer me at age thirteen when my cousin Deirdre had died of leukemia. Reeling in deep existential pain since that day of lost innocence, I could never reconcile the idea of God with the seemingly needless suffering I saw around me.

"Give me one reason why I should not abandon this meaningless world?" I asked, sitting at the kitchen table.

"Go into the living room, close your eyes and take the first book you come to in the bookcase," I heard a very clear, firm voice say in my mind.

I was astounded. I wasn't expecting an answer. Then, I thought, "What do I have to lose?" So I got up and walked into the living room. I closed my eyes, put my hands out and let them move toward the bookshelf. I pulled out a single book and opened my eyes. It was I *and Thou* by Martin Buber.

I opened the book to the first page and began reading. After the first paragraph or two, it became clear that I had my answer. I sank down into the book, hearing each word spoken into my ears, drinking the truth with a profound thirst I did not know I had.

I wanted an answer and I got one. Life was not just the shell of sadness I was seeing. It was more.

"There are two worlds," Buber told me, "the world of I-It and the world of I-Thou." The world of I-It I knew only too well. It was the world of exploitation, struggle, greed, selfishness, layers upon layers of suffering. That was the world I wanted to escape.

But there was also another world, Buber maintained. It was the world of union, relationship, trust and grace. It was the world of unconditional acceptance and love. Even though I had experienced only brief glimpses of this world of "I-Thou," I knew of its existence.

I had to admit the fact that the world was not all suffering. It was perhaps 99 percent suffering, and 1 percent grace. Was I willing to stick around for that 1 percent chance of unconditional love? I didn't think so.

But then the voice in the book spoke into my opening heart and said: "It's up to you which world you want to see!"

With just a single sentence, my self-pitying, state-of-the-world-bemoaning attitude was stripped of its artifice. Now the emperor had no clothes. Suffering was not a dictum, but a choice. It was up to me which world I chose to see.

You mean I could choose to see grace all of the time? You mean the quality of my experience did not depend on what was outside of me, but on the attitude I brought to it? You mean the "I" in "I-Thou" was my responsibility, not somebody else's, not even God's?

I reeled from the words even as they resonated like waves inside of me. I knew they were truth, but letting them in would change my entire life. Never again would I be able to play the role of victim or innocent bystander.

If the world I inhabited depended on how I saw it and stood in relationship to it, then I had homework for the rest of my embodiment. I had to stop looking outside at what others were doing, and begin looking inside, at the contents of my own consciousness.

I was responsible for whether my "I" was the "I" in the relational event "I-Thou" or the "I" in the non-relational, manipulative event "I-It." Every moment I made a choice for joy or sadness, love or fear. My dialogue with God depended on which "I" approached Him/Her. If I approached as "I-It," S/He could not hear me or answer me, because S/He did not live there.

That explained the stony silence I had encountered at age thirteen when I begged God to give back Deirdre and take me instead. At that time, I came to God not as the lover comes to the beloved, but as the victim comes to the executioner to beg a few crumbs. I did not come for understanding to a God of love, one who cared for me and for Deirdre too. Instead I came to a God of fear, who capriciously gives and takes away. I came to the Grim Reaper with a grisly proposition fitting only for such a being: "Take me, you cruel, bloodthirsty ogre and give Deirdre back instead."

At thirteen the "I" that came to God was the "I" in the non-relational event "I-It." At twenty-three the "I" addressed by the powerful, resonant voice within was the "I" in the relational event "I-Thou." The Beloved was calling. How could the Lover not respond?

When we feel unworthy, it is hard to believe that we are the one chosen by God to bring love into this world. Yet every despairing man or woman who gets on his or her knees and asks for help is a chosen one.

By repudiating the world of suffering, we ask for a better way. And asking, we are not only given the way, but asked to walk it, asked to bring the light we find in the darkness of our own hearts to others who are calling out for it. Our God works in strange and magnificent ways, always lifting us up, always giving the gift through our hands.

We are the ones who must learn to bring affection to the love-starved children of our hearts and minds. If we don't bring it, who else will bring it? And if we can bring it to ourselves, then we can also bring it to all of the sons and daughters of God who do not know that they are loved and cherished just the way they are.

In my living room, I was given my homework for the rest of my incarnation. I was not here on this earth to be a victim of a callous, uncaring world. I was here to give birth to love in my own heart and to carry that love to everyone in my experience. I was not the victim or the executioner, but the king offering the stay of sentence. I was the savior, pointing the way of redemption. I did not know it then, but Christ had taken hold of me and wherever I walked from that day on, He walked with me hand in hand. (RTG)

Seeking and Finding

My life from that day forward was not particularly eventful. I read many books by Martin Buber. I devoured the words of the Baal Shem Tov, Rabbi Nachman and the great Hasidic rabbis. I discovered a joyful and soulful vein of love teaching within the core of Judaism which enabled me to embrace the Jewish side of my heritage.

I became thirsty for knowledge. I studied the Kabbalah, the Egyptian Tarot, esoteric astrology and psychology. I studied Buddhist, Hindu and Taoist scriptures, humanistic, transpersonal and Jungian psychology. I developed my intuition and used both left-brain and right-brain approaches to understanding human behavior. I did charts and readings and counseling sessions.

My clients were happy, but I wasn't. It seemed that the more I learned the further I got from the truth. I began to realize that I had become preoccupied with my tools. There was no joy in them. The intellect, try as hard as it could, would never be able to fathom the meaning of human experience or the way in which the divine intersected it.

It was at this time that I picked up *A Course in Miracles*, a book written by Helen Schucman, a research psychologist at Columbia University in New York. This book claimed to be written by Jesus through Helen.

When I picked the book up, I had the same experience I had when I read *I and Thou*. I heard the words spoken in my ear and felt them resonate like waves throughout my body. I knew this teaching was the next step on my spiritual path and that it came from the same source as the previous material.

But I felt very uncomfortable with the idea that Jesus wrote the material and I didn't like the Christian terminology or the archaic style of prose in which the book was written. Why would a book which I knew intuitively to be the truth come in a form which was so distasteful to me? Why did we need 1,100 pages to express the truth when Lao Tzu needed only 81?

It took several years for me to realize that only *A Course in Miracles* could have brought me to Jesus. I may not have liked how it was written, but I did like what it said. It was the real teaching of Jesus, the one I knew in my heart. It had psychological depth and intellectual consistency. It could stand up alongside the most sophisticated teachings of the East.

It spoke to my skeptical side. And even though I had a little trouble at first using terms like "Holy Spirit," I knew that I could substitute the word "Tao" without changing the meaning. Holy Spirit was still the impersonal God energy that manifests equally through each one of us, just as the Tao does.

The most important aspect of this material was its focus on our own relationship to the divine and its contention that each one of us could have an ongoing relationship with God in our hearts and minds. We could ask for help and receive it. We could bring our problems to God and S/He would guide us in a way that would honor everyone in our experience. A *Course in Miracles* was not just a theology, but a practical method for living in the consciousness of God.

Unfortunately, the majority of the people I met who were working with the *Course* were trying to understand it or teach it. They weren't letting the material come into their hearts and their lives. They weren't practicing it. And without practice, this was yet another system of knowledge that points in vain at the truth. To take the truth in, practice is necessary.

During this period, I began working with the material in a heart-centered, experiential way. I invited people to conferences and workshops where they could practice the material. I published a magazine encouraging diversity and open discussion, and discouraging dogmatic approaches. I wanted our community to walk its talk, to be the embodiment of love in action.

Then, I began hearing a voice within that said, "I want you to acknowledge me." Whenever I would teach, the voice would remind me, but I ignored it. There was only one person I was not acknowledging and I didn't want to acknowledge him. I didn't want to get up and say, "Jesus is my teacher." I didn't want to say, "Jesus is the author of *A Course in Miracles.*"

But the more I resisted, the louder the voice got. I began having dreams in which Jesus would speak to me. These dreams were surrealistic and strangely lifelike. In one dream I was in a large cave. There were several figures dressed in brown hooded robes. Out of the corner of my eye, I saw one of them bend down to pick up a gleaming broadsword. Then he turned, carrying the sword in front of his heart, and walked directly toward me. As he came close, I looked into his face, and I knew that this was Jesus. We looked deeply into each other's eyes, and then He placed the sword flat against my heart. I felt unbelievable energy go through my body. I was catapulted back against the stone wall and fell to the ground. Jesus came to where I was lying and looked down at me. "You see," he said. "This energy is real and you will use it to heal as I did."

He made a gesture toward his third eye and said, "You must have the absolute conviction of the innocence of the other person here and"—pointing to his heart—"unconditional love and acceptance for the person here. Then, these mental and emotional energies triangulate with the hands, so that healing energy flows through the hands to the other person. If that person can receive the truth that you are thinking and the love that you are feeling, then they can also receive the extension of that truth and that love: the energy which is flowing through your hands."

Later in the dream, Jesus answered several of my questions. In particular, I asked Him about sections of *A Course in Miracles*, in which he supposedly claimed that our physical bodies and the world that we live in were actually creations of our ego structure.

"It is true," he said, "neither the body nor the world are ultimate reality, but they are not to be denied or denigrated either. Everything can be lifted up through the power of unconditional love."

The body could be a vehicle through which love expresses. The world could be a place where love and compassion make their home. To say that they are created by the ego is to miss the point. It is how they are used that matters.

Are they used by ego or by the true Self? Buber had taught me earlier, the "I" in "I-It" was not the same "I" as the "I" in "I-Thou." The body used in a loving way was not the same as the body used in an angry or fearful way. The problem was not "the body" or "the world." It was what we put into them.

Sex, for example, is neither good nor bad. If there is love in it, then sexuality becomes an expression of that love. If there is no love in it, then sex becomes empty and unfulfilling.

"Everything can be lifted up," he told me, "by the power of unconditional love." It is not what you do so much as how you do it.

Jesus is teacher of love. He does not want to tell us what to do in every situation. He does not favor 613 commandments, such as we have in the Talmud. Even ten commandments are probably more than we can handle. He gives us just two: "Love your neighbor as yourself" and "Put no other Gods before Him."

Let God come first in your life and love your neighbor. A very simple teaching, but a very challenging practice.

As I began to feel the energy of Jesus come into my life, I experienced a deep kinship toward him and his teaching. It was so simple, so pure.

Clearly, we had lost sight of the pure teaching. What we had was not what he gave us, but what others gave us in His name.

What was clear to me in reading A Course in Miracles and what was viscerally clear now that I was in dialogue with Him was that the fear- and guilt-based teachings of the church had nothing to do with Jesus.

Anyone who knows Jesus in his or her heart knows this as an inner certainty. Jesus is an uncompromising teacher of love. His ferocity comes from His commitment to love and His insistence that love is the only answer to our problems.

Shortly after I had the cave dream, hands-on healers began to come into my life. At the time, I was putting on large conferences for students of A Course in Miracles and I invited many of these healers to come to these events as speakers and workshop leaders. This pushed the buttons of Course purists who had adopted an anti-body attitude.

At one conference, there were a number of healings that took place. In fact, during the whole conference I could feel Jesus' presence behind me. Energy would be pouring through my heart. And, whenever I hugged anyone, I could feel that there was a transmission of energy through my heart and hands.

My heart was on fire. My body was burning up. I didn't think I could stand it. I was riding in a cocoon of energy. It felt so delicious, I didn't want to come out of it, yet it was so intense I wondered if I could stay in it without exploding.

People would come to these conferences, experience this energy, and then go home and crash. That didn't feel right to me. I knew that we had to give people a way to feel connected to the Christ energy when they got home. So we began to develop the *Affinity Group Process*. Jesus concurred. "The time for these large conferences will soon pass," he said. "Before long, you will be working more deeply with smaller groups."

At our conferences, people would be able to feel the Christ energy, but they didn't know where it came from or how they could stay connected to it. Where it came from was very simple. When people were willing to put their judgments aside and live from a place of trust, they would go into ecstasy. They would look into the eyes of total strangers and fall in love. They could feel this kind of love, not just for a few people, but for everyone. It was the kind of love that happens when you let yourself fall into the heart. Anyone standing before you would receive that love, because as long as you stayed in your heart, you could not stop giving it.

But as soon as the judgments came back and were entertained, as soon as fear came up and got a foothold, then the defensive shield would come down over the heart and the flow of love in and out would stop. You could see this happen for individuals. Someone would push their buttons and they would retreat to their rooms. Then, the fear and judgment would pass, and they would come back to the group to recharge.

People didn't realize that the experience of ecstasy originated inside themselves, in the dropping of their judgments and expectations. They did not know that their ability to become an open channel through which love flowed unimpeded depended on their own internal surrender. So they were not able to carry this experience home.

They kept coming back to the conferences to "fill up" their empty tanks with love. But that love would always be short-lived because it was not fueled by their own surrender.

As we began to shift the responsibility from the presenters and entertainers to each participant, the conferences got smaller and smaller. "You are the only subject of this gathering," we told people. "Nobody else has the answers for you. Your connection to love is an internal proposition, not an external one." As we integrated the *Affinity Process* more and more into our gatherings, people began to get it. They began to realize that they were the light and the love of the world. They were the vehicle through which wisdom and love could express. Not just one or two of them. But every one of them. Christ was not just something experienced by Jesus. It was in all of us. (RTG)

The Master Teacher

It was always amazing to me that students of *A Course in Miracles* could believe that Jesus spoke through Helen, yet doubt that he could speak through others. As I began to acknowledge and surrender to my own connection to Jesus, I realized that he spoke to so many people in different ways. I recognized his energy and guidance behind the Twelve Steps of Alcoholics Anonymous. I heard him speak through "born again" Christians. I saw his presence in the simple acts of caring and service done by hundreds of individuals with no religion to preach nor any ax to grind.

Anyone embodying unconditional love, acceptance and forgiveness was his messenger, his disciple. Some knew it. Some did not. But that was not important. What was important was that, through them, love was offered. And having given love, they could not help but receive it. The more they gave, the more they received. There was no deficiency of love in the world. Love lived in the heart of every human being. As it was trusted and expressed, love became present in the world. Through this process, everyone and everything would "be lifted up."

In my conversations with him, Jesus has never claimed to be the only son of God. He has never claimed to have died for our sins, to have walked on water, to have been born of a virgin or to have physically resurrected his body. Instead, he maintains that we are all sons and daughters of God, that we can all die to our sins and reclaim our innocence. Just as he was, we too are crucified by our egoic experience, and we too can be uplifted by the power of love to realize our true nature even while we are here in this body in this world.

Jesus has always told me, "What I can do you too can do, if you are willing." He has always considered himself to be an equal. When I have sought to raise him up, he has lowered himself down to look me squarely in the eyes. And whenever I have tried to raise myself up above any of my brothers or sisters, he has told me: "Lest you love the least of them, you do not love me."

Jesus does not speak for one man or woman, but for all human beings. He holds each one of us dear, and refuses to let anyone think s/he is better or worse, higher or lower than the next. In Jesus' eyes we are all equally spiritual. The pope is no holier than the prostitute or drunk on the street. Clearly, we have many biases and opinions to surrender if we would see each other as Jesus sees us.

While Jesus does not suggest that this body or this earth represents ultimate reality, he would have us treat the body and the earth with respect. In respecting the forms in and through which we live, we also respect the breath that gives life to them and uplifts them.

Love itself is ultimate reality. It is the beginning and the end, the alpha and the omega. It is the original creative spark, its fullness, and its self-containment. It emanates from itself, expresses itself and rests in itself. Whether rising or falling, waxing or waning, ebbing or flowing, it never loses touch with what it is. In the same manner, when we are in communion with love, we never lose touch with who we are.

While we live in this body and this world, we can commune with ultimate reality. We can give love and receive it. We can also get attached to this body and this world and close down our connection with ultimate reality. When that happens we experience pain. We suffer.

This wakes us up. It helps us remember that we cannot be happy unless we are in communion with love. Fortunately, we are never more than one thought away from love. When we lose touch with love, we have only to think a loving thought and love comes flowing into our hearts.

Death may dissolve the body and the world, but it cannot dissolve love, because love is eternal. It is not dependent on a particular body or personality.

Jesus may not be present here in a body, but He is present in the love. When we tune into the love, we tune into Jesus. It is that simple.

If you are looking for the historical Jesus, it may be hard for you to find him. That body/mind construct ceased to be ages ago. But if you are looking for the loving, contemporary presence, then you do not have very far to look. Whenever you speak to him, he is there. You just need to be quiet to hear His voice. You just need to be still to feel his energy.

Having a personal relationship with Jesus is the essence of Christianity. Unless you feel the presence of Jesus, unless you receive his love and his guidance, it will be difficult for you to follow his teaching.

Jesus is not some abstract image from the past, but a living reality. He is not in a separate body but he lives in the love that uplifts all bodies, all hearts and all minds. You can think with him, feel with him, breathe with him.

The compassionate presence that gave us the teaching of love and forgiveness two thousand years ago is still giving it to us now. The voice of God is still speaking to us, through Jesus and other great beings who have joined with him in this great work of At-One-ment.

Every time one person wakes up to the truth about himself or herself, a great sun rises in the heart of the archetypal human, radiating its light and its love to all of us. No wonder we feel His love. No wonder we feel the love of all beings who have our greatest good at heart. (RTG)

The Divine in the Human

The life of Jesus is a metaphor for the highest spiritual teaching. As such, it retains all the power of Myth. We believe that Jesus had a divine origin, that he was sent by God to redeem us. To highlight his divine origin, we have the story of the virgin birth. We believe that Jesus did not come from the human milieu, that he was not conceived by a sexual act, but was a divine gift given to Mary as acknowledgement of her chastity and her faith.

If we believe that this divine origin was true only for Jesus or perhaps Mary too, then we set them apart from us. We put them on a pedestal. They are divine and we are human. They are the beloved of God and we are mere sinners. Needless to say, this is not a teaching of empowerment.

If you look at the life of Jesus, you will see that he never placed himself above others. He sought out the poor, the ill, the disenfranchised. He kept company with lepers and prostitutes. He carried the teaching wherever he went. His was not a gospel for the rich and famous or the spiritual elite. It was a gospel for every man and woman. It empowered even the lowest of the low with dignity and respect.

Jesus did not attempt to put himself on a pedestal. He sought to raise everyone up. If he was of divine origin, then so were we. Whatever he could do, we could do and more. He did not want special status. He wanted to show us the way that we too could walk. He led not just by words, but also by example.

If we want a personal relationship with Jesus, it must be with the man, not with the Myth. He fit the archetype of the Godman, the divine in the human. As such he is larger than life. How can one have a relationship with the only Son of God? Surely, this is as difficult as having a relationship with God Himself. Any such relationship is bound to be special, privileged. Of course, specialness and privilege were part of the conceit of the Jewish tradition. Were they not "the chosen people"?

Did Jesus come to continue the tradition of specialness or to destroy it once and for all? Did he come to remind us of our equality with each other and our inner connection with God or did he come to create yet another spiritual elite? Was he a teacher of universal truth or parochial dispensation?

In truth, his teaching was the most radical to come to the planet. "Love everyone, even your enemies . . . turn the other cheek . . . judge not lest you also be judged." He was not Milquetoast, but the fire in the oven.

He came to create a revolution within Judaism, to turn it away from narrow parochialism and specialness, to open it into a universal teaching available to all. He did not come to create another narrow religion.

Were he here today in body, Jesus would be neither a Jew nor a Christian. He would live and teach beyond labels, beyond prejudice, beyond ideas that separate one person from another. Were he here today, his teaching would threaten those in positions of power and privilege just as it did in his day. And it is likely that he would be plotted against, betrayed and handed over to the very authorities he threatens. Perhaps he would not be crucified, but he might spend his life in prison or perhaps await a more clinical execution on death row.

So long as we deny the potential of our own Christhood, we will continue to crucify the Christ outside of us. That is why Jesus is not here in body today. He does not need a repeat performance of the Passion play, nor do we.

We need to realize that where Jesus once walked so now do we. The Passion play is not his now, but ours. We need to decide whether we want to continue to carry our cross up the hill, or put it down. If we insist on carrying it, we will not be the only ones to be crucified. Others will follow dutifully in our footsteps.

But if we lay our cross down, those who follow us can be spared their journey of fear and guilt and a new day can dawn on earth, a day when the Christ is celebrated in each one of us, rather than crucified upon a cross. That day is coming. And Jesus is doing everything he can to help us bring it. If we will listen to him and practice his teaching, if we will model it in the world by embodying love and compassion, then it will not be long. Once we put down our burden of guilt and fear, our load is lighter and we can work more lovingly and confidently.

The journey to the cross, the crucifixion and the resurrection is not history, but Myth. Just as Jesus returns to his divine home unscathed by the brutality of the world, so do we.

By loving and accepting our humanness as Jesus did, we begin to connect to the essence of love, our divine origin. We meet the essential Self that was not born and will not die, the Self that cannot be hurt or compromised, even though this Passion play might lead us to believe otherwise.

Accepting our humanness is the way to the divine presence within. For the human was made in the divine image. There is nothing bad about it. There is nothing bad about our fear or anyone else's. Our fears simply need to rest inside the love they are seeking. Otherwise, we go about seeking love through our fear. And that doesn't work. When fear seeks love, it only finds itself.

Inside the man Jesus is the Christ. When Jesus is okay with Jesus, including all his pain and all his fear, he becomes the Christ. It is no different for us. When we have accepted all the aspects of self of which we were once ashamed, when we are holding our fears and those of others compassionately, we too become the Christ.

A true Christian does not worship Jesus and place him on a pedestal. S/he internalizes his teaching and becomes the Christ.

In the Jewish tradition, the Messiah cannot come as long as one man or woman attempts to live outside the embrace of love. Jesus brought us the teaching that will enable all of us to return to the arms of love. We have only to practice that teaching.

In that sense, the decision each one of us makes is crucial. For the Messiah does not come from on high. S/he comes in the hearts of each one of us. (RTG)

God's Mouthpiece

I once received a letter from a woman who told me that she had been very moved by these Christ Mind materials, but because of her upbringing she needed to understand how I could speak for Jesus. The truth is that Jesus came into my life. I did not ask for a relationship with him, at least not consciously. I simply experienced a profound resonance with this teaching. In my heart, I knew I was being called into this work.

My ego was not too happy with this direction. I didn't have much respect for Christianity, so it was hard to open to Jesus. I had to let him speak to me directly. I had to realize that all of the injustices perpetrated by the Christian church had nothing to do with Jesus, his energy or his teachings.

I simply became willing to listen to him. I opened to a relationship that brought me not only clear understanding, but boundless acceptance and love. I knew in my heart of hearts that my purpose in this embodiment was to embrace these teachings fully and to be a mouthpiece for them.

Early on, Jesus made it clear to me that my job was just to show up and he would do the rest. In the beginning of this work, I was self-conscious. When I gave a talk or a workshop, I tried to prepare for it, make notes, think it through. One day, I kept hearing this voice inside that said, "No notes. Your job is just to show up." I tried to ignore it. I went back to my room and began writing notes about the material I expected to cover in my workshop the next morning. I was quite pleased with myself and went to bed feeling prepared. The next morning I woke up and read over my notes. I was amazed. They were utter gibberish!

I went to my workshop with my mind totally blank. I kept hearing the words "Just show up. It will be fine." And so I went to my workshop and even when I opened my mouth to speak, I did not know what words would come out. As I needed them, each word and sentence came into my consciousness and I spoke them.

After the workshop, people came up to me and thanked me enthusiastically. I felt strangely detached. I didn't feel that I had done anything. And I hadn't.

Increasingly, he made it clear to me that my ego was to step aside when I spoke or taught. The way I could do that was by just showing up and having no idea what was about to happen. By surrendering to the moment, I could meet it with open arms.

In truth, he was training me to do what he had learned to do: to surrender the part of the mind that wants to be in control so that I could rely on God within. He was there as a kind of gatekeeper, helping me open the door to the divine presence within.

So what is the authority that enables me to speak the words of the teaching that I know in my heart comes from Jesus? It is not an outer authority, but an inner one. It is the same authority that enabled Jesus to say, "I and the Father are One." It is the same authority Moses claimed when he brought down the tablets of the law.

All prophets are attuned to the voice of God. And that voice is not outside of them, but within their consciousness, in their heart of hearts. You might not believe it, but that voice is in your heart too.

Jesus belongs to the prophetic tradition. I may have come to it kicking and screaming, but it is my tradition too. It is the path to God that begins with the rejection of idols. It is the path that asks us to turn to the mystery within.

The question "By whose authority do you speak?" can only be answered: "By the authority of the God Within." If you ask Moses or

Jesus or Mohammed, this is what they will tell you. And they are the way-showers, are they not? Would they then expect us to give a different answer?

I speak to you therefore not as someone who has a special relationship with Jesus or with God, but as someone who has discovered the Christ within. And in that discovery, I am one with my teacher, Jesus of Nazareth. You can be one with him too, if you open your heart to his teaching and his presence in your life.

The word "channeling" as it is commonly used cannot do justice to the relationship event we speak of. Therefore I prefer not to use it. However, I recognize the truth that we are all potential prophets or channels for truth in that we are capable of stepping aside and letting the voice of God (in whatever form we hear it) speak to us and through us. (RTG)

The Renewal of the Covenant

In every generation, the truth must be encountered directly by prophets, mystics and visionaries. Becoming one with that truth, they can express it in the language of their times.

When prophets, mystics and visionaries express the truth, they often challenge the institutions, dominant beliefs and the authority figures of their society. That is what Jesus did.

These people claim an inner authority, not an outer one. They oppose and expose all forms of hypocrisy and injustice, even when they are institutionalized. As such, prophets, mystics and visionaries are not very popular with the powers that be.

The teachings of these inspired people often ignite the hearts of their contemporaries. People feel empowered to ask questions and to challenge old customs and laws that no longer serve the greatest good. The impact of such teachings is an awakening within the consciousness of individuals and revolutionary within the collective consciousness.

Through the authentic life and teaching of such individuals, truth remains a living force. It is modeled in their actions. Through their humor, their compassion, their courage, we see Spirit at work in the world.

In contrast to the prophets, mystics and visionaries, there are the fundamentalists: people who like to live their lives based on a past authority. They look at the Bible or some other holy book as literally true. They are concerned about the letter of the law, not the spirit of it. When Jesus was born, the Pharisees were the fundamentalists, but fundamentalists can be found within every religious tradition. Now, we have fundamentalist Christians and Muslims too. We even have fundamentalist *Course in Miracles* students.

Fundamentalists tend to feel that there is only one truth and they alone have it. They are often intolerant of other paths and work hard to convert others to their beliefs. They often profess their beliefs with great zeal, but this zeal in itself seems to hide an inner insecurity. Were they secure about their own relationship with God, they would not be threatened by others who hold different values and beliefs.

In every generation, fundamentalism opposes the rediscovery of truth within the hearts and minds of human beings. It emphasizes an outer authority, rather than an inner one. It establishes hierarchies and creates new idols. It substitutes elaborate rules and rituals for the authentic practice of God-communion and sacrifices the freedom of the individual to the tyranny of the group mind.

It is into this narrowing focus of consciousness that Christ is born today, as he was two thousand years ago. And as he is realized in the hearts and minds of people today, the prophetic tradition is renewed. New scriptures are received and brought through by mystics and visionaries. The eternal truth is understood in the context of the time in which we live.

In some respects, this is a confusing time to be on the planet. Today, there are hundreds of thousands of books, tapes, lectures and workshops claiming to point the way toward truth. Every path you can imagine is being offered, from angel guidance to satanic rituals, from witchcraft to the new physics, indeed from the ridiculous to the sublime. It is hard for some people to discriminate.

The old, hierarchical religion is in its death throes. The patriarchal God of retribution is done in. There are no more chosen people. Now, every one of us is chosen.

We can no longer take our direction from churches or gurus. We must find it in our own hearts. We must try new ideas and experiment with new practices, learning what works and what does not. We must learn to discriminate. We must take responsibility for our own path and learn to honor the path of others.

It is an exciting time. It puts the responsibility squarely on us.

Will we make mistakes? Absolutely.

Will we try some ideas that don't work, perhaps hurting ourselves in the process? Very likely.

But we will learn from all this and move on. We will struggle with layers and layers of shame and guilt until we come face-to-face with our own innocence. And when we do, we will fall back into the heart, and realize that nothing we have ever thought, said or done can ultimately condemn us. Because right now, we have a choice. And right now, we choose to be gentle with ourselves and each other.

Compassion is not born overnight, nor is responsibility. But you can be sure that both are being born in us right now. (RTG)

Return to the Garden

When we left the garden of our innocence, we began a quest for knowledge outside of ourselves. We sought truth in the ideas and philosophies of other people. We read books, traveled to faraway places, sought esoteric and unusual experiences. All this took us away from our inner connection with God. We tried to find outside of us what we already had within. Indeed, the more we sought truth without, the more we forgot the inner connection with truth. Our relationship with God, which once had been intrinsic, became extrinsic. We made idols and worshiped them. The more we searched outside of us, the more empty we felt within. And the more empty we felt, the more our search was fueled.

For some of us God became a large bank account, an exquisite house or a fancy car. For others it became an expensive education or a successful career. Still others found idols in a bible, a teaching/belief system or a preacher/guru. And of course, a few made idols of a bottle, a recreational drug, casual sex or the promise of love.

All these things seemed to offer us satisfaction, but none of them delivered the love or the comfort they promised. Instead, they left us feeling empty, wanting more and more.

We became over-stimulated without and lost our capacity to feel and connect within. Our relationship to love became inverted. We became needy, dependent, alone. We forgot how to offer love. We could only ask for it.

We desperately wanted relationship, yet we could not handle its demands. We had become too selfish, too defensive. We had driven ourselves into a corner. The very thing we wanted most was the thing we could not have, or at least this is what we believed.

The search for God outside of us led to a wall we could not climb or get around. It was too tall and too wide. We were at an impasse.

The journey outside of us had come to an end. There was nothing left to do but turn around.

To turn authentically, we had to recognize the utter futility of the search for love outside ourselves. That moment of recognition would be the beginning of our spiritual path. It would be the end of our descent from grace, and the beginning of our return to the garden.

The Jesus who died on the cross spoke more to our suffering than he did to our connection to God. He represented our relentless attack upon ourselves.

We thought it was our brother who was pounding the nails into our hands and feet. But now we know we were the ones doing it.

Everything we ever did to anyone else, we did to ourselves. We are the victims of our own actions.

It is not easy to learn to take total responsibility for our experience. It is not easy to give up the game of shame and blame. Yet, if we want to turn our lives around, that is what we are asked to do.

We must look at the hell we have created within our own consciousness and take responsibility for it. We must understand once and for all time that we are the ones who walk to the cross, the ones who are crucified, and the ones who perform the crucifixion. There is no one else to blame.

But if we can torture and abuse ourselves in this way, can we not also be the ones who bring love and compassion? Can we not also be the peacemaker, the Christ, the one who comes with arms extended?

If we can create hell, can we not also create heaven? Is our creativity essentially distorted, prejudiced toward error/evil, or is it simply misdirected? Are we like Adam or Eve—men and women condemned to suffer for all eternity for our mistakes—or are we the fallen angels who once sat at God's side, the ones suffering from pride who need but to surrender to regain their celestial seat?

Do we have a choice? Can we create with God, instead of against him?

Lucifer means light-bearer. The anointed one is not outside. S/He is mythic. S/He can only be found within.

When we learn to find light in our own darkness, we can become bearers of that light. When we learn to bring love and acceptance to our own wounded psyche, the Christ within steps off the cross and walks free of shame and blame. When we can do that for ourselves, we can offer the same hand of love to others who are crucifying themselves. Then, the resurrection is at hand. Then, the Messiah can come.

When each one of us takes total responsibility, there is no one left to blame. There is no enemy to be found outside self, and the enemy within has been forgiven. That is the path back to the garden, the path of forgiveness, the one that Jesus showed us, and the one he offers to us, even now. (RTG)

Sin and Redemption

When I sat at the kitchen table contemplating suicide in 1973, I did not know that I was responsible for my experience. I thought that I was a victim of pain in a meaningless world. I did not know that my pain belonged to me and was my responsibility to transform. I did not know that I was here with specific lessons to learn about loving myself and others.

Life wasn't showing up positively for me, because I demanded that it be a certain way. My expectations and demands were the cross on which my experience manifested. Until I changed my attitude toward life, everything I experienced would be filled with pain and suffering.

Trying to change the external events and circumstances of life without addressing my internal beliefs and attitudes had proved to be a waste of time. If I wanted change in the outer circumstances of my life, I needed to accept things as they were and begin to look at the contents of my own consciousness. What meaning was I giving to the situation that presented itself? Was I suffering because of what happened or because of my interpretation of it?

In my own way, I discovered the principle that "thought is creative." The way I look at something influences the way I experience it and what I attract to me in the future. If I stop resisting and struggling, life gets easier. Events that support my life begin to occur naturally. I don't have to try to make them happen.

The truth is that I can change my experience. But that change begins with a shifting of my own perceptions. Therefore, it can never be mechanical. My heart must be in it or I am powerless to shift any external condition in my life. The inner work always comes first.

The law of grace operates from the inside out. As changes are made in the way I hold my experience, my experience begins to shift.

I do not push my experience away just because it shows up differently from the way I expect it to. When it shows up different from what I expect, I take a deep breath, let go of my expectations, and try to get my arms around what is happening. I know that my job is to embrace everything that happens to me, and that the more difficult it is for me to embrace something, the more deeply I will learn from it.

I learn to stop resisting, to stop distrusting. I begin to surrender into life. I begin to trust. In so doing, I shift my consciousness. And as consciousness shifts, so does the external reality that reflects it.

Since I never know how life will show up, I have to keep surrendering my demands and expectations. That is a perpetual process. Surrender just doesn't happen once or twice. It happens continually, day to day, hour to hour, moment to moment.

The outside aligns with the inside. This is the law of grace.

But it can't be quantified. It can't be precisely described. It can't become a technology of transformation.

Consciousness is poetry in motion. It is a dance of form, embodied for a moment and then empty again. It comes into being, changes shape, disappears and reappears. It is playful, spontaneous, always new. You must be in the moment to see it or appreciate it. It has nothing to do with the past or the future.

Understanding what our responsibility is in life is the invitation to the dance. The rest is practice: the dance itself . . . dancing with self, with other, with life unfolding and the indwelling God.

I received that invitation in 1973. When did you receive it? When did Christ make Itself known to you? When did the voice of the living God speak to you in your time of fear, distrust and pain?

Jesus has told us, "Knock and it will be opened." When we ask for help, we will receive it.

But it never comes unless we ask. Have you asked for help, or are you still trying to do it alone?

It is easier to find the source of love when the Friend comes into your life. Have you asked the Friend to join you?

This is all a game of hide-and-seek. First I hide and you seek me. Then it is your turn to hide.

The truth is that you are better at hiding than I am at finding you. I am willing to concede. I am willing to end the game. Are you?

The Friend is with us, but we cannot see Him. He leads us beside the still waters. He speaks deeply to our souls. In our communion with Him, we know that goodness and mercy follow us throughout all our nights and our days, and that we will live in His house forever.

In my time of terror and disbelief, the Friend came to me with a booming voice. "There are two worlds," he told me, "the world of pain and the world of surrender, the world of struggle and the world of grace. Choose which world you want to see. For the world you choose to see is the world you will live in.

"As you sow, so shall you reap. As you believe, so will your beliefs be embodied."

I send you my blessings on your journey. May the Friend walk beside you. May the love of God be ever-present in your heart. Namaste. (RTG)

Paul Ferrini is the author of numerous books which help us heal the emotional body and embrace a spirituality grounded in the real challenges of daily life. Paul's work is heart-centered and experiential, empowering us to move through our fear and shame and share who we are authentically with others. Paul Ferrini founded and edited *Miracles Magazine*, a publication devoted to telling miracle stories offering hope and inspiration to all of us. Paul's conferences, retreats and Affinity Group Process have helped thousands of people deepen their practice of forgiveness and open their hearts to the Divine presence in themselves and others. For more information on Paul's workshops and retreats or the Affinity Group Process, contact Heartways Press, P.O. Box 99, Greenfield, MA 01302 or call (413) 774-9474.

NEW TITLES FROM
HEARTWAYS PRESS

I Am the Door
288 pages hardcover
ISBN 1-879159-41-4
$21.95

Years ago, Paul Ferrini began hearing a persistent inner voice that said, "I want you to acknowledge me." He also had a series of dreams in which Jesus appeared to teach him. Later, when Ferrini's relationship with his teacher was firmly established, the four books in the Reflections of the Christ Mind series were published. Here, in this lovely, lyrical collection, we can hear the voice of Jesus speaking directly to us about practical topics of everyday life that are close to our hearts such as work and livelihood, relationships, community, forgiveness, spiritual practices, and miracles. When you put this book down, there will be no doubt in your mind that the teachings of the master are alive today. Your life will never be the same.

The Way of Peace
256 pages hardcover
ISBN 1-879159-42-2
$19.95

The Way of Peace is a simple method for connecting with the wisdom
and truth that lie within our hearts. The 216 oracular messages in this
book were culled from the bestselling Reflections of the Christ Mind
series by Paul Ferrini. Open this little book spontaneously to receive
inspirational guidance or to ask a formal question, and follow the simple divinatory procedure described in the introduction. You will be
amazed at the depth and the accuracy of the response you receive.

Like the I-Ching, the Book of Runes, and other systems of guidance, *The Way of Peace* empowers you to connect with peace within
and act in harmony with your true self and the unique circumstances
of your life. Special dice, blessed by the author, are available for using
The Way of Peace as an oracle. To order these dice, send $3.00 plus
shipping.

Taking Back Our Schools
212 pages paperback
ISBN 1-879159-43-0
$10.95

This book is written for parents who are concerned about the education of their children. It presents a simple idea that could transform
the school system in this country. This book does not pretend to have
all the answers. It is the start of a conversation. It is Chapeter One in a
larger book that has not yet been written. If you choose to work with
these ideas, you may be one of the authors of the chapters to come.

THE RELATIONSHIP BOOK YOU'VE
BEEN WAITING FOR

Creating a Spiritual Relationship: A Guide to Growth and Happiness for Couples on the Path
144 pages paperback
ISBN 1-879159-39-2
$10.95

This simple but profound guide to growth and happiness for couples will help you and your partner:

- make a realistic commitment to one another,
- develop a shared experience that nurtures your relationship,
- give each other the space to grow and express yourselves as individuals,
- communicate by listening without judgment and telling the truth in a non-blaming way,
- understand how you mirror each other,
- stop blaming your partner and take responsibility for your thoughts, feelings and actions, and
- practice forgiveness together on an ongoing basis.

These seven spiritual principles will help you weather the ups and downs of your relationship so that you and your partner can grow together and deepen the intimacy between you. The book also includes a special section on living alone and preparing to be in relationship and a section on separating with love when a relationship needs to change form or come to completion.

OUR SURRENDER INVITES GRACE

Grace Unfolding: The Art of Living a Surrendered Life
96 pages paperback
ISBN 1-879159-37-6
$9.95

As we surrender to the truth of our being, we learn to relinquish the need to control our lives, figure things out or predict the future. We begin to let go of our judgments and interpretations and accept life the way it is. When we can be fully present with whatever life brings, we are guided to take the next step on our journey. That is the way that grace unfolds in our lives.

Return to the Garden: Reflections of the Christ Mind, Part IV
124 pages paperback
ISBN 1-879159-35-X
$12.95

"In the Garden, all our needs were provided for. We knew no struggle or hardship. We were God's beloved. But happiness was not enough for us. We wanted the freedom to live our own lives. To evolve, we had to learn to become love-givers, not just love-receivers.

"We all know what happened then. We were cast out of the Garden and for the first time in our lives we felt shame, jealousy, anger, lack. We experienced highs and lows, joy and sorrow. Our lives became difficult. We had to work hard to survive. We had to make mistakes and learn from them.

"Initially, we tried to blame others for our mistakes. But that did not make our lives any easier. It just deepened our pain and misery. We had to learn to face our fears, instead of projecting them onto each other.

"Returning to the Garden, we are different from how we were

when we left hell-bent on expressing our creativity at any cost. We return humble and sensitive to the needs of all. We return not just as created, but as co-creator, not just as son of man, but also as son of God."

LEARN THE SPIRITUAL PRACTICE ASSOCIATED
WITH THE CHRIST MIND TEACHINGS

Living in the Heart: The Affinity Process and the Path of Unconditional Love and Acceptance
112 pages paperback
ISBN 1-879159-36-8
$10.95

The long-awaited, definitive book on the *Affinity Process* is finally here. For years, the *Affinity Process* has been refined by participants so that it could be easily understood and experienced. Now, you can learn how to hold a safe, loving, non-judgmental space for yourself and others which will enable you to open your heart and move through your fears. The *Affinity Process* will help you learn to take responsibility for your fears and judgments so that you won't project them onto others. It will help you learn to listen deeply and without judgment to others. And it will teach you how to tell your truth clearly without blaming others for your experience.

Part one contains an in-depth description of the principles on which the *Affinity Process* is based. Part two contains a detailed discussion of the *Affinity Group Guidelines*. And part three contains a manual for people who wish to facilitate an *Affinity Group* in their community.

If you are a serious student of the *Christ Mind* teachings, this book is essential for you. It will enable you to begin a spiritual practice which will transform your life and the lives of others. It will also offer you a way of extending the teachings of love and forgiveness throughout your community.

WITH ITS HEARTFELT COMBINATION OF
SENSUALITY AND SPIRITUALITY,
PAUL FERRINI'S POETRY HAS BEEN COMPARED
TO THE POETRY OF RUMI.

*Crossing the Water: Poems About Healing and Forgiveness in Our
Relationships*
96 pages paperback
ISBN 1-879159-25-2
$9.95

"The time for healing and reconciliation has come," Ferrini writes.
Our relationships help us heal childhood wounds, walk through our
deepest fears and cross over the water of our emotional pain. Just as
the rocks in the river "are pounded and caressed to rounded stone," the
rough edges of our personalities are worn smooth in the context of a
committed relationship. If we can keep our hearts open, we can heal
together, experience genuine equality and discover what it means to
give and receive love without conditions.

 With its heartfelt combination of sensuality and spirituality, Paul
Ferrini's poetry has been compared to the poetry of Rumi. These luminous poems demonstrate why Paul Ferrini is first a poet, a lover and a
mystic. Come to this feast of the beloved with an open heart and open
ears.

Miracle of Love: Reflections of the Christ Mind, Part III
192 pages paperback
ISBN 1-879159-23-6
$12.95

In this volume of the Christ Mind series, Jesus sets the record straight
regarding a number of events in his life. He tells us: "I was born to a

simple woman in a barn. She was no more a virgin than your mother was." Moreover, the virgin birth was not the only myth surrounding his life and teaching. So were the concepts of vicarious atonement and physical resurrection.

Relentlessly, the master tears down the rigid dogma and hierarchical teachings that obscure his simple message of love and forgiveness. He encourages us to take him down from the pedestal and the cross and see him as an equal brother who found the way out of suffering by opening his heart totally. We too can open our hearts and find peace and happiness. "The power of love will make miracles in your life as wonderful as any attributed to me," he tells us. "Your birth into this embodiment is no less holy than mine. The love that you extend to others is no less important than the love I extend to you."

Waking Up Together: Illuminations on the Road to Nowhere
216 pages paperback
ISBN 1-879159-17-1
$14.95

There comes a time for all of us when the outer destinations no longer satisfy and we finally understand that the love and happiness we seek cannot be found outside of us. It must be found in our own hearts, on the other side of our pain. "The Road to Nowhere is the path through your heart. It is not a journey of escape. It is a journey through your pain to end the pain of separation."

This book makes it clear that we can no longer rely on outer teachers or teachings to find our spiritual identity. Nor can we find who we are in relationships where boundaries are blurred and one person makes decisions for another. If we want to be authentic, we can't allow anyone else to be an authority for us, nor can we allow ourselves to be an authority for another person.

Authentic relationships happen between equal partners who take responsibility for their own consciousness and experience. When their buttons are pushed, they are willing to look at the obstacles they have erected to the experience of love and acceptance. As they understand and surrender the false ideas and emotional reactions that create separation, genuine intimacy becomes possible, and the sacred dimension of the relationship is born.

The Ecstatic Moment: A Practical Manual for Opening Your Heart and Staying in It
128 pages paperback
ISBN 1-879159-18-X
$10.95

A simple, power-packed guide that helps us take appropriate responsibility for our experience and establish healthy boundaries with others. Part two contains many helpful exercises and meditations that teach us to stay centered, clear and open in heart and mind. The Affinity Group Process and other group practices help us learn important listening and communication skills that can transform our troubled relationships. Once you have read this book, you will keep it in your briefcase or on your bedside table, referring to it often. You will not find a more practical, down-to-earth guide to contemporary spirituality. You will want to order copies for all your friends.

The Silence of the Heart: Reflections of the Christ Mind, Part II
218 pages paperback
ISBN 1-879159-16-3
$14.95

A powerful sequel to *Love Without Conditions.* John Bradshaw says: "With deep insight and sparkling clarity, this book demonstrates that the roots of all abuse are to be found in our own self-betrayal. Paul

Ferrini leads us skillfully and courageously beyond shame, blame, and attachment to our wounds into the depths of self-forgiveness . . . a must read for all people who are ready to take responsibility for their own healing."

Love Without Conditions: Reflections of the Christ Mind, Part I
192 pages paperback
ISBN 1-879159-15-5
$12.00

An incredible book from Jesus calling us to awaken to our Christhood. Rarely has any book conveyed the teachings of the master in such a simple but profound manner. This book will help you to bring your understanding from the head to the heart so that you can model the teachings of love and forgiveness in your daily life.

The Wisdom of the Self
229 pages paperback
ISBN 1-879159-14-7
$12.00

This groundbreaking book explores our authentic experience and our journey to wholeness. "Your life is your spiritual path. Don't be quick to abandon it for promises of bigger and better experiences. You are getting exactly the experiences you need to grow. If your growth seems too slow or uneventful for you, it is because you have not fully embraced the situations and relationships at hand. . . . To know the Self is to allow everything, to embrace the totality of who we are, all that we think and feel, all of our fear, all of our love."

The Twelve Steps of Forgiveness
128 pages paperback
ISBN 1-879159-10-4
$10.00

A practical manual for healing ourselves and our relationships. This book gives us a step-by-step process for moving through our fears, projections, judgments and guilt so that we can take responsibility for creating the life we want. With great gentleness, we learn to embrace our lessons and to find equality with others. A must read for all in recovery and others seeking spiritual wholeness.

The Wounded Child's Journey: Into Love's Embrace
225 pages paperback
ISBN 1-879159-06-6
$12.00

This book explores a healing process in which we confront our deep-seated guilt and fear, bringing love and forgiveness to the wounded child within. By surrendering our judgments of self and others, we overcome feelings of separation and dismantle co-dependent patterns that restrict our self-expression and ability to give and receive love.

The Bridge to Reality
192 pages paperback
ISBN 1-879159-03-1
$12.00

A heart-centered approach to *A Course in Miracles* and the process of inner healing. Sharing his experiences of spiritual awakening, Paul emphasizes self-acceptance and forgiveness as cornerstones of spiritual practice. Presented with beautiful photos, this book conveys the essence of the *Course* as it is lived in daily life.

From Ego to Self
144 pages paperback
ISBN 1-879159-01-5
$10.00

One hundred eight illustrated affirmations designed to offer you a new way of viewing conflict situations so that you can overcome negative thinking and bring more energy, faith and optimism into your life.

Virtues of the Way
64 pages paperback
ISBN 1-879159-02-3
$7.50

A lyrical work of contemporary scripture reminiscent of the Tao Te Ching. Beautifully illustrated, this inspirational book will help you cultivate the spiritual values required to fulfill your creative purpose and live in harmony with others.

The Body of Truth
64 pages paperback
ISBN 1-879159-02-3
$7.50

A crystal-clear introduction to the universal teachings of love forgiveness. This book traces all forms of suffering to negative attitudes and false beliefs, which we have the ability to transform.

Available Light
128 pages paperback
ISBN 1-879159-05-8
$12.00

Inspirational, passionate poems dealing with the work of inner integration, love and relationships, death and re-birth, loss and abundance, life purpose and the reality of spiritual vision.

POETRY AND GUIDED MEDITATION TAPES
BY PAUL FERRINI

The Poetry of the Soul
ISBN 1-879159-26-0
$10.00

With its heartfelt combination of sensuality and spirituality, Paul Ferrini's poetry has been compared to the poetry of Rumi. These luminous poems read by the author demonstrate why Paul Ferrini is first a poet, a lover and a mystic. Come to this feast of the beloved with an open heart and open ears. With Suzi Kesler on piano.

The Circle of Healing
ISBN 1-879159-08-2
$10.00

The meditation and healing tape that many of you have been seeking. This gentle meditation opens the heart to love's presence and extends that love to all the beings in your experience. A powerful tape with inspirational piano accompaniment by Michael Gray.

Healing the Wounded Child
ISBN 1-879159-11-2
$10.00

A potent healing tape that accesses old feelings of pain, fragmentation, self-judgment and separation and brings them into the light of conscious awareness and acceptance. Side two includes a hauntingly beautiful "inner child" reading from *The Bridge to Reality* with piano accompaniment by Michael Gray.

Forgiveness: Returning to the Original Blessing
ISBN 1-879159-12-0
$10.00

A self-healing tape that helps us accept and learn from the mistakes we have made in the past. By letting go of our judgments and ending our ego-based search for perfection, we can bring our darkness to the light, dissolving anger, guilt and shame. Piano accompaniment by Michael Gray.

PAUL FERRINI TALKS AND WORKSHOP TAPES

Answering Our Own Call for Love
A sermon given at the Pacific Church of Religious Science in San Diego, CA, November 1997
1 Cassette
ISBN 1-879159-33-3
$10.00

Paul tells the story of his own spiritual awakening: his atheist upbringing, how he began to open to the presence of God, and his connection with Jesus and the Christ Mind teaching. In a very clear, heartfelt way, Paul presents to us the spiritual path of love, acceptance and forgiveness.

The Ecstatic Moment
A workshop given by Paul in Los Angeles, CA, at the Agape International Center of Truth, May 1997
1 Cassette
ISBN 1-879159-27-9
$10.00
Shows us how we can be with our pain compassionately and learn to nurture the light within ourselves, even when it appears that we are walking through darkness. Discusses subjects such as living in the present, acceptance, not fixing self or others, being with our discomfort and learning that we are lovable as we are.

Honoring Self and Other
A workshop at the Pacific Church of Religious Science in San Diego, CA, November 1997
1 Cassette
ISBN 1-879159-34-1
$10.00

Helps us understand the importance of not betraying ourselves in our relationships with others. Focuses on understanding healthy boundaries, setting limits and saying no to others in a loving way. Real-life examples include a woman who is married to a man who is chronically critical of her, and a gay man who wants to tell his judgmental parents that he has AIDS.

Seek First the Kingdom
Two Sunday messages given by Paul Ferrini: the first in May 1997, in Los Angeles, CA, at the Agape International Center of Truth, and the second in September 1997, in Portland, OR, at the Unity Church.
1 Cassette
ISBN 1-879159-30-9
$10.00

Discusses the words of Jesus in the Sermon on the Mount: "Seek first the kingdom and all else will be added to you." Helps us understand how we create the inner temple by learning to hold our judgments of self and other more compassionately. The love of God flows through our love and acceptance of ourselves. As we establish our connection to the divine within ourselves, we don't need to look outside of ourselves for love and acceptance. Includes fabulous music by the Agape Choir and Band.

DOUBLE CASSETTE TAPE SETS

NOW FINALLY OUR BEST-SELLING TITLE
ON AUDIOTAPE

Love Without Conditions: Reflections of the Christ Mind, Part I
The book on tape read by the author. 2 Cassettes, approximately 3.25 hours
ISBN 1-879159-24-4
$19.95

Now on audiotape: the incredible book from Jesus calling us to awaken to our own Christhood. Listen to this gentle, profound book while driving in your car or before going to sleep at night. Elisabeth Kübler-Ross calls this "the most important book I have read. I study it like a Bible." Find out for yourself how this amazing book has helped thousands of people understand the radical teachings of Jesus and begin to integrate these teachings into their lives.

Ending the Betrayal of the Self
A workshop given by Paul Ferrini at the Learning Annex in Toronto, Canada, April 1997
2 Cassettes
ISBN 1-879159-28-7
$16.95

A road map for integrating the opposing voices in our psyche so that we can experience our own wholeness. Delineates what our responsibility is and isn't in our relationships with others, and helps us learn to set clear, firm, but loving boundaries. Our relationships can become areas of sharing and fulfillment, rather than mutual invitations to codependency and self-betrayal.

Relationships: Changing Past Patterns
A talk with questions and answers given at the Redondo Beach, CA, Church of Religious Science, November 1997
2 Cassettes
ISBN 1-879159-32-5
$16.95

Begins with a Christ Mind talk describing the link between learning to love and accept ourselves and learning to love and accept others. Helps us understand how we are invested in the past and continue to replay our old relationship stories. Helps us get clear on what we want and understand how to be faithful to it. By being totally committed to ourselves, we give birth to the beloved within and also

without. Includes an in-depth discussion about meditation, awareness, hearing our inner voice, and the *Affinity Group Process.*

Relationship as a Spiritual Path
A workshop given by Paul Ferrini in Los Angeles, CA, at the Agape
International Center of Truth, May 1997
2 Cassettes
ISBN 1-879159-29-5
$16.95

Explores concrete ways in which we can develop a relationship with
ourselves and learn to take responsibility for our own experience, instead of blaming others for our perceived unworthiness. Also dis-
cussed: accepting our differences, the new paradigm of relationship,
the myth of the perfect partner, telling our truth, compassion vs. res-
cuing, the unavailable partner, abandonment issues, negotiating
needs, when to say no, when to stay and work on a relationship and
when to leave.

Opening to Christ Consciousness
A talk with questions and answers at Unity Church, Tustin, CA,
November 1997
2 Cassettes
ISBN 1-879159-31-7
$16.95

Begins with a Christ Mind talk giving us a clear picture of how the divine spark dwells within each of us and how we can open up to God-
consciousness on a regular basis. Deals with letting go and forgiveness
in our relationships with our parents, our children and our partners. A
joyful, funny and scintillating tape you will want to listen to many
times.

HEARTWAYS PRESS

ORDER FORM

Name _____

Address _____

City _____State _____Zip_____

Phone/Fax_____

E-mail _____

BOOKS BY PAUL FERRINI

Taking Back Our Schools ($10.50) _____

The Way of Peace Hardcover ($19.95) _____

Way of Peace Dice ($3.00) _____

I Am the Door Hardcover ($21.95) _____

Reflections of the Christ Mind: The Present-
    day Teachings of Jesus Hardcover ($19.95)
    (available June 2000) _____

Creating a Spiritual Relationship ($10.95) _____

Grace Unfolding: The Art of Living a
    Surrendered Life ($9.95)   _____
Return to the Garden ($12.95)   _____
Living in the Heart ($10.95)   _____
Miracle of Love ($12.95)   _____
Crossing the Water ($9.95)   _____
Waking Up Together ($14.95)   _____
The Ecstatic Moment ($10.95)   _____
The Silence of the Heart ($14.95)   _____
Love Without Conditions ($12.00)   _____
The Wisdom of the Self ($12.00)   _____
The Twelve Steps to Forgiveness ($10.00)   _____
The Circle of Atonement ($12.00)   _____
The Bridge to Reality ($12.00)   _____
From Ego to Self ($10.00)   _____
Virtues of the Way ($7.50)   _____
The Body of Truth ($7.50)   _____
Available Light ($10.00)   _____

AUDIO TAPES BY PAUL FERRINI

The Circle of Healing ($10.00)   _____
Healing the Wounded Child ($10.00)   _____
Forgiveness: The Original Blessing ($10.00) _____
The Poetry of the Soul ($10.00)   _____
Seek First the Kingdom ($10.00)   _____
Answering Our Own Call for Love ($10.00)_____
The Ecstatic Moment ($10.00)   _____
Honoring Self and Others ($10.00)   _____
Love Without Conditions ($19.95) 2 tapes   _____
Ending the Betrayal of the Self ($16.95)
    2 tapes   _____

Relationships: Changing Past Patterns
   ($16.95) 2 tapes   _____
Relationship as a Spiritual Path
   ($16.95) 2 tapes   _____
Opening to Christ Consciousness
   ($16.95) 2 tapes   _____

POSTERS AND NOTECARDS

Risen Christ Poster 11" x 17" ($10.00)   _____
Ecstatic Moment Poster 8.5" x 11" ($5.00)   _____
Risen Christ Notecards 8/pkg ($10.00)   _____
Ecstatic Moment Notecards 8/pkg ($10.00)____

SHIPPING

$2.50 for first item, $1.00 each additional item _____
(Add additional $1.00 for first-class postage _____
and an extra $1.00 for hardcover books)   _____
Massachusetts residents please add 5% sales tax ____
Please allow 1–2 weeks for delivery   _____
TOTAL   _____

Send order to Heartways Press
P.O. Box 99
Greenfield, MA 01302-0099
Phone: 413-774-9474
Toll Free: 1-888-HARTWAY (Orders only)